AMERICA'S MASSACRE

The Audacity of Despair and a Message of Hope

TEWHAN BUTLER

ISBN: 0692281827
ISBN 13: 9780692281826
Library of Congress Control Number: 2014915684
Raise UP Media, New York, NY

If you are interested in publishing with Raise UP Media visit: www.RaiseUPMedia.com

DEDICATION

To Pamela Butler, my loving mother; throughout it all you have climbed the highest mountains to display a mother's love; and to my children Tewhan Jr. and Zamel—with this story do I accept the dimming of my light and the awakened brilliance of yours; to my grandparents John Q. Butler Sr., Maxine Butler, and Nellie Smith, may you all rest in peace, and to my grandfather R.D., the still-standing symbol of strength; and last but not least to the man who made me who I am, my father John "YahYah" Butler, may you rest in peace. I love you all!

"American society as a whole can never achieve the outer-reaches of potential, so long as it tolerates the inner cities of despair."

—Jack Kemp

FOREWORD

By KAMAAL BENNETT, New York City, July 2014

America's Massacre is truly a powerful message from a powerful messenger— Tewhan Butler, also known as Massacre, the man the United States government largely holds responsible for the rise and spread of street gangs on the East Coast.

For those who ever wonder, maybe even worry, what leads an alarming number of inner-city children to choose street life and gangs, this book is a must read. Cover to cover it is an intimately personal and interesting blend of anthropology, criminology, history, sociology, and swag.

Tewhan and I were neighbors. As young kids, we didn't view our section of East Orange as the ghetto. It was simply home. It was all we knew. Our lives had very similar beginnings and along the way took different turns that led to drastically different outcomes. Like Tewhan, I was a high honor roll student in East Orange public schools through elementary school. After elementary school, through my mother's awareness, effort, and sacrifice, I gained admission to Newark Academy, a prestigious private school in suburban Livingston, New Jersey, twenty minutes from where we lived. Newark Academy introduced me to life outside our neighborhood and to the reality of two different Americas. It is a reality many in America's ghettoes and suburbs do not fully understand. Through private school I gained new friends and was introduced to a quality of life unknown to my neighborhood friends. I saw parents of my schoolmates who had a quality of life that far exceeded any drug dealer's from our neighborhood and wealth that outlived an entertainer's or athlete's career. I came to know the common denominators of success: education, hard work, faith, patience, and perseverance. I also came to know privilege and entitlement—that regardless of education, skills, abilities, and work ethic some would always have more than others could ever earn.

My educational experience taught me to interact with and embrace people and cultures outside our neighborhood. Many people rarely venture outside their communities and social circles, and that limits life experiences. The distance between cultures and communities, suburban, urban and rural, poor and affluent, black and white, creates deep division. Division leads to a silent apathy and even fear and mockery of culture and people not our own.

And while my world began to open up at a young age, Tewhan remained in the failing local public schools with a near-uniform racial composition and cultural experience. Different perspectives led Tewhan and me to make different choices. Our paths split. I fell away from the streets and went hard in school and ultimately went on to graduate from Loyola University. Tewhan fell away from school and went hard in the streets and ultimately graduated to a life of isolation in a Federal penitentiary.

Since we were kids, I honestly believe we were in pursuit of the same outcome— a better life. I can literally say, but for the grace of God, a mother who is a teacher and a relentless champion of education, and some neighborhood old heads who helped keep me on the straight and narrow, I would be dead or in prison. That's why after college, I started an educational organization to galvanize community involvement and support to help schools best serve students and families, starting where Tewhan and I grew up in Essex County, New Jersey.

Once I started, my work with schools reinforced what I already knew from the plight of my childhood friends, just how many school-age kids there are in America with incarcerated parents. I saw bright kids in failing schools, and I saw some progressive educators doing great work who gave me great hope for those kids in their schools. But I realized the kids who are most in need and most at risk are not in school. They are on the streets with a different set of values and different priorities following the mis-lead of rappers, fake gangsters, and other false rolemodels. Disgusted with the deceit and tragic loss of potential in America's inner cities, I reached out to Tewhan, who was silenced in prison, and sought his help in reaching those kids lost in the streets. It had been years since we had spoken but I knew the authenticity of his character and his great potential to effectively engage a pedigree of people others, including myself, could not. He was eager to do what he could to help others and that was the inception of this project.

This led me to ponder the dichotomy of my life and the people and places in it:

How in the twenty-first century do America's inner cities resemble ghost towns and war zones? Some abandoned. Some still under siege. Living in a war zone, it should be no surprise inner-city children are growing up like soldiers—complete with a combat-like mentality and post-traumatic stress by the time they become teenagers.

These neighborhoods are controlled by gangsters, their community resources hijacked by corrupt politicians and other ignoble opportunists who prey on their undereducated residents and exploit their lack of means for personal and political gain. The oppression-for-profit business model is real. Let's be clear. It's not just the "man" oppressing these communities. Black leadership, what little there is, is also to blame and oftentimes their constituency is complicit.

Resources meant for the people aren't reaching those people and it is not just them who suffer, it is America. Generations of ignorance impede American innovation and prosperity. Able bodies trapped in a labyrinth of social services where the most vital social institutions are failing: government, families, schools, houses of worship, and prisons. Dilapidated homes and empty lots sink real estate values, depress urban economies, and pare down the local tax base, leaving less money where it is most needed and others to foot the bill.

If you dare go beyond the trendy dining and shopping districts surrounding many new pro sports stadiums and arenas and into the shadows of America's cities, you will find ignorance, low self-esteem, prolific drug abuse, extreme violence, frequent death, and utter despair. In some neighborhoods, it's near Third-World conditions. The only difference may be running water. Residents are lucky to find decent housing, quality schools, peace of mind, and the optimism that tomorrow offers a bright future for their young. Drive-by shootings and roadside Rest in Peace memorials are art and culture—and what could potentially be trendy shopping districts are transformed in the inner city into open-air drug markets. All the while, corporations fund multimillion-dollar sponsorships of stadiums and arenas, patrons shell out hundreds of thousands of dollars on luxury boxes, and politicians tout landmark economic development while their constituents languish in poverty. If you are a real estate developer or a politician, the investment must be the same—in communities and in people. There is more at stake than tax incentives and abatements and another ribbon to cut. In the end, whose investment is really at risk?

Because the large portion of the inner-city body politic is disengaged—if not totally disenfranchised, with little or no economic power—the problems of America's inner cities sit quietly outside the doorstep of national concern. And the exploitation of inner-city residents continues. Check the litany of recent noteworthy public corruption in some of America's largest cities, including Atlanta, Baltimore, Chicago, Cleveland, Detroit, Los Angeles, New York, New Orleans, Newark, and Washington, D.C. These also happen to be cities with fairly new arenas, stadiums, or both, at the heart of highly touted economic development plans. Often the remainder of those plans never goes beyond a press release and the poverty remains.

Again, let's be clear, the "man" is not solely to blame. Black leadership, what little there is, is also to blame. Just look at the majority of corrupt officials who were players in the abuse of public office and misuse of public funds in the cities named above. And please don't try to compare corrupt public officials to scheming Wall Street bankers. One group does not absolve the other. The underlying problem is when lawless and oppressive behavior becomes the norm.

Poverty, desperation, exploitation, and exclusion spawn a harsh reality in America's inner cities. This reality gives way to an unorthodox value system among the youth devoid of spirituality and faith. This distorted value system and despair often lead to actions, events, and headlines that baffle the mainstream psyche.

Policymakers and law enforcement continue to focus their efforts and resources to address the symptoms—drugs, gangs, violence, and the curb appeal of urban communities. And while this may create the illusion of change, it does not eradicate poverty's root causes—ignorance and division.

A big change demands everything from God's humanity. In justice's kingdom learned men never oppress people. Quarrels rouse suspicion. Truth unveils virtue. Wanton xenophobia yields zilch.

The American paper chase and the commoditization of society has birthed a culture where the individual is paramount—where people have come to define themselves by bank statements and worldly possessions, oftentimes viewing themselves as omnipotent. This dynamic has led to an arrogantly secular and morally bankrupt society that lives outside of universal natural law in a man-made system that casts judgment and projects fear and division based on the prejudices and pretexts of its architects. The harmonies in the common spirituality that vibrate throughout all humanity are muted or perhaps even drowned out by the discord and rancor of despair and the voids of vanity. Absent of faith, the wealthy too lack fulfillment and know despair. An old head who helped keep me focused as a child once told me, "In today's world, money is the God and sex is the religion; it's all vanity." What a sad truth.

Today's youth must stop sacrificing their morality and potential for quick chances at monetary gain. Instead, today's youth must come to identify their true selves and realize the abundant potential of their innate talents, then use those talents positively and productively to prosper.

Without prejudice, humanity must join forces to end poverty's massacre and restore civility and promise to American cities.

Government must work with constituents to foster fair and pragmatic policy and programs that level the playing field—that integrate not marginalize and empower not pacify. Government must work to ensure there no longer exists a two-tier educational, legal, and healthcare system—one for the rich and one for the poor. Government must work to foster universal access to quality education, equitable healthcare, and a living wage for all. The answer is not robbing Peter to pay Paul. The answer lies in self-determination and in helping people to become self-sufficient.

The many successful people who were raised in the inner city and who have abandoned their roots for the allure of affluence must recognize those humble roots are what make them who they are today. And they must reconnect to find effective ways to pay it forward.

Residents of America's inner cities must assume responsibility for their communities and their future, build economic power and political clout, and stop relying solely on government and charity to solve their problems. Ultimately, resources must be of the people and for the people in the communities where they live and not funded by and under outside control.

The inner-city body politic can no longer afford to lend blind support to profiteering politicians and charlatans who gallivant as community leaders but who in reality obstruct others' development and prosperity.

Residents of inner cities cannot remain absent from the political process and without a seat at the economic bargaining table for America to prosper in the 21st century.

A driving force behind the decision to publish this book is the need for diverse and authentic voices in the media, which have a major influence on morality, perception, and the zeitgeist. Media must recognize and appreciate its critical role in shaping the development of society. The media can either continue to sensationalize the superficial and fuel mindless materialism and crass consumption, conjure fear, and deepen the divide, or it can be an integral force in building understanding and a more tolerant, compassionate, and responsible global community.

Poverty's massacre will continue as long as America remains divided and Americans side-step personal and social responsibility. Most of all, as long as we are not one nation under God, divided we fall. There may be glimmers of hope, yet unknown potential is forever lost.

The world's future is at stake.

(Kamaal Bennett is president of Raise UP Media)

ACKNOWLEDGMENTS

I HAVE GREAT respect and appreciation for my editor Tom McCarthy, my publisher Raise UP Media, and the many who read, read, and re-read the many versions of the pre-published manuscript along the way, most notably Jade-Addon Hall. Just when I thought I was done, your experience in Hollywood blessed me with unparalleled insight and gave me the encouragement to take this story to the next level. You truly added many new dimensions. Special thanks. Now let's take it to TV and the Big Screen. To the one and only Anne-Valerie Bernard from Paris, France, whose feel for my story helped deliver the book's title, I am forever grateful. And to the many who have written me letters and supported my work on www.livefromlockdown.com and aided in my struggle, thank you. From the bowels of the darkened prisons that hold America's socially rejected hostages . . . I acknowledge the struggle.

Lastly, but with no less significance, the man, along with the most high, who made it all possible: Kamaal "KB" Bennett. Your vision, your drive, your relentless dedication, and your refusal to let me surrender during an at-times grueling process exacerbated by the reality of life in many of the worst United States penitentiaries, control units, and long stints in solitary confinement is what got us here. I salute you!

The entirety of my neighborhood, I love you 235%.

It is the pulse of the people that gave me the courage to share my truth.

INTRODUCTION

I SHARE IN this book my past in the hope that you recognize it is our future.

This is my story. They call me Massacre, a name that helped engrave this reality in stone. Much of my trouble, in hindsight, I could have prevented. I'm not pointing any fingers, nor do I place blame. But does my acceptance of responsibility remove the responsibility of others?

I cannot point only to the injustice that I felt the system served me, because I too was responsible for what happened with me and to me. I was always the controller of self. Though choices were limited, I still had choice. Truthfully, I grew up wanting the best, and felt I deserved the best. But I didn't know how to attain the best. Poor judgment pushed me further from life's treasures. The potential was always within me, but over time my struggles got the best of me, and I lost hope and faith. Then, it didn't seem to matter. But today I realize that with faith possibilities are endless. I hurt not only for those close to me but for all who share similar hardships. I want something greater for our future. Why now? Time establishes understanding. As they say, better late than never.

As a man still finding my way, I feel it is time to own up to my shortcomings and all the past injustices I served my own by not being a better example, by not being their motivation to better themselves in ways that would someday amount to something other than prison and death. I doubt I will ever discover if they secretly blamed me, but as the elected "big homie" I knew I had failed them—and that was in part and majority my fault.

As leader of the gang, the burdens of my brothers were mine to bear. My leadership and the example I set proved to be flawed. Without clarity I ran from the truth and watched others live out a lie. Lives were destroyed, families torn apart, and violence and poison riddled my very own neighborhood and far beyond. I take responsibility—and not with pride.

As a kid, I remember hanging up my football cleats and trading in blissful childhood superstardom for the attractiveness of street dreams. Instead of using The Oval as a steppingstone amid a hardened road, I used it as a means to endorse exactly what led me and those who vowed to walk alongside me to prison.

If I could take center stage and have one more meeting in the same 'hood with the same group of homies in the same park at the same time and under the same set of circumstances, the only thing I would change is the example I set.

I understand being sentenced cannot take back the wrong I helped create. But it makes for an example from which we all can emerge. Through my trial and error may others discover a more fulfilling life.

With what I know now, it's evident that our first course of action in exacting excellence is self awareness. Greatness lives everywhere, yet it is rooted from within. Circumstances need not ruin hope but are essential in cultivating change.

My thirty-year sentence is more than a term to be served. It is time, time for introspection, time to identify the person I was, the person I am, and the person I aspire to be. It is time to make use of myself and my story as a tool to awaken the many who started out just like me but who do not have to finish like me.

I call out to the street corners in every ghetto, to the suburban living rooms, the school buildings, the community centers, courthouses, the cells of every jail, prison, and penitentiary, and to all legislative chambers and ask:

Who will join me and accept responsibility for the current state of disaster in America's cities? Who will accept responsibility for the hundreds of thousands who are starving within America's borders? Who will take responsibility for the millions said to be living below the poverty line? Who will take responsibility for millions of fatherless children? Who will accept responsibility for a culture that persuades many into a life of crime and ultimately to prison and early death?

These questions are rarely asked and never answered. It is easy to paint the picture of a twenty-seven-year-old Massacre, yet it has proved more difficult to address the audacity of America as it quietly dismisses the back-breaking effects of despair, which have been disabling our people well before my time on this planet.

What is despair?

Despair is America's failing public institutions.

Despair is economic iniquity, unemployment, and illiteracy.

Despair is drugs, guns, gangs, crime, and early death.

Despair is the girl next door turning tricks to feed her newborn.

Despair is orphans and runaway kids.

Despair is the homeless, the hungry, and the helpless.

Despair is mass incarceration instead of education.

Despair is a system that wants to punish, not rehabilitate.

Despair is prison's revolving door.

Despair is the psychological slaughter of those who do not fit society's mold.

Despair didn't end with emancipation or integration.

Despair didn't end with the rise of the black fist.

Despair didn't end with a black president.

Despair is hopelessness.

Despair is people stuck in perpetual poverty.

What can WE do about it?

First, we must Raise UP!

See, you don't rise awareness, you don't rise the level of consciousness within the community, and you don't rise new standards. You must *raise* a generation before that generation can rise. We can't afford to sing the same old song, nor do they want to listen.

We must break the chains of our addiction to mediocrity and the mindless monotony of misery. The moment we accept mediocrity as a way of life, misery becomes us.

Perhaps, together, we can raise a generation of politicians and businessmen who give a damn and have the integrity to lead by example. Perhaps, together, we can build a new and more relevant skills-based approach to education, one that it is a gateway to prosperity as opposed to a pipeline to prison. Perhaps, together, we can evolve a more compassionate criminal justice system that can provide alternatives to human warehousing. Perhaps, together, we can endow social incentives instead of social services. Perhaps, together, we can embody a more just society. Perhaps, together, we can build a stronger America.

This deluge of despair in which we are drowning can be undone if we believe, open our eyes and take suitable action. Sound the alarm for those trapped in darkness. We must strengthen the weak and educate the unknowing. Together let's take responsibility for our families, friends, communities, and society at-large. Let's acknowledge the commonality of our struggles and place humanitarianism above politics. Let's accept that we are one regardless of location, appearance, and social status. As members of a global community, let's forge unbreakable bonds and build bridges to prosperity.

There is no denying that poverty is also a result of ignorance. Prior to looking for alternative avenues, we must first look within and seek to better understand ourselves. Our dreams are only figments of our imagination not to be made true when we fail to pursue them. Through right action, all is possible. We must remove our own limitations and RAISE UP!

Indeed, struggle and hardships have been inherited by one generation from the last and have left future generations burdened with the ill fortunes of the past. Yet the illusion that we are doomed to fail is totally untrue. Our truth is in how we answer the calling. The mode in which we own up to and accept responsibility for ours is what will bring us closer to a unified collective. Excuses are blinders and the result of narrow-mindedness. It is time to open not only our eyes but our minds. We are too strong to leave life to chance.

It is our choice if we want to accept defeat or claim victory. It is up to us to change our circumstances. Let's take action that will manifest national advancement. Let's make it clear that our intent was and remains to bring about a better today and tomorrow. In life there exist absolute truths and wavering lies. The truth we desire may never be found alone.

I hope you understand.

1

MY BEGINNING

THE DAY WAS Monday, October 1. The year 1979. Saint Michael's Hospital on High Street in Newark, New Jersey, was filled with a mixture of screams—screams that if listened to carefully, told a story all their own. Through all of the commotion, hooting and hollering, Pamela Smith could be heard frantically yelling at the top of her lungs, as doctors coached her through labor. "Push, push!" coached the doctors. Pam wondered how a moment meant to be filled with overwhelming happiness could arrive amid such pain. In an attempt to erase the discomfort, she closed her eyes and returned to a moment in time.

Pamela Smith was a small-town, country girl, born to parents Nellie and R.D. in Opelika, Alabama, in 1958, when Alabama was knee-deep in the Civil Rights Movement and just two years after the historic Montgomery bus boycotts. Pam was the youngest of four children. She was raised in a home where religion set the tone. When she was just a child, her parents were very much aware of the racial tension and lack of opportunity for African Americans in Alabama in the 50s and 60s. Pam's parents were determined to keep their "baby" protected from the injustice of those days and decided to pack up what little belongings they owned and move their young north in pursuit of more productive living. This trip north led the family to New Jersey in 1966. They left Alabama to escape the racial divide and inequality of the South. But they arrived in New Jersey at the dawn of Newark's race riots, which resulted in countless injuries and twenty-six deaths and changed the face of a community forever.

Pam attended Kentop Elementary School in East Orange, New Jersey. Little did she know a few city streets away lived John Q. Butler II, also known as YahYah. I guess you could say YahYah was the typical young black male, struggling to find his place in society.

YahYah was raised in a section of East Orange named Arcadian Gardens, the one and only housing project in East Orange that became known as Little City. Little City was not your average run-of-the-mill project. If one hovered over Little City, it could have been easily mistaken for prison complexes. Little City was a maze of metal-and-brick hallways littered with syringes, glass vials, burned spoons, clouded crack pipes, and bullet casings—evidence of the drug addiction and violence that infested its courtyards. Crime and drugs hid within the buildings of Little City and did their best to pick apart resident after resident. You could find everyone from priests to pimps in Little City. Though a dark cloud seemed to hover over Little City, there remained those with the determination to make it out and—be it by hook or by crook—YahYah was one of those few.

Pam and YahYah lived just minutes apart, yet they lived in two totally different worlds. While Pam's part of town rested with what many may have considered to be the "Haves," YahYah's part of town was filled with government hustlers—the "Have Nots." It's amazing how they were so close, yet so far away.

Growing up in the projects YahYah was taught to fight to get what he wanted from life, and he took it literally. In an era when fair fights between neighborhood crews still existed, nine out of ten issues in Little City were settled with a hands-on approach. It wasn't long before YahYah took his street-fighting skills to the gym and hit the boxing ring. Was there anything wrong with a young kid from the projects who dreamed of becoming the next Ali or Frazier? The struggle to maintain a balance between the streets and the gym began to take its toll on YahYah. Then, YahYah's trainer informed him he was to begin training for the Golden Gloves, the championship of amateur boxing.

The Golden Gloves news excited his Little City crew and others. However, for reasons still unknown to me, YahYah's dreams of boxing faded and he found himself ripping and running in and out of Little City, up and down Sussex Avenue trying to make a living, all while he attended East Orange High (one of two high schools in East Orange at the time). Even though YahYah ran with what many considered the "bad boys" from Little City, he managed to keep his head in the books. He knew very well no matter how bad he was, or how well he boxed, he was no match for Maxine, his mother.

Maxine was a short, pudgy, brown-skinned lady who was rough, tough, and took no shorts. If you crossed that line she would undoubtedly bring the hammer down.

Far from dummies, YahYah and his crew would hit school, knock out their school assignments early, then ditch the last few classes so they could make their way over to Clifford J. Scott High School, the other high school in East Orange at the time, to rough up the boys and try their luck with the ladies. It was during one of these many trips that YahYah first laid eyes on Pam, or "Lateefah," as her high school running mates, Candice and Donna, called her.

Candice, Donna, and Pam were said to be classy, yet a little flashy with a hint of 'hood spice. Though YahYah and his crew were popular in the projects, they barely blended in on the other side of town among the Haves. So in attempt to capture the ladies' attention, they did what they knew best—they fought.

Day after day of beating and chasing the local boys away left plenty of females around for YahYah and his crew to have their pick. But for YahYah, the plan seemed to backfire. The more he did, the less attention Pam paid to him. When YahYah found out Pam was originally from the South, he was quick to switch his approach. YahYah now began to hit Clifford J. Scott with one thing on his mind: Pam.

One day, YahYah approached as smooth as can be and caught Pam off guard. After a few minutes of conversation, they promised to stay in touch. Pam didn't want to let on she fell for the young bad boy from the projects and tried to keep it a secret, thinking it would pass. But you know how the saying goes: a person's eyes tell tales of buried truths. Needless to say, Candice and Donna caught on quick. They were more hip to the fast-paced city life and made it clear that "cool" was in, and from what they heard, YahYah was as cool as cool gets. Pam was confused as she weighed her "likes" against her parents' "likes," figuring they would never accept a young man whom many believed to be a young thug.

It wasn't long before Pam and YahYah officially became a couple. There were walks home after school and trips to the projects to meet his family—all while high school breezed by. Before you knew it, they heard, "*Congratulations! It's a boy!*"

That baby boy was me, Tewhan Hakim YahYah Smith. My last name was Smith because at the time my parents were yet to marry. I was born out of wedlock and into the struggle of two who were so deeply in love. The challenges of parenthood would set out to test just how deeply in love my mother and father truly were. On the date of my birth, my parents had just turned twenty years old. They lived apart and were basically broke. They had to deal with the whispers of "I told you, you weren't ready for a baby" and "How would they be able to provide for not only themselves, but a little one as well?"

My father still lived in Little City and managed to save money from side hustles and whatever else came his way. My mother, with the support of her parents, was basically covered. That didn't sit well with my father. My father knew it was time for him to step up and become a provider. A man who couldn't provide for his family was considered weak, one thing YahYah was definitely not. He definitely wanted to do right by my mother and me, and he put hustling on the back burner and went on the job hunt. YahYah finally landed a job as a card dealer in Atlantic City. The job was cool and provided enough funds to tuck away, but the commute was too time-consuming and left few if any hours to spend with his family. He found a place to move the family under one roof and put down the first month's rent and security deposit. He still had enough money saved to cover a few months' rent and decided to quit his job and find another as soon as possible.

Our first apartment landed us *up the hill* on Harrison Street in East Orange. The part of Harrison Street where we lived was a pretty nice area. At the time Harrison Street was middle class—high-rise apartment buildings, freshly built condos, and quiet compared with other parts of town. But this part of Harrison Street was all too close to streets, like Halstead and South Orange Avenue, whose young and middle-aged desperados wreaked havoc on the streets and terrorized the 80s under crew names such as Halstead's Finest and SOAP (South Orange Ave Posse).

In the 80s, and still today, South Orange Avenue was a place laced with everything you could dream up—community centers, fast food spots, dollar stores, bodegas, homeless shelters, a dozen or so liquor stores, crack dealers, and prostitutes.

Halstead Street was equally dangerous. Although the drug market was not as open as in other areas, the boys on Halstead hustled hard and certainly had the remedy when it came to rocking people to sleep.

The bottom side of Harrison Street, between Central Avenue and Freeway Drive, was deadly. Its many apartment buildings made it difficult for the law to get a grip on the peddling of the infamous 80s drug of choice—crack rock. Cooked here, bagged there, and sold on every inch of pavement where a dollar could be made.

Our apartment on Harrison was as far away from the projects as you could get and definitely a step up from the world we knew. But the apartment didn't last long. The bills began to pile up and money was tight. My parents packed up in favor of a more affordable part of town. We found ourselves right back *down the hill*, on the corner of New Street and Maple Avenue. A step up then a step down.

I guess keeping up with the Joneses wasn't as easy as people would believe.

While on New Street, we learned my mother was expecting again. Well, only the second time, but, yes, once again. It was good news, but still a tough pill to swallow with regard to their financial situation. Though my parents both graduated from high school—Pam, from Clifford J. Scott and YahYah from East Orange High—it seemed their diplomas held little value as they went on countless job interviews.

YahYah genuinely didn't want to turn to the streets. He put pride to the side and went to holler at my grandfather, Pam's father R.D. After their discussion, R.D. told YahYah he was glad he decided to come and speak with him and he would put in a good word for YahYah at his job. In fact, their conversation even helped my father realize that regardless of his ambitions, without the right knowledge, it was like using a boat on dry land. He would never get anywhere. This conversation seemed to reinvigorate my father with newfound energy and a sense of urgency. Shortly after, with my grandfather's help, my father got a job with the State of New Jersey. And before you knew it, my mother and father met at the altar.

My parents were still young, with a new job, a new marriage, and a few new house guests—me and my new little brother Steven Butler. Stevie, as he was known among family, was born August 16, 1983. He was an 80s baby and a blessing to the family, but certainly another financial weight as my mother and father struggled to make ends meet.

One night my mother hopped out of bed to fulfill a late-night craving and strutted into the kitchen and turned on the lights. With the flick of the lights, in the middle of the kitchen floor stood New Street's newest houseguest—one of the biggest mice she ever saw. The type that felt it ran the household; the type that stood still and stared back at you. The type that would eat you out of your Zoom Zooms and Wham Whams that you waited all month to purchase with your food stamps. The fat bastards expected you to move before they budged. I'm sure if you're from the 'hood you share a similar experience of hearing your mother scream at the sight of a mouse in the house.

My mother darted back to the bedroom and shook my father from his sleep and made it clear she wanted the mouse caught immediately, and that this would be her last night sleeping in a house with these unwanted guests. My father grew up in the projects and was no stranger to mice and rats and didn't really see the big deal. My pops would do anything for his family, but on this night he bargained with my mother to let him sleep and promised to begin looking for a new apartment in the morning. Shortly after my mother's encounter with the four-legged furry friend, we moved to Carnegie Avenue.

Carnegie Avenue was still in East Orange. It was about halfway between where we were living on New Street and where we lived before on Harrison Street. Carnegie was home, and home wasn't always the prettiest. Our two-bedroom apartment was laced with Rent-A-Center's finest. There were no leather living room sets, or big screen TVs, but our cloth couch, beige recliner, and thirteen-inch color TV positioned atop the kitchen counter was a lot more than most. My brother and I not only shared a room, we also shared bunk beds. There were Hulk Hogan posters on the walls, along with stars from the Dallas Cowboys and New York Giants. Filas, Etonics, and Lotto sneakers were thrown in milk crates and stashed in the closet. Clothes stuffed our wood-grain paneled dressers. The house smelled of Lysol and ammonia at all times. The old wooden floors would leave splinters in our feet if we dared to walk around barefoot. Mom and pop's bedroom was decked in your typical 70s décor, with the famous painting of dogs sitting around the poker table. Their king bed sat on crates. Their dresser was covered with gold-plated jewelry, my mom's hair rollers, and dad's loose change that I would sneak and pocket whenever he wasn't around. Outside the house sat a half of a patch-grass yard and our late-70s model Gremlin Hooptie. This was home on Carnegie.

Even in dog years, I was still a puppy when we moved to Carnegie Avenue. But Carnegie gave me my first taste of street life. Carnegie was a real incognito strip. You could drive through and, if not paying close attention, you would never believe the things that took place on this block. Though it wasn't much violence, other crews from other areas knew Carnegie Avenue Posse (CAP) wasn't deep in numbers, but if crossed in any way, deep was where they took you. Six feet, that is. In the mid to late 80s, Carnegie Avenue was a clinic, a street pharmacy for real. While protecting the privacy of those from that era, let's just say when Jay-Z rapped about "still spending money from 88," these dudes knew exactly what he was talking about.

Still on the porch, watching the fast life in slow motion, I would sit and stare as kids fresh out of junior high school pulled up driving kitted-out rides with a fly chick in the passenger seat. They would pop their trunk to show off their car's sound system, which more than likely was their entire trunk. Eighteen-inch speakers and multiple amplifiers knocked KRS 1's "Black Cop," Eric B & Rakim's "Paid-n-Full," and, of course, Kool G Rap and DJ Polo's "Road 2 Riches." The music was a clear indication of art imitating life. During this time in the 'hood it was "niggas with attitudes" on the "road to the riches" trying to get "paid in full" while "black cops" wanted to bury you. I remember Soul-to-Soul telling me to be steady, while asking if I was ready.

The old heads on Carnegie would hop out of their rides and throw me a head nod, or sometimes even holler, "Lil T, what up?" Lil T was what I was called in those days. To be acknowledged by guys of their caliber meant a great deal to me. You may wonder why, but for me, this was my reality. When I wasn't attending Nassau

Elementary School on Central Avenue, my life consisted of listening to music, watching music videos, and sports. From what I could see, things portrayed in those music videos were right outside my front door, live, in color and 3-D. So while most kids sat in their living rooms and idolized Slick Rick, L.L. Cool J, Big Daddy Kane, and a host of other rappers, I grew up wanting to be like members of the Carnegie Avenue Posse.

Carnegie Avenue in the 80s was Cross Colors outfits, goose down coats, and the red, black, and green medallions. Public Enemy had everybody ready to fight the power. I remember the pretty girls with the doorknocker earrings, biking shorts, and lollipops in their mouths—playing hard to get doing their best to be chosen by a hustler.

The hustlers in the 80s were "those guys." The ones up the block who donned "Cool Ass" in front of their names. Cool Ass T. Cool Ass Moe. Cool Ass Hass. What made them cool was a list of things: the way they flashed the big LEE patch on the back of their jeans, their Kangol hats, their four-finger gold rings, herringbone chains, and Big Daddy Kane and Run DMC-style gold dookie ropes.

Cool on Carnegie in the 80s were Acuras, Honda Accords, Honda scooters, Audi 5000s, Volkswagen Jettas, Nissan Maximas, Suzuki Samurai jeeps with five-star rims, Alpine audio systems, pull-out radios and custom interiors. Everyone wasn't a hustler but those who were made it look damn good.

As a child in the 80s, I learned hustlers varied in rank. You had your nickel and dimers, the eight-ball and ounce pushers and then you had those "who supplied the suppliers"—shout out to Dip Set's Hell Rell. Whenever they came around everything stopped. There were no more Acuras and Accords. Whips upgraded to BMW and Mercedes Benz. Bosses sported fur coats and mink hats with the earflaps. Their jewelry glistened with diamonds and rubies, and they rolled with an entourage to protect them from the area's famed stick-up boys.

In the 80s, the housing projects in the neighboring city of Newark held the area's most vicious stick-up crews. Dayton, Grafton, Prince, and Hayes were all projects with their hustlers, but also an even share of men who wore all black year round and saw everyone—dirty or clean, young or old—as potential victims. The stick-up boys back then didn't know what it meant to hold a 9 to 5 or stand on the corner battling for drug sales. What they did know was others were getting paid off crack and there was money to be taken.

Growing up as a kid in the 80s in East Orange and Essex County, New Jersey, little did I know I was on the front lines of America's War on Drugs. I was an innocent bystander of sorts. I was a child. I had yet to be introduced to the game but I was familiar with those around the way already in the streets and privy to the recipe. Raw coke, powder form, stretched with boiling water and baking soda. What you had on your hands was the next best thing in the 'hood since penny candy—crack rock.

Crack was powerful. It made its distributors rise and its users crumble. The pros and cons of the drug game played out around me on a daily basis. I did my best to keep my eyes glued to reality.

On Carnegie Avenue as a young'un I did plenty besides watch the flash of the 80s drug game, which lit up my block like a disco ball. We found ways to find trouble. The younger version of Carnegie Avenue Posse was Oop, IB, Don, Mean, Naim, and I. I can't forget the other homies from Carnegie Avenue like Shakoor, his little brother Rashad, and my main man Jamil "Urk Dog" Rollins. Although there wasn't much for us to do in the neighborhood, that which we could do, we did together. We used the Laundromat on Central Avenue between Shepard Avenue and Burnett Street for much more than washing clothes. We would sit around the folding tables in the back of the Laundromat like Mafioso crime bosses and plot our day's activities.

"Ay T," Oop shouted overtop loud spinning washers and dryers.

"What's up?" I asked, sipping my quarter water trying to savor the flavor.

"So what's your plan?"

"To be big like John Gotti and the rest of them mob niggas."

No clue as to who the rest of them "mob niggas" were. But one thing I knew, John Gotti's name rang throughout precincts, courthouses, the suburbs, and the 'hood.

"John Gotti? Nigga, what you know about John Gotti?" Oop shot back, sounding almost offended.

"All I need to know is that nigga doing big things," I replied.

The word *nigga* back then took over our vocabulary, and every other word that came out of our mouths was nigga this, and nigga that. The only thing of importance when it came to using the word was pronunciation, n-i-g-*g-a* or n-i-g-g-*e-r*. Saying it with the "er" would get anybody an ass whipping, but the "ga" in the hood was sort of like a term of endearment.

"Big things? Nigga, my brother doing big things," Oop shot back without delay.

Indeed he was, but the comparison between Oop's brother and John Gotti, well, there was none. But Oop could never and would never allow anyone to disrespect his brother's name, or his pockets for that matter.

"Yeah nigga, I'm Carnegie Avenue to the end, but them mob niggas be wilding. They be tying mothafuckas up and the whole nine yards. You fuck wit them mob niggas and your ass is grass," I said with excitement in my voice and the whole bit.

"Man, fuck you and the mob. Nigga, you keep talking Imma have my brother and them tie yo ass up! Matter fact, nigga just last week I heard Cool Ass Moe and them in my backyard talking about how they chopped a nigga head off from cross town. Now what, nigga?"

At the Laundromat table things always grew tense. The streets had to be ours and whenever we talked about them, ran in them, and finally joined them, we did it with tons of emotion.

"Aight ya'll take a chill pill," interrupted Cool Ass Ib, who was always the voice of reason among the crew.

"Oop right. I did see 5-0 [police] in the park a few days ago." Ib looked my way so Oop couldn't see his face and winked.

"Fuck all that. Right now we need to find out how we going to hit Papi's ass again. Nigga, I'm starving."

"I got the door," hollered Na Bills.

"I got Papi," Don chimed in. Both were tired of the back and forth between Oop and me.

"Well, Oop, you and T gotta get the shit."

In unison, Oop and I looked toward one another and mouthed, "Aight." The minor feud was over and our dreams of being big-time drug dealers and mob bosses faded. At the moment we were nothing more than petty thieves going to shoplift out of Central Avenue's bodega.

Little did we know, sports and video games had already begun to lose their appeal. I guess you can say at this age, we discovered the distinction between needs and wants. According to our parents we needed to be good and we wanted to be bad. It wasn't strange for us to be referred to as little bastard kids by the elders who watched us run circles around Carnegie Avenue.

At this point, we weren't jail bad, but we were definitely bad enough. What our parents did not know was we had seen the backseats of many police cars on different occasions. Sadly, that was how we began to describe fun. We would squat on the police, do something to get their attention, and then take off like bats out of hell. Convinced age was nothing but a number, we found a thrill in trying to outrun the screaming sirens and uniformed officers hot on our trail. Often times, we would lose them with our youthful speed. Other times, they lucked up and caught one or two of us. They'd quickly realize we were just "bastard kids" (the police weren't exempt from calling us names), hold us for a few, dole out a few meaningless threats, then release us. This process must've been a joke for the police. It certainly was for whoever in our crew got caught. Still, we were all wet behind the ears. I guess you could say we were already rehearsing for a life of crime. Although running from black and whites (cop cars) was not considered a crime, it was a misdemeanor (obstruction of justice). We did exercise Crime Pays 101 in other areas. The most twisted were our weekend bike heists.

We would bike-hunt around the neighborhood, targeting blocks like Chestnut Street, Beech Street, and Lenox Avenue surrounding Carnegie. We would steal bikes or build bikes from scrap parts we found around the neighborhood. These bikes were only used to get us to the nearby suburb of Bloomfield. Specifically, to Bloomfield Avenue, which was their downtown center.

Bloomfield Center held stores like Economy Sneakers, sporting goods and clothing stores, the Royal and the Center movie theaters, arcades, bike shops, and Tony Soprano types. After all it was Jersey. I always felt uneasy in Bloomfield. Maybe it was because we were far from our neighborhood, or maybe it was the fact we were up to no good. The looks we received from the adults in the area screamed, "I got my eyes on you." The stares from their children were of pure fear. The stares were always from a distance. Still, we were there to get what we came for. We wanted the BMX dirt bikes with the stunt-pegs and the Diamond Backs with the goosenecks.

The plan was always pretty much the same; simply put, get bikes and haul ass. We'd spot two or more bikes to our liking, trash the ones we came with, and leave town on the stolen bikes. Most often, banging a few heads in the process. A chase was sure to follow. With our heart-rate thumping, sweat pouring from our foreheads and into our eyes, we were cool on the outside and mixed and mingled on the inside. Our minds focused on one thing and one thing only—pedaling like our lives depended on it. We knew better than to look back. Entire families would be clawing at our jackets and the straps of our book bags, which held our emergency repair kits—air pumps, pliers and tire patches. The beatdown we'd receive if caught was sure to be Soprano style too. Getting caught was never part of the plan. A beatdown, arrest, and another beatdown from our parents was out of the question. A few blocks into the chase and our pursuers would be long gone. Our faces would be covered with devilish grins as we downplayed any earlier concern. At this young age, this was a long day of hard work.

Before you knew it, we were back in the 'hood trying to ease into the house unnoticed before the streetlights came on. My mother, always the attentive one, would creep up out of nowhere and hit me with, "Tewhan, where have you been all day? Why are you so dirty? Whose bike is that you're dragging into my house?" That was the million-dollar question to which I would reply, "Nobody's ma, just Don's. He let me ride it home to catch the lights."

"Whose bike?" she would ask again.

"Naim let me borrow it."

Feeling interrogated, I showed signs of agitation without realizing I just went from Don to Naim. Moms would hit me with a "You know you done fucked up don't you?" stare from the movie *Menace to Society* with a snarl her own. My mother would wave her hand and brush me off knowing good and well I had told a boldface lie.

"Don't take your dirty ass in my kitchen," she would say.

"Whatever," I'd mumble under my breath.

With the best ears in Jersey she would go in, "What you say, boy?"

"Nothing, dang," I would reply.

"That's what I thought. Now go and wash up."

"Aight ma, I love you." These were my code words for thanks for not tripping.

"Yeah, I love you too."

While trekking mischievously through Bloomfield's suburbia on our bike heists, I took notice of the differences between their clean and polished neighborhoods versus the repulsive and repugnant roadways of our 'hood. In Bloomfield there wasn't a hint of worry in the air. There were no walls spray-painted with graffiti. People didn't appear to be disgruntled and mad at the world, with their faces twisted for no reason. In the suburbs everyone seemed to be friendly and wore welcoming grins, at least until they saw us. Empty refrigerators and growling stomachs did not appear to be of any concern in their neck of the woods. Their sidewalks were smoothly paved, unlike our uneven sidewalks with grass sprouting in the cracks. The sprinklers on their lawns hissed as they quenched the thirst of their professionally landscaped lawns. It may sound simple but in the 'hood if you lived somewhere with a lawn big enough for sprinklers, you were no doubt far above the majority. In Bloomfield homes had room for driveways with two car garages and NBA-style regulation basketball hoops that looked like they were never used. In the 'hood we wore out garbage cans and milk crates and played basketball in the street. Their driveways were packed with late-model foreign cars with vanity plates. These cars lacked the tinted windows, shiny rims, and loud sound systems trademark of the 'hood. I suppose the folks in the suburbs had more important things to spend their money on, like home mortgages and college tuition.

In the 'hood most people didn't own their homes and more kids seemed to be making their way to prison rather than college, so in most cases neither a mortgage nor college tuition were of concern. In the 'hood folks would blatantly dismiss the month's rent and utility bills to upgrade their ride, for the latest in fashion, or just on a wild night on the town.

The farther along we rode into Bloomfield, and at times the neighboring town of Glen Ridge, the more exotic the homes became. We were amazed by the double-framed glass doors, the columns, and marble trim. We would ride down the street screaming "*Daaaammmn*" as we played "My Car," a 'hood game where if you were the first to call it, you claimed it as your own. We'd claim cars and houses we could only dream of. For us, it really was a different world; a totally different reality many did not realize existed.

Seeing the pretty little safe world of the suburbs only enraged us. I was definitely too young to really understand our ill will. But now, subconsciously, I believe us taking what they had emanated from us wanting what they possessed and our resentment over, for whatever reason, not having it.

Many years after our crime boss-style meetings around the Laundromat folding table and trips to Bloomfield, Naim, Don, Oop, and Mean (Pac) were all later convicted as co-defendants in Essex County Superior Court and each sentenced to nearly a decade in New Jersey's prison system. Following their convictions, Cool Ass Ib was arrested and convicted for a serious act of violence. And while I remained on the streets, only time would tell.

As a kid, I so wanted to be one of the cool ones. My neighborhood was full of fly guys, and those who weren't stood out like sore thumbs. For me, my time to be cool was during school. While attending Nassau Elementary School, though we were basically "innocent" children, we were well aware of the cool kids, the nerds, the pretty boys, the bullies, the Barbies—the little girls with a million different color barrettes in their hair, the color-coordinated socks, and the latest kicks. Then you had the rough chicks with barely enough hair to fit in a ponytail, ashy faced and denim cut-offs, who preferred to run with the young aspiring street thugs. The pretty boys and the bullies were sort of like the same crowd. That was until the pretty boys had something the bullies wanted. It could have been anything from a Nintendo game to candy or a girl. The nerds were simple. They minded their own business and kept their faces in the books. Me? I was a mixture of cool, nerd, pretty boy, and bully.

In school I was always smart enough to mingle, to a degree, with the nerds to keep myself ahead in the books. If a subject ever presented too much of a problem, I would gladly use what I knew of bully tactics to press those better prepared and in a position to help.

Even though all the boys wanted a Barbie, the rough chicks were the best. After school, at an age when all were curious about sex and the haves and have nots of the opposite sex, the rough girls were the ones you could sneak off with to the house or the back of an abandoned building and convince them to let you cop a feel, a kiss, or a two-minute pants rub. The prissy Barbie chicks wouldn't dare. I would still try my hand with the Barbies. It usually began with a folded note passed in class with the words "Will you be my girlfriend? Circle yes or no." Most often I was shot down. Maybe I was not as cool as I thought.

Even though my circle-yes-or-no notes were repeatedly rejected by the school Barbies such as Hassana and Sabrina, those notes frequently garnered me attention from the older girls who didn't hesitate to mention how cute I was and how they couldn't wait till I got older and that I would be a heartbreaker. Certainly, those remarks had me feeling myself in a cool pretty boy sort of way, but I was never fully convinced. So, for validation I did it all. I tried my hand at basketball via Nassau's Little League, played the drums in music class and concerts, was one half of a group of Kid-N-Play impersonators and, if you ask me, I had one of the best Michael Jackson "Thriller" performances the 80s had to offer. If that wasn't enough, I was an honor roll student, and nice with a switchblade thanks to my grandfather, John Q. Butler Sr. aka Cutty Saw. So nice, I managed to put three cuts in my eyebrow. My father beat my ass for that but the three cuts in my eyebrows remained. I was also one hell of a big brother. I would provide my younger brother Stevie with all the encouragement he needed to stand up on the sun porch after school and yell, "Stupid dummy bisch" to passing females. He was too young to properly pronounce bitch.

As I reached for confirmation with respect to who and what I was and who and what I was to become, I remained keen on what the nobodies and somebodies had going on. I figured this way I would know what to do and what not to do to secure mine. Simply because I was advancing from addition and subtraction to multiplication and division didn't mean my dreams of capturing a king's ransom were too early to be decided. Even while I ran through the fourth, fifth, and sixth grades with teachers like Ms. Cool, Ms. Burnett, whom I had a huge crush on, and Mr. Santoro, who was the only male and only white teacher I had come across at this age, I knew I would soon move on in the direction of a life I deserved.

We ran circles around Mr. Santoro during the first few months of class. He was a new teacher, definitely not from the 'hood and, did I mention, he was white? I used to sit in the back of the class as cool as can be, or so I thought, cracking jokes, scribbling on the desk, or fantasizing about the day when everyone would know my name. That was until Mr. Santoro got the hang of things and figured out how to keep us badass kids interested and excited about learning, which was a harder task than it might seem. Mr. Santoro turned out to be one of the best teachers I ever had. I remember seeing his smiling face as proud as can be amid the auditorium's crowd the day I crossed the stage to receive my elementary school diploma.

Far from a fool, I schooled at an all-time high, making the honor roll through-out elementary school. However, I must admit my grades didn't stem from a stellar education courtesy of the East Orange Board of Education. My classmates and I all sort of felt cheated, because school went something like this: show up, complete your assignments (right or wrong, individually, collectively, copy, whatever; just complete it), sit up straight, and no talking if the principal entered the class, then you passed.

With Nassau Elementary School's Principal Imp, *aka* Dr. Weaver, who was a bullhorn-blowing Bill Cosby look-a-like disciplinarian with zero tolerance, the teachers were pleased not to be put on the spot by a misbehaving student and get chewed out by Dr. Weaver as if they were children themselves. As a reward for the temporary good behavior, little gold stars were placed by our names, and we would go in the "history" books as Student of the Week. I guess we could have called this the Award for Fakers. Today's remedy proved to be tomorrow's recipe for disaster, and they have the nerve to wonder why.

This culture of social promotion created the illusion of progress and achievement. It also kept my mother and father off my back. It allowed me to bounce back and forth between Carnegie Avenue and Little City, trading one evil for a lesser.

My many nights spent at my Aunt Ann's house in Little City kept me sharp. I would sit in front of Building 17 with my cousin Sheyeast, a gang of her girlfriends, and the local hustlers who broke night attempting to put the play on her and her crew. Though this was my relative they were trying to bag, I didn't trip; I just sat back, played my position, and soaked up game. All her girlfriends adored my "innocence." They would tease me and call me their little boyfriend and all that nonsense. All the hustlers in Little City knew my father and knew I was their way in with my cousin Sheyeast and her girlfriends, so they looked out for me and kept me with enough change in my pocket to splurge as much as I wanted for a kid my age. I couldn't wait for the next day, when the ice cream parlor would open so I could buy my Aunt Ann's favorites—a sixteen-ounce Pepsi and a pack of Newports. I'd take them to her and head back out to spend my earnings on video games, hustling the hustlers. Most say it ran in my blood, but I had yet to figure out why or how. Everywhere I turned, I would hear "YahYah this" and "YahYah that." Either they had the wrong guy, I was hearing wrong, or my dad was a damn good actor. Too young to pry, I kept my questions to myself, but decided to see if I could figure him out. This not only led to me becoming more observant of his ways but the ways of the streets as well.

When I was about ten years old, if we weren't playing basketball in Mean's dirt-patched backyard or playing football on the grass in front of Nassau School, we would gather around Enoch's pad, mixing on turntables and practicing dance moves for school concerts and talent shows. *House Party* the movie had just come out and Oop and I were something like the next Kid-N-Play.

On occasion, which wasn't often, I was able to convince my father to give the OK for me to sleep over a friend's house. On these nights, we would hit Club 88 Teen Nights and burn up the dance floor. We wouldn't get into too much. Our reputations were pretty much solidified from the groundwork laid by the old heads from Carnegie who just so happened to be Oop's older brothers and my relatives.

There were days when they lined us up and made us fight each other until we could go no longer. You could tell in our eyes we didn't want to go at it with one another, but turning down a fade could not and would not be tolerated in the 'hood. We were told these matches would make us tougher and prepare us to defend our block when they decided to pass the torch. These minor bouts would cause some to stop talking, but a few hours later, when the ice cream truck made its rounds, or we were treated to Stuffy's Restaurant, everything was right back to normal.

This was the life. Everything seemed picture perfect, at least from a 'hood perspective. The few mishaps somehow always worked themselves out or you just learned to cope.

Some mornings, I would see police cars lined up and down Carnegie. By now, I learned whenever the police were deep like that, it was a raid—a raid where everyone had to go. Hell, even at my young age I had to duck to make sure I wasn't snatched up. It didn't matter if something was found or if someone owned up to their product, it was like everybody had to pay for the inconvenience of making the police department work. Local police didn't believe in simply taking down the bad guy, it was take down the bad guy, his friends, and his family. And if his neighbors didn't like it, take them down too.

On these days, I would rush past the drama and make my way to school, only to sit in class and think about what I just witnessed and pray for the day to speed up—hoping by the time school was over everyone would be home. It didn't always happen as fast as I'd like, but within the next couple days, after being released on their own recognizance or bail, I would see Carnegie's old heads strolling down the block with their sneaker tongues flopping and pants sagging as a result of East Orange Police Department's suicide prevention policy: No Shoe Strings and No Belts. I guess for some, taking their own life beat sticking around smoking their soul through a pipe or living unable to explain how brutal of a beating life bestowed upon them.

I would conceal any worries with a smile and play like it was nothing. But if you knew like I did, you would have been worried too. I saw people get pulled over during routine traffic stops, and taken on year-long vacations, courtesy of New Jersey's Department of Corrections. So to see my family return gave me a good feeling deep down inside, like it was Christmas.

· The police tactics and the way they attacked the innocent and deliberately destroyed homes and abused those they arrested—all while donning a smile—is what I would say completely turned me off about the law. I couldn't stand to see them smile, as if tearing apart yet another family symbolized winning. Even as a kid, I could feel and understand the mentality behind such devious grins. One game we never played in the 'hood was Cops & Robbers because you could never find a kid trumped up enough to play the role of a cop. There were always more than enough robbers to go around.

After these raids, my next-door neighbor Colby would sit me down to warn me of the dangers of the streets. When Colby would sit me down, his normal all-too-cool demeanor faded, and I got the impression the life he was living was one he didn't take pride in. I learned the lifestyle was more a necessity than anything. One conversation, well, lecture, I recall went like so:

"What's up lil man?"

I was a little shy and still unsure how the older homies on the block viewed me and replied with a simple head nod. Colby sensed my apprehension and told me to come over and kick it with him for a few.

Colby's house was only two houses away from my house, so I knew my parents wouldn't trip if they came out and found out I was gone. I strolled over with a light ditty-bop. Instantly Colby began telling me how he would watch me as I watched the streets with thirst in my eyes. He told me he used to do the same thing when he was my age and his older brother and his crew would nickel and dime in Dapper Dan crocodiles and big-framed Gazelles. I was all into his story and then he lost me when he started talking that old-school fashion. I remember asking, "What are Gazelles?"

Colby chuckled and answered, "That's them big ass glasses you see Run DMC and them wearing in videos."

I couldn't help but feel slightly embarrassed.

Colby continued, "Listen, I know you, Rockeem, Marty, and Bo know what's going on out here but y'all are not paying attention to the things you don't see."

As I grew older I realized that Colby was talking about the extensive criminal records that hold us back and the ugly intentions of pretty girls who leave as soon as the cuffs are put on and the so-called friends who turn their backs on you with an out of sight out of mind attitude.

Colby then explained how I should be thankful that I had two parents and how most had no father around and their moms got high and had sisters who turned tricks. Colby knew my mother and father were living paycheck to paycheck and were welfare recipients and Section 8 residents. The struggles of urban America had long since been accepted as the norm. How dare the audacity of despair? My lone blessing was that my struggling family remained together.

With a bit more emotion Colby made clear, "The game don't change, only the players. If you don't man up and do something different nine times out of ten the same situation you see today will be your own."

I thought to myself man up and do something different? There wasn't anything different to do. I was still young but old enough to know that the 'hood didn't change either. Looking around it wasn't hard to tell that nobody really cared about us. In school I would hear teachers complain about not being paid enough. I would see my mother and father argue over backed up bills. Even with all of this on my mind I kept it simple and to the point.

"I see y'all, big rims, big chains, and even bigger smiles, so doing something don't really seem to fit the bill," I replied.

"Nah, it ain't out the question. It's the only answer," Colby clarified.

Before Colby could finish his beatdown, a burgundy TransAm pulled up smoking like it was one block away from conking out. Inside were two white females with pockmarked faces, runny noses, and sagging eyes.

"I got to go lil man. I'll catch you later."

"Yeah, later Colb," I replied.

Apparently Colby's something different would have to come later as well because it didn't take a drug dealer to see the two women inside the car were all-day rock smokers. Still, I looked up to Colby and the life. I looked up to him a great deal, so I would take it all in. However, at the end of the day, for a kid my age, seeing was believing. I'm unsure if I was simply blind to the facts or just flat out ignoring the warning signs, but what I saw was what I wanted and what I wanted was to *be*. I didn't realize forcing a play normally resulted in someone dropping the ball until the day I almost lost my life nearly taking another's.

I can't say it was just kids being kids because I must admit we were reckless. I can't remember how or where, but my crew and I stumbled across a sawed-off shot-gun. Yes, it went and does go down like that in the 'hood on the regular. On days we were overcome by boredom, we would slide to a homie's crib just to show off the pump shotgun and do our best impressions of Clint Eastwood. I can't really say "we," because I was not only the youngest, but the smallest of the bunch, so usually the pump would pass right over me and its barrel pointed in my direction. Even though it wasn't loaded, this would piss me off to the max. I couldn't wait until I got my hands on it.

One day, Oop and I were scheduled to DJ a cookout and needed to pick up the equipment. I found the shotgun hidden behind one of the speakers while packing. I took this opportunity to exact my revenge. Oop ended up as my target. I raised the pump and pointed it straight at him.

"What's up now?" I said. "Ain't no fun when the rabbit got the gun, huh?"

"Stop playing. Get that shit out my face," Oop responded, not really paying me much attention.

We both knew I wasn't going to shoot him, but pointing a gun at a person was like marking them for death and could get you killed in the 'hood. It goes back to one of the original principles of street life: "Don't pull your strap, if you ain't gonna use it." But among the best of friends, it wasn't that serious. Still, I figured I must've had nine lives, as many times as the barrel was pointed at me. It took nearly all my might to cock the shotgun, and all you heard was "Clack Clack!"

At that exact moment so much adrenaline rushed through me, it was unbelievable. After feeling enough was enough, I laughed and lowered the pump. I wasn't prepared for its hairpin-trigger, and BOOM! The gun went off.

It damn near knocked my shoulder out of socket. Oop and I stood in a daze. Out of all the days we went through these same motions the gun was never loaded, but when my chance finally arrived, a slug was slammed in its cradle and was a split second from rocking my relative to sleep, forever. It was definitely a wake-up call, a true story of how serious things can actually get. I was only a ten-year-old kid, and I was seconds away from trashing my life. After this reality check, I decided to slow down for a minute and take a look at my life. I re-evaluated my priorities and tried my hand at sports.

2

HARDENED INNOCENCE

I<small>T WAS ALWAYS</small> a childhood dream of mine to become a star in the NFL. My father and grandfather were both diehard Dallas Cowboys fans, so I felt it was my birthright to become Dallas's next star running back. After school and on weekends, picture scenes from the movie *Boyz n the Hood*, I would bring out my football and go house to house to recruit enough of my homeboys to start a game of hold football in the street or tackle football in the front field of Nassau Elementary School. I was pretty much the smallest of the crew, so I had to use my speed to avoid the pounding of the bigger homies, who couldn't wait to put a lick on anyone who crossed their paths. It was on the football field where my physical talent was first recognized.

As a family, we weren't starving, but kicking out extra money wasn't part of the script either. I procrastinated as long as I possibly could until my childhood best friend Ibn (Cool Ass Ib) Hassan pressed me to ask my father for football equipment. Ibn was maybe two or three years older than I and, from where I stood, a genuine friend. Finally, when I asked my father, to my surprise, it wasn't hard for me to convince him to purchase the equipment I needed to sign up for one of the local Pop Warner teams.

We still lived Up the Hill on Carnegie Avenue not too far from Elmwood Park, where the local Pop Warner team, the East Orange Oilers, practiced. Back in the late 80s and early 90s, the Oilers were pretty good, though to me, they lacked that grit and 'hood camaraderie. So, in search of the good old down and dirty fun you experience when playing football in the 'hood, I made my way to Oval Park in a section of East Orange known as Down the Hill, where the East Orange Rams grinded it out. Oval Park played a significant role as it relates to my current condition. The Oval was the place where it all started and partially ended.

The first time I stepped foot in The Oval I felt like I walked into the circle at the Coliseum. Its many gladiators positioned throughout with a hungry look in their eyes as if each day was a fight to the death. This was exactly where I wanted to be. The Oval was not your ordinary park. For those in the neighborhood The Oval was where everything would come together and sometimes fall apart. Good and bad. Summer time community events in The Oval usually ended with brawls or shootouts. Neighborhood touch football games turned into tackle and usually ended with the same result—a beatdown or flying bullets. But there too were many days when all was cool and the family vibe permeated The Oval. You can't talk about The Oval and not mention the Civic Center, a recreation center adjacent to the park, and its parties where as preteens we rubbed pants all night. Some even adopted an Oval Park bench of their own. Somewhere they could call home and you know . . . everyone loved The Oval. It's where boys turned to men and the good girls turned bad.

In pursuit of my dreams for football stardom, I set out to be the best the Rams had ever seen. After my rookie year of riding the bench, my coaches, Jerry Jew and Hass, finally put me in the game. I was determined to make my mark and join the Oval Park Greats such as Fabian "Big Bear" Thorne, Shy-Meil and Dy-Meil Simpkins, and Nikosi Brown. I hit the field with a vengeance. Our team unity made it easy for me to fit in and do my thing. We set records and broke others, enjoyed undefeated and unscored upon seasons, but after a while my excitement for the game started to die down. So to create a thrill I, and a few of my teammates, would slide off before games and puff on a few blunts. This became a ritual after demolishing yet another team. We would smoke behind the school, under the bleachers, or wherever we couldn't be caught. We entertained ourselves by clowning whoever dropped a pass or fumbled the ball, while giving props to whoever made it into the end zone or knocked somebody on the opposing team out of the game.

Since my rookie year of being beat up on by such players as Nasir "Nasty" Johnson, James Pickard, Zaki Jones, and a few others, my first challenge wasn't presented until

1990. I strolled in The Oval, late as usual, so I could skip the warm-up portion of practice. I noticed the team already started hitting drills. I was known as one of the hardest hitters on the team, and this was one of my favorite parts of practice. The coaches seemed to be overly excited, so I wondered who was over there "bringing the noise," as we would say.

After I slow-poked my way around the track for two laps, I brought it in and was confronted by my coaches and teammates. They were all hyped to tell me they had somebody ready to go head up in a drill we called "the Nutcracker"—where the team makes two parallel lines with two players lying on their backs on opposing ends. The coach blows the whistle, they jump up and run at each other full speed and collide with full impact. This particular drill usually lasted until someone quit, something that would get you punked for the rest of the season, or if somebody was laid out with the wind knocked out of him. I was always up for a challenge; after all I was "Big Daddy," a nickname that stuck from me sporting my father's old Mean Machine football jersey. Mean Machine was a perennial powerhouse in the area's adult touch football league. This league was highly competitive among the old heads in the 'hood. Nevertheless, me and this other person lay down, waited for the whistle, and went at it. Both of us refused to fold. I didn't yet know the name or even the face of this kid who refused to quit. One thing I did know was he had heart. Although we were just kids at the time, we all knew heart was definitely a must if you wanted to survive in the 'hood.

After drills, we stood on the side and chopped it up for a few and exchanged names and such. I came to learn my new teammate's name was Quadree Smith. He was a slim kid, maybe ninety pounds with football equipment and all, with a flattop haircut, and the heart of a lion. In those days we called him Qua. However, as time passed he would run through other names. One I remember best was "Bugs," a handle he carried from his days as a 40-Ounce Gangsta (a local crew in the late 80s and early 90s). Ultimately, the name he would settle with was Troub, short for Trouble, which suited him well. He too had previously played for the Oilers and decided to switch teams for similar reasons. From that day on, we basically became inseparable. We stayed over each other's houses and swapped everything from video games to sneakers. Since we shared the same last name, we even adopted one another as cousins, which was something a little bit of everyone did in the 'hood. Once you developed a close enough relationship, it became so and so is my family. The yearning for family always existed no matter how big of a household one came from. In the 'hood we identified and adopted.

At this stage of my life, everything seemed sweet, but there was one thing that left a bitter taste in my mouth. Individually, all was intact, but collectively, I couldn't ignore the hardships faced by those around me. Reality became clear when I slept over teammates' houses on the nights before our Sunday Pop Warner games. There were times when teammates insisted sleepovers be held elsewhere so we wouldn't see their living conditions. It was poverty to the extent of nothing but buttered rice for dinner and window curtains made out of bed sheets. Steaming radiators evicted roaches from their hiding posts and kept the rodents warm. Parents so strung out on drugs they couldn't care less who witnessed them in their "element." This was the environment my peers attempted to hide. Not that any of it was their fault, but as kids most would use another's misfortune to ridicule without remorse. I couldn't blame them for not wanting others to see. I mean, these were kids with great potential, but life had worked and over-worked some families, homes were broken down, refrigerators were empty, and dreams were slowly fading. When your house is not a home, shelter is usually sought in the streets.

I was only a kid myself, but I wanted so badly to be of some sort of assistance. I lacked the means, but came to the conclusion I would endure and embrace their struggle as if it was my own until I figured out a way to make something happen. Growing up in a household with two parents, a younger brother, and a sizeable amount of extended family, the core values of family were embedded into my upbringing— values such as commitment, loyalty and a willingness to sacrifice.

Early on I faced a choice to be selfless or selfish. Friends never came a dime a dozen, so I promised myself I would display my loyalty to those I considered to be friends. My quality of life wasn't much better, but I would willingly sacrifice it for someone whose only means of survival was to struggle. Not for long, but at least until we found our way.

It should be crystal clear while I was one of the few blessed to have both parents around and food in the refrigerator, I was still burdened with the same struggles, for the most part, of those around me. Let us not be fooled into believing a two-parent household meant all about better days. We were a working-class family living paycheck to paycheck and in no way whatsoever rolling in the dough. I recall plenty of days in the grocery store, ashamed as my mother would pay for items with food stamps and the fear of what my friends would say if I was caught going to buy a loaf of bread or carton of milk with what we called "Broke People's Money" back then. Even if two parents meant more, does it mean one was not poverty-stricken? Money didn't cure all problems, especially those outside the home. The fragile stability in my household was not peace from the storm, but shelter from adversity's downpour.

I wasn't really sure if the few tricks of the trade I picked up in Little City and on Carnegie would work long term; I continually brushed off scheme after scheme and stuck to football. However, the thrill of smoking weed and playing football continued.

Our "weed missions," as we liked to call them, would lead me to the Teen Streets, the heart of Down the Hill, aka Illtown. The Teen Streets were a whole new world. Down the Hill was densely populated. Homes were tightly squeezed next to one another with just enough room for adult shoulders to pass between. These alleyways, or "cuts" as we called them, ran a maze through the 'hood that could carry you from the top of the hill to its bottom, if you knew your way around. But you didn't dare walk through Down the Hill if you weren't from the 'hood, never mind venture into its cuts. Lookouts and shooters occupied our rooftops, overseeing filthy, unkempt yards and disheveled people slaves to a mixture of drug abuse, crime, and reckless sex. Abandoned homes with boarded-up windows and only two steps out of a flight of six stayed crowded with hustlers in the cut ducking the law, with runners out in front pushing packs and serving their clientele. Empty lots were littered with condom wrappers, dirty Pampers, empty beer bottles, blunt guts, drug paraphernalia, and stolen car parts. Not all homes were abandoned. This was the life and environment residents were accustomed to. All corners were flooded with lost potential. Those who aspired to be Michael Jordan lost their edge as the War on Drugs ran them off local playgrounds and into a more dangerous game. They were replaced by young boys out day and night sporting menacing grins, perched atop mailboxes and milk crates in thug apparel in front of graffiti-tagged storefronts. Rundown tennis shoes dangled from illegally run cable wire and crimson-red blood crusted to the sidewalk. The streetlights were shot out. At night the entire block was pitch-black, making it easy to maneuver in and out of alleyways and backdoors. Pay phones were blown up with M-80s by someone seeking a payday. There was no calling for help.

There wasn't anything going on Down the Hill I never saw before but for some reason I couldn't figure out until years later, everything felt so different. It wasn't just the style of dress. Back then, everybody from Down the Hill seemed to sport Dickies suits and Timberland boots, or Naughty Gear from head to toe. But to me, Down the Hill represented freedom. It was a neighborhood where I knew no one and no one knew me. I was free to be my true self without worrying about someone running back to tell my parents, something that seemed to happen on the regular whenever I thought I was getting over in Little City or on Carnegie.

Our smoke sessions were our private time when we would ignore the outside world—no football, no school, and no supervision. In the clouds of weed smoke nothing existed but the moment. Children attempting to be adults, following behind adults who themselves had no clue on the direction of their lives. We would huddle in abandoned homes adorned with milk crates and other "furniture" of the sort. In addition to Phillies Blunts we would rotate forty ounces of beer, bottles of Cisco, cipher loose cigarettes, and anything else to enhance the high. Almost every weed cipher led to a rap cipher. Our eyes would be bloodshot, fingertips burnt, and not a worry in the world until the weed was gone and our bottles emptied. That's when a mix of humor and paranoia set in as we questioned whether we looked high. Believed to be rebels without a cause, nobody was willing to take the chance of getting busted by our elders. As youngsters, it was understood our involvement was to be limited. This made our weed missions all the more thrilling.

As we mobbed down to 15th and William Streets to get a sack, I noticed a few kids who played for the Rams but only seemed to show up for games or had quit earlier in the season. While we waited for the "Weed Man" to return, it dawned on me I was in the heart of the 'hood, a 'hood, technically, I had no business in. Born in Little City and living Up the Hill on Carnegie, I was definitely out of pocket. Up the Hill and Down the Hill always had beef since our parents were kids. In the midst of these thoughts, two kids walked up and asked the teammates I was with (Stickman Gangsta, Skrap G, and Troub) who I was and where I was from.

Stickman Gangsta was the quiet type. It was rare to hear him speak unless he was tore down on one of the many intoxicants we tampered with at the time. Much of his vocal abilities went into spitting hot sixteens (rap verses) that were out of this world. His laid back but gangster drawl was similar to Snoop Dogg when he first stepped foot on the scene as the legendary Dr. Dre's protégé in *Deep Cover*. Take a few years off the D-O-double-G and there sat Saadi Davis, aka Stickman Gangsta.

Skrap was the youngest of his brothers, Evol and Damu. Growing up he was one of the smallest, light skin with braids, and like many boys in the 'hood, his passion was torn between the streets and sports.

"A yo who dis nigga?" questioned Kwasi, an older homie from Down the Hill who was dark skin with a slim build and looked to be five years older than us. His man who I came to know as Loonatic was in the background shooting me rocks.

I was determined to stand my ground and opted to remain silent unless someone directed the questioning to me. They gritted and I gritted back, although it was a little hard to look like a young gangster suited up in football equipment.

Gangsta stepped up and replied, "That's my homie, why?"

"That ain't ya mothafucking homie. He ain't from round here," Loonatic erupted. Loonatic was in the same age bracket as us, but was much bigger in size. He wasn't fat, but he wasn't all muscle either. Let's just say he was stocky and big for his age.

"Well, he is now!" Skrap made clear.

Wow. Were they serious? I wasn't blind to drama but not too familiar with the crew. I didn't know how to take the whole ordeal. Things appeared hostile. It was if all were imperfect strangers. When Troub, Skrap, and Gangsta stepped in and vouched for me, it made me feel welcome and, honestly, made me want to get down even more. Regardless, I knew I had to be prepared to defend myself. It was clear holding it down in the 'hood had no limits. In that instant I learned another important lesson of the hood—you never turn your back on one of your own.

"Man, get the hell outta here. He ain't going nowhere, and we ain't going nowhere," Skrap and Gangsta let it be known.

At the time, I didn't know if I was ready for what nearly happened. I was lost and wondered, damn, what about football practice? We only came to get a quick bag of stress weed, smoke, and get back to The Oval before we were missed. Now, here I was stuck. I couldn't let them down, especially after how they just put it down for me. Kwasi and Loonatic stared at me and walked off.

When the Weed Man returned, we slid off and Gangsta told me Kwasi and Loonatic were his relatives and not to worry because they were just feeling me out. I was far from tripping; I just wanted to smoke and head back to practice to bust a few heads.

(As I wrote this book I was informed Loonatic was murdered. May he rest in peace.)

My first smokeout was me and a few of the homies in a back alley, arguing over who was going to get to roll. If you couldn't roll, you were best off deferring, rather than sabotage the cipher with a blunt that didn't smoke properly and deprive everybody else of the five dollar high they chipped in on. Within the cipher everybody had a role, so and so would be the roller and someone else would break the weed down. At this age, dirty fingertips always picked out the many seeds and heavy saliva sealed the Philly blunt. Everybody else most likely provided entertainment with jokes or making beats and freestyling.

We spent all our money on the essentials, the weed and the blunt, and were left without enough money for even a lighter. We struck the matchstick, the flame rose, and I inhaled deeply, not sure what to expect. What came next were chest-rattling coughs, followed by a series of loud laughs. I damn near choked myself to death. Instantly, it seemed I was high. My eyelids got heavy and dropped. My mouth grew dry, and my head was spinning. I was most definitely high and, in the back of my mind, I knew I was hooked.

After practice, my mother picked me up from The Oval. She was still over-protective and did not want me to walk home alone at that age. I remember pulling off in the car, all I did was think about everything I just experienced on my short walk from The Oval through the Teen Streets to 6th Avenue, the borderline where William Street in East Orange turns into 6th Avenue in Newark. I did not want to leave the darkness of Down the Hill like most kids don't want to leave Disney World. Back then it was like I was in a movie. Ghettos around the world resembled each other. The rigors may differ yet the pulse of the people is always the same. Still Illtown, Down the Hill was the School of Hard Knocks. I wanted to graduate with honors.

On this ride home, as fate would have it, my mother informed me life was taking us to a new destination. We were moving again. It would not be too far from where we currently stayed on Carnegie Avenue. However, we were about to move even closer to the streets I couldn't wait to get back to, Down the Hill. My mother was under the impression I would be disappointed and asked if I was OK. I looked toward her as she continued to drive and with a straight face nodded "yes," not wanting to let on to my menacing joy.

When I returned to Carnegie and got up with my CAP crew, I put them on that I would be moving soon, but didn't know exactly when. Up until then, Carnegie Avenue was where I spent most of my life, so it was a little emotional, as emotional as a crew of youngsters on the rise could display. We all vowed to stay tight no matter what; after all, it wasn't like I was moving a million miles away. It was only about a ten-minute distance, though we all knew the separation a few short blocks could create. To leave the neighborhood and my childhood friends up to this point was a change that could easily have led to major differences.

A person could live around the corner, and if for any reason a beef broke out between neighborhoods or blocks, there would be no more talking. Kids who were once friends quickly became sworn enemies. It may sound cold to many, but your block, street, avenue, 'hood, or turf was your home, your family. And no matter what walk of life you originated from, it was always taught family first.

The kids who were raised somewhat sheltered or "on the porch," as we called them, were raised to give respect and not to tolerate disrespect as it pertains to their *household,* while kids growing up in the *streets* were pumped up with lessons like "Respect must be earned" and "Never let anyone disrespect the neighborhood." When disrespected you fought; you didn't run home and tell mommy and daddy—who would wait for you to finish your story before they dragged you right back to the streets to find whoever it was to handle your business. So, while the "on the porch" kid loved on a household basis (parents and siblings), the kids in the streets displayed their love collectively for the neighborhood, their turf, which at the end of the day was their family.

I was around eleven years old and my parents were still as strict as could be. Not so much my mother as it was my father, with his attempts to keep me away from the streets he knew all too well. Troub and I had already grown tight and our parents knew it. Come to find out our parents knew each other from the same streets my road-dawg and I now planned to run. This was not to say that Troub or I were only out to make a way in the streets, because that was the furthest thing from the truth. We still had our dreams of going pro and playing in the NFL and taking care of our parents. However, we were already playing peek-a-boo with reality. Still, we hoped for the best and planned for the worst.

A few weeks breezed by as we tried to familiarize ourselves in the new apartment on Oraton Parkway. My side of Oraton Parkway was right off Central Avenue, and Troub lived directly down the street on the corner of Oraton Parkway and William Street. The new place was definitely a step closer to where I wanted to be. They say everything happens for a reason, and as I woke up each day, I was determined to find mine.

Oraton Parkway rewarded me with my own room and therefore a little more privacy, and I could keep my indiscretions under wrap. The last beating I received was by my mother after a few bad grades on a report card. I contemplated whether to give the report card to my parents or trash it, and I balled it up and tossed it on the side of the house. My luck, the report card didn't make it in the garbage can and blew directly in front of the house by the time my mother came home.

The things I was doing on Oraton Parkway would have got me a million more beatings had I been found out. In fact it was on Oraton Parkway I allowed the pressure of my peers to tempt me to turn my parents' house into a smoke shop. One of the many foolish things brought on by puberty.

My life began to change when we moved to Oraton Parkway. I became more exposed to the disease that crowded the city's streets. I realized things I saw on Carnegie were taking place everywhere. The hustle, bustle, and struggles of Carnegie weren't in the least bit unique. Everyone everywhere was out to soothe their struggle and find a way.

On my morning treks from my house on Oraton Parkway to Vernon L. Davey (VLD) Middle School the harsh realities of the city became even more noticeable. Before we moved my world consisted of Carnegie Avenue and Little City, two zones of ugly. Football practices at The Oval educated me to the sullen sections of Down the Hill. Now, as I walked to school to gain academic instruction, I was coached by corruption with each step I took. The erroneous exploits of those around me began to erode the little self-control I had.

Down the Hill was already becoming my new stomping ground. I was getting high as a hobby and my somewhat sheltered life vanished. I remember walking home after a long day of smoking the world's worst weed. I mean pure grass. I was still too young to maintain, and I walked home with my eyes wide open in attempt to let the breeze clear the redness from them. The closer I got to home everything wasn't as funny. That's when all of a sudden my nerves began to kill my buzz. Mommy and daddy might be at the door to get a good look at their child. Most times I passed the test and, after a clear landing, I would head straight to my bedroom to chase the high with deep inhales of Newport cigarettes, exhaling right out my bedroom window.

I wasn't taking penitentiary chances yet, but the consequences would have been just as bad if I was caught. I was a pre-teen with a weed habit out of this world. While most my age were hooked on phonics, I was hooked on chronic. Everyday of the week there was a different weed cipher, from sessions with my man Fat Sal from Prospect to smokeouts with the homie KB.

KB was the homeboy from the 'hood heavy on his chief (smoking). He worked in the barbershop on Grove right behind The Oval. He stumbled on a legit hustle through some old heads and cut hair to earn a dollar. KB lived right around the corner from my Oraton hut, and our sessions outside the 'hood made for a better high. KB and I would grow apart. KB left the weed alone, retired his skills at rolling blunts, and invested his time, effort, and energy into the books. In fact he was the only homie from the 'hood in the same age bracket who went to college and didn't go to prison. KB went on to graduate college and become a successful businessman. Not everybody from the 'hood falls short. His will and determination got him through. While KB never lost focus, I was teaming up with other homies and hotboxing the interior of my landlord's disabled pickup truck, which just happened to be parked in my backyard.

The drug of choice was weed and no one saw it as a habit or a problem. Although, being it was a usual mode of action, it was a habit. And given the things we would do to get high or while high, it proved to be a problem. We didn't care. We would rob, steal, and even skip school. We would wait until our parents left for work and sneak back into the house with a few "friends" and get white-boy wasted. Somehow, we, or at least I, believed the cloud of smoke and the potent smell of weed would disappear before my parents returned. My mother couldn't believe it when she opened my bedroom door and was licked by the contact. She phoned my grandmother all hysterical. To me that was a low blow. I could live with disappointing others but I couldn't see letting down Grandma Nellie. My grandmother spoiled me since I was a toddler and gave me everything I wanted and more. Under one condition—Do right!

By the time I finished middle school, the person I wanted to become looked a lot more promising. Still, I was not above feelings of vulnerability. My parents said it was natural. I was a nervous wreck when I entered VLD's hallways, but I had to go. It was either go or cut and be caught and ultimately feel the wrath of Big YahYah.

On my first day of school, I maintained 'hood tradition and walked into school looking what our parents called "sharp" and we called "fresh to death." The big LEE patch on the back of your jeans was now history. Respectfully, I rocked a pair of deep blue crispy Levi denims, a striped Le Tigre shirt, the latest Nike Air Jordans, and, of course, a fresh haircut. The fade was still in and mine stayed highlighted with my signature hook part.

Already, I was in school because I had to be. I saw no use for school. In my eyes it was a complete waste of time. If you asked me then, a diploma only decided if you worked fast food or pumped gas. My mind was already set; I wasn't doing either. Sad to say but school did little to nothing to show me how the lessons in the classroom applied to real life and the success I dreamed of. So I carried on with the belief football would surely propel me up and out the ghetto and, if it didn't, I believed the lessons the streets gave would get the job done.

Junior high at VLD was the least bit of what I thought it would be. It was just like the 'hood. You had your cliques and so on. It wasn't long before I was running to school.

I was already familiar with the clicks that frequently bumped heads on school grounds like the South Orange Avenue Posse, Halstead Boys, and the Harrison Street Crew. The members of these clicks were adolescents who had barely reached puberty, yet they were already vying for dominion. The only things childish about their quarrels were the grounds where they occurred. I wasn't part of any of these crews. I was neutral in their beefs. This made me plenty popular. I could kick it with members of all sides when they could, yet most were unable. That's because they weren't attending school. VLD became nothing more than a battlefield. For me everything worked out fine. My attention was on the females, and the absence of the bad boys left plenty time to mingle and little competition.

As much as I socialized with the Barbies, my eyes were on one in particular, an eighth grader named Della Gathers. She was a pretty petite somebody out of *Essence* magazine. Her hair was done up in a bob. Della wore fitted jeans with the $54.11 Reeboks. She must've had every color with the socks to match. To me Della was simply gorgeous. It was puppy love from the first day I laid eyes on her. I was just a seventh grader and certainly nowhere near qualified for the real deal of boyfriend and girlfriend, and Della paid me little attention. Yet, I was optimistic. Around mid-school year I caught another cool kid break. I bumped into one of VLD's hippest students, or at least I believed him to be a student. His name was Mylee Cottle.

School was really just a hangout for Mylee. A fitting description for Mylee back then would be a thugged out Fonzy from *Happy Days*. I turned out to be Mylee's protégé. Though Mylee always seemed to have a million other things to do, he always made time to shape and mold my game as a youngster. Mylee even helped me to get my first real girlfriend.

From what I knew of Della, she was a quiet, reserved type. She didn't socialize with many besides her best friend Tahira. Tahira was chocolate and stallion-like for that age, somewhat loud mouthed, and had an attitude and temper like Naomi Campbell. The day Mylee gave me the boost of confidence I needed to approach Della at the far spot in the playground I still didn't know what to say. I had no idea. Game was not my strong suit, so I opted to keep it simple. My nervousness must have been apparent. They both broke into light chuckles before I could say anything. I swear I wanted to turn around and run, but I knew I would have embarrassed not only myself but my middle school mentor Mylee as well.

"I was wondering if I could call you sometime." I finally did it. Now, the only thing left to do was receive my yes or no.

Still giggling, Della replied, "Do you have a pen?" The sound of her voice was a summer's breeze.

I dropped my head, looked up at her, and replied with a smooth Billy Dee/Big Daddy Kane drawl, "Yeah, I have one."

The seven digits were mine and shortly thereafter so was my first love Della Gathers.

Della and I lasted until the summer I was on my way to the ninth grade. For kids this love was real, so it hurt like hell when she called me while I was watching Ralph McDaniel's *Video Music Box* on Channel 31 and told me she was moving miles away to Atlanta. I was heartbroken and filled with anger. I cursed her over and over. Though it wasn't her decision, I was still upset. I blamed her and nearly hated her for it. Just like that, it was over for Della and me.

Eventually, Della moved back to New Jersey, and we even tried to rekindle our puppy love. But by that time my affair with the streets had become my first love. I don't know what ever happened to Della. I truly hope she found the love she deserves.

I was still in school at VLD and playing football. I refused to let that discourage me from learning the ins and outs of street life. My weekends were spent, in full, at

Troub's, Gangsta's, or even J. Black's cribs. Some nights, we'd even say we were staying at one place and ended up at another, or simply running around the Teen Streets until day broke.

On our nights spent Down the Hill before football games the gloves came off. We took to the 'hood as if we owned it. We were twelve-year-old kids with pocketsful of lint and barely enough weed to make it to the morning. If we couldn't scrape up the funds for more weed and intoxicants from the older homeboys, we would resort to whatever measures came to mind. Fearless, heartless, stupid, maybe a blend of them all—when we broke nights, we broke laws.

We would break into the bodegas after they closed at ten o'clock. It didn't matter if we spent the afternoon playing Papi's arcade games or negotiating beef patties on coco bread on credit. Breaking and Entering wasn't our thing but getting money was. With flashlights, a crowbar, two lookouts, and two homies crazy enough to slip through the drop door, hit the register, snatch a few goodies, and do the hundred-yard dash back to our abandoned house in a minute flat, we found ways to quench our thirst for the life. Some nights we would call the Chinese food store or local pizzerias and place a large order and when the delivery arrived, we bumrushed and took what would get us through the night. This slowed down when the law pinched the homie "O" from 4th Avenue and charged him with the death of a pizza deliveryman.

The reckless behavior we delighted in was pure insanity. Playing back the early 90s, though we were old enough to know the difference between right and wrong, I hold the belief the reality of our community, our schools, and our homes created a black cloud that made it hard for us to see clear skies, let alone sunny days. I don't recall a compassionate or optimistic soul in the group. None of us knew what it was to feel. We just hit our teens and were already emotionally numb. Love wasn't about encouragement. It was more or less demonstrated through common struggle. Love was rolling on the enemy for disrespecting a homeboy. Love was spending nights together in abandoned homes and cars. Love was splitting $1.50 turkey sandwiches, without the cheese, from corner store bodegas. Love was breaking down quarter ices. Love was giving your homeboy a fair fight. Like it or love it, this was who the 'hood made us.

On a trip through the Teen Streets with a few homies from Down the Hill, we bent the corner of 18th Street and for the first time I saw Treach of Naughty by Nature in what could be considered all his glory—a pearly white kitted out Benz with a state-of-the-art sound system. A crowd was gathered around blazing rhymes while Treach sat bopping his head, chains swinging and diamond rings glaring.

From what I could see Treach had it made. This was a dude I saw on TV. I was already so infatuated with the grit of Down the Hill, I forgot this was the 'hood where stars were literally born. Especially in the 90s, not too many 'hoods across the globe can attest to having a platinum selling, Grammy Award-winning artist not only grow up in their 'hood but stay in their 'hood even after the fat checks started rolling in. Treach was one of the Grammy Award-winning rap music trio Naughty by Nature— baseball bat carrying, skull cap and lock and chain wearing Down the Hill old heads. Naughty had recently broken into the music industry with their smash hit *O.P.P.* and that led to nearly everyone Down the Hill wanting to be rappers.

Rapping and being a rapper even became another dream of mine. I'd never rapped a day in my life, but seeing firsthand the glitz and glamour it attracted, I secretly began writing rhymes in my spare time.

I was always confident, but when it came to rapping, I was shy as ever. I still remember the day I finally decided to put my rap skills to the test. The day before at football practice, Troub, Gangsta, and a few others told me after school they were going to pop off with some kids from the other side of town—whose crew went by the name NSKG, which stood for North Side Killer Gangstas. NSKG represented most of East Orange's north side by Park Avenue, Walnut Street, Arlington Avenue, and other back blocks. In the early 90s—from 1990 to 1992—NSKG was not yet gang-affiliated.

Troub was already attending Hart Middle, the other middle school in East Orange, with most of the homies from Down the Hill, so he was pretty much "in." I attended VLD and was not all the way "in" with the 'hood. Nevertheless, I promised I would be there when school let out. I left school early and hit Hamilton Street where Hart Middle School was located.

Hart Middle was comprised of three buildings for grades six through eight. Just the sight of this supposed educational complex brought to mind prison. The security guards and beat-walkers from the local police department patrolled a bunch of eleven-, twelve-, and thirteen-year olds like convicts. And like convicts we carried on. It's ironic we would become what? Prisoners.

I saw Gangsta, Mad Dog, and a couple more homies from Down the Hill posted up outside the school. Mad Dog was a light-skin and light-eyes basketball-playing bad boy with a little weight on him from his many trips to the Youth House. Mad Dog would much rather get into some shit than utilize his gift on the court. The things the ghetto did to the young I will never understand.

Some knew I would be there, others looked surprised to see me. At this point, to most, I was just a kid from the football team. I was determined to show I was "down," and I was ready for whatever. We stood around kicking it until school began to let out. All the homies seemed so cool and collected, as if this was a regular occurrence. Later, I would learn it was. My adrenaline was pumping. My heart was racing, not from fear but from feeling this would be the day I didn't simply get in where I fit in, but I'd fit in wherever I went.

After all the anticipation, only three to five dudes exited the school. The others decided to slide out the back exit. Good for them, I thought, but bad for those who stayed. Before I could even blink, Mad Dog recognized one of them and rushed to get his man and chaos seemed to erupt. We chased the remaining few until we caught them and laid down our muscle game. Overall, the brawl was simple; it wasn't the kind I thought it would be—Braveheart style, where dudes went blow for blow and everywhere you turned someone was getting up after being knocked down. Still, after these sorts of scuffles we bragged about and compared our war wounds. If you came out with none, you probably weren't in as deep as you were supposed to be.

I see now just how far I was willing to go to belong. There was no limit, because I saw no consequences. The feeling of belonging took precedence over anything else in my world. I loved my parents and knew they wouldn't see my actions in the best light. However, as a child, I was in search of a different form of love. The love I received at *home* could never compare to the love of my *homies*. Neither outweighed the other, but there were many differences—differences many failed to realize.

With home being the main source of influence for a child, in most cases, it is home where the good, the bad, and the ugly will be discovered. Influence in the home is major. In instances where it is not, examples are set directly, indirectly, or both, in the streets. With no guidance, children become lost in the wilderness when home fails. What is spilled in and out of the home is soaked up by our children or cleaned up on the corner. Numbers don't lie. Statistics show "broken" homes produced the most children with ill will. My home wasn't broken but my community was in need of repair and its ills seeped into my residence and my curiosity trickled into the streets.

It was hard to establish your own identity within your home. Parents believed they had it all figured out and knew exactly what was best for you based on what they went through. It's true that education and morals play a major role in one's upbringing. But at home, they tried so hard to deter you from the evils of the world we'd eventually still grow up to see that they ended up handicapping us. The struggle was inevitable and couldn't be escaped. You were affected either directly or indirectly. Parents did their best to hide you from the real world, while the homies pumped you up to confront it. Homies didn't believe in running; either you faced your fears and overcame them or you fell flat on your face attempting to escape them. Parents' desperate attempts at being protective were exactly what pushed us kids in search of reality, which most often led us to the homies. And that's where I ended up, right back with the homies.

After the light scuffle and a brief police chase, we mobbed back in the direction of the 'hood. When we hit Park Avenue and Oraton Parkway, we ran into a rap battle. Out of all of us, the only ones who ever rapped were Gangsta and Bad Newz.

Bad Newz was bad news. Most said he resembled a young Treach of Naughty by Nature. Seven days a week Newz was dressed in sagging Dickies khakis, flannel shirts, cornrow braids down his back, and a red rag draped from his right pocket. At heart, Newz was a born rapper. At least until the ugly of a crime- and drug-infested neighborhood wore on his aspirations of some day owning a crowd with one of his many straight off the top verses. His dreams of becoming the next best thing were almost answered when he made his debut on a Naughty by Nature album, spitting a verse that not only gained him 'hood notoriety but added fuel to the raging fire with our beef with the Little City Ruffnecks from the Little City Projects. These were the same projects where my father was from and I was partially raised. All it took was one line, "little cities get mashed out," and the beef was on. I think it's safe to say that one line brought out the big guns, literally; big guns that would never be put away. As I write this book from the clutches of Federal prison, so sits Bad Newz for possession of an illegal firearm.

I told homies about my rhyming, but had yet to step out there. After our scuffle with NSKG, I was feeling good, as if I was one of the crew, so I decided to jump in. After a few bars, I was amazed as the bystanders gave a few oohs and ahhs. Following the session, Gangsta told me he and a kid who recently moved down South were in a group called The Gutter Ratz and he felt I had what it took to be down. At the same time, Bad Newz made it clear he and Treach's relative Headache had gone their separate ways and he didn't mind collaborating. By the time we reached the 'hood, it had been established that me, Gangsta, and Newz would hold it down as The Gutter Ratz until the fourth member of our group returned.

Contrary to what many believed, The Gutter Ratz wasn't established to be a gang or anything of the sort. Still it was labeled as such very early on. The Gutter Ratz was simply a group of kids who decided to take rapping seriously, in hopes of making it to the top of the charts.

To many, inking a rap deal wasn't one of the easier things to do, sort of like making it as a professional athlete. But we dreamed big. We also had an advantage, since our old heads weren't your average old heads. Our old heads (Naughty by Nature) were already established artists, making their impact on the music industry. The blueprint wasn't hard to follow: write rhymes, write rhymes, and write more rhymes.

The Gutter Ratz gradually became more than a music group. It also became the name of the click we formed as juveniles. Among the click you had those who formed the rap group.

Growing up, The Gutter Ratz as a click was always bonded, at least for the most part. Still, there were groups within the click. As with anything, those who identified better with one another tended to run together, and in the 'hood this often equated to those who robbed robbing together, those who hustled hustling together, those who loved to get high, getting high and doing nothing else together—and then of course you had the rappers. I wouldn't call them separate clicks or subsets like others in the neighborhood. Regardless of similarities or differences GRatz were always GRatz. The three or four GRatz here and five or six GRatz there was normal in the 'hood and never seen as separation.

Anywhere Down the Hill there rested a grimy looking and scheming pack of GRatz always into something. We traveled near and far, sporting our custom nylon jackets embroidered with our name and our click (GRatz), so we could be easily identified. We wanted you to know who we were and what we represented. Thanks to the homie Headache who lived with Treach and was able to get his hands on Naughty's contact for an Adidas rep, the GRatz even had official Adidas t-shirts (logo, label, and all). I highly doubt Adidas was aware its brand name was attached to a group of juvenile delinquents.

Little did Adidas know, GRatz were running the town sticking up cab drivers, breaking and entering, and beating up fiends. We would do anything in the day to ensure we could party at night. Party meant a boom box, at least forty ounces of Old English, and two-for-five dust bags of stress weed.

It was 1992 and we were still young, though a lot of the homies already took to the corners and began hustling just to get by. Back then the hustle wasn't major. You'd come up with a couple dollars by robbing, stealing, bagging groceries, or saving lunch money—you name it. Those funds went straight to the Weed Man to make a quick flip.

During those times, coke and heroin were a big man's game. And although we were now established as the youngsters around the way, we had yet to earn enough stripes to enter that lane. Gangsta, Bad Newz, and I had yet to pick up a pack. It was very tempting, seeing homies with pockets full of money, while we walked around broke writing rhymes, rhymes, and more rhymes.

Truth be told, it seemed as if we were getting no closer to our dreams while everyone around us was living the life. Other GRatz who didn't rap sensed our frustration and promised to look out for us who did rap as much as possible, if we stuck to our guns. They financed studio sessions and the proper stimulants (weed and alcohol) to keep us content while in the studio for hours. The homies would pay for countless studio hours, and we all used the studio as an escape—an opportunity to get away and release all the pinned-up emotions and frustrations. Though it seemed small, just weed, alcohol, and studio money, the homies' intentions were good and it meant a lot to me. They were sacrificing and doing whatever to feed their families and themselves, while taking our dreams into consideration as well. The little they did kept us out of harm's way and enhanced our chances of success.

The summer of '92 hit and Naughty by Nature was about to hit the road and tour. As bad as we wanted to go, the GRatz were shot down. Was Naughty by Nature not taking us on tour really just another excuse and example of the youth being brushed off and not taken seriously? Just like the outside world, Naughty either failed to acknowledge our potential or altogether ignored it. That "work on your demo and keep writing" shit were lines dropped by industry A&Rs to artists they barely knew or did not know at all. Yet, here were the older homeboys from our 'hood who made it in the industry feeding us that garbage. It couldn't be. Was "not right now" all we were worth?

Even at twelve, thirteen, and fourteen years old, the 'hood schooled us well, we knew "not right now" meant never. After continuously catching these foul balls, members of the GRatz such as Snoop, Boot Rat, and Skrap set caution to the wind and began voicing the truth we had been avoiding. If we were to make it, running around looking for a handout wasn't going to do it. At one point, we were so frustrated tension boiled over and for a short period of time members of the GRatz began physically beefing with Naughty and members of their inner circle.

In the early 1990s, my generation witnessed the rise, success, and global fame of rap stars. It was only natural many from the 'hood began to look at rap as the ticket out. Rapping was one of few and for some the only example of success they knew. East Orange was the home of superstars such as Whitney Houston, Naughty by Nature, Queen Latifah, The Fugees, and others. Their success raised the bar in terms of how my generation viewed success. We yearned for the opportunity to take the stage and show our older homeboys and the world what we had in store.

Nevertheless, we were left behind and told to work on our demo and to have it ready upon Naughty's return. Crunch time! We were no longer in the studio recreationally. We were now officially attempting to get things on and popping. We began including homies who didn't rap on hooks, skits, and ad-libs. Within every song, we screamed, "Gutter Ratz." It was our movement. After all, it was the homies' encouragement and financial support that got us to this point. We didn't have just one demo ready—we had about three or four demos lined up, including beats we'd constructed on our own.

While we waited for Naughty's return—whenever we weren't in the studio—we were down on the Avenue. Gangsta would mack with his relatives, while I continued to get familiar with the 'hood and began to see firsthand the money that fattened homies' pockets and financed our studio sessions. We most definitely had to develop callousness in order to endure the sights we would see on a daily basis. Life would wear and tear, and eventually found a way to destroy the best of them.

In the 'hood we called this hustlers and habits. Over time, many got addicted to the fast life, but believe me when I say this: Most began playing the game because they could no longer take the game playing them.

Some of the purest intentions became obscure in the fight to *survive*. So while Troub and I prided ourselves on being *survivors*, we would not close our eyes until we both had truly *lived*.

The truth hurts, but where I'm from, poverty was everywhere and opportunities were scarce. Inner-city schools dumbed down the curriculum and played on the intelligence of urban youth to receive some sort of grant or bonus in the name of the schools and their supposed achievements. The money never seemed to make its way into the schools; at least as students we did not see any notable changes. The community would see no after-school programs intended to keep children focused and enthusiastic about education. These monies were most likely awarded then re-routed in some slick way to adults, not children. Overall education became a watered-down process. Without challenge, kids found themselves in search of alternatives. Sad to say, if you lacked a wicked jump shot, chances were you had a pocket full of crack rock. Without a pot to piss in or a window to throw it out of, the means were disregarded as the end drew closer.

Throughout the summer, The GRatz grew thicker, brutalizing the back blocks and claiming our turf. Some of us still played football for the Rams but no longer went to practice. We used that time for smoke sessions and to construct more songs. We were so consumed with writing rhymes and doing what we had to do to support our growing weed habit the only time we saw the football field was for game time.

It wouldn't be long before Naughty's tour ended, and our music business seemed straight. But as a member of the GRatz, I had yet to find my stage name. We threw names back and forth while playing a game of H-O-R-S-E (a basketball shoot-around game) when Bad Newz yelled, "I got it! Massacre! That's it! That's your name. I'm going to call you Massacre."

I never really gave it much thought. I was just honored to have a homie who spit rhymes the way Newz did bless me with an alias, and so I ran with it. Instantly, my life changed. I was no longer Lil T, T-Broke from Carnegie, Lil YahYah, or even Tewhan. I was now Massacre, the rapper. My next mission was to make sure the rest of the world knew it.

Armed with a can of spray paint, I tagged "Massacre" everywhere I went. I rapped it in every song. I dropped it on every girl I met. In the 'hood more often than not people called themselves something other than what was listed on their birth certificate, so it didn't come across as too crazy. But to be honest, it did take me some time to build up the heart to say my new name when asked, "Who's calling?" by a female friend's parents. There were times when I was thought to be a prank caller and hung up on. Nevertheless, Massacre was here to stay.

3

LET'S GET IT STARTED

I HAD BEEN AROUND hustlers my entire life in one form or another and though I was only thirteen years old and still developing my street smarts, I felt it was time to see if I had what it took to make the game go good. I knew the most important part would be to secure a "connect" (a supplier). I already had that piece of the puzzle. The same guy I'd meet on a regular basis to cop my weed always talked about the amounts of "weight" he sold. I always wondered why he made it his business to tell me this every time I popped up. I knew what the deal was, but I was barely coming up with the five dollars it took to purchase a nickel bag. But the day I arrived and pressed him about this "weight," he told me: "I knew your day would come, Lil Rude Boy. I see the hunger in your eyes. You gon' be big."

I took it in stride. I remained silent and waited to conduct business. I wanted to be the best at everything I did, and the game would be no different. Still, at the time, this wasn't a career move for me; it was just something to keep me flying high until The GRatz blew up. Still dreaming big, I went from dreams of professional football and rap super stardom to picking up a pack!

I was a bit naïve at the time to comprehend the full extent of the consequences of the life I was choosing, but the reality was, right at that moment when I made the decision to get in the game, the streets began to dictate my potential. It wouldn't be long before I began telling myself every day, "Just one more flip, and I'll be good." I wasn't purchasing pounds or anywhere near. I kept the baggage as light as possible. But I remembered a jewel dropped on me a while back: "It's all in the flip."

After every $50 or so I made, I was back at my man's doorstep to purchase another half-ounce of weed. Some days were so good I was able to flip my money two to three times. Sitting on work wasn't what hustlers did, and they call it grinding for a reason. You didn't always double your money, but the pace with which you turned your money over determined your earnings. And your earning potential was only as great as what you could supply. The more you could supply the more customers you could serve. There was no shortage of demand. These quick flips were key to accumulating profits. It was always important to stay on top of inventory and keep stock replenished as it flew off the shelves like a good sale at the local Walmart. A true businessman knows when to place his order and knows there must be supply to satisfy the demand or risk losing his customer to the competition.

Compared with what I had seen going on around me, I considered myself smooth. When I was on the block, I didn't do crowds and never kept anything on me. It was straight grind mode. Running back and forth to the stash was tiring, but it kept me out of the Youth House. Sometimes I would watch fights jump off after one homie stunted as if he didn't see another run to his stash to get product and instead served the customer while the other was gone. I never tripped. I wasn't on the corner for problems. I was out there for a dollar.

Money and murder might go hand in hand, but they damn sure don't mix. And if it didn't make dollars, it didn't make sense. Besides, I understood that no matter how deep I'd gotten in, I wasn't originally from the Ave and my rites of passage would always be an issue, so I kept my mouth shut and stuck to the script—a script that read *Money, Money,* and *Mo' Money.*

While out nickel and diming I watched out not only for police and customers, but I paid close attention to the old heads and the way they moved. One in particular always caught my attention. He was small in stature, but big in heart. His distinctive qualities were like none other. Girls and guys alike would flock to him as if 6th Avenue was a reservation and he was the Chief—Malik Triplett *aka* Whip Wop, the big homie of the 'hood. Whip just sat around, shot dice, and kicked it, while directing traffic and collecting money. For those who wanted to be hustlers, Whip had the blueprint. Watching him, I knew if hustling was what it was going to be, that was the way to do it.

Whip was of a different caliber, with a low-key demeanor. He stayed in designer garb but never really wore jewelry. Honestly, he did not need jewelry to shine. His aura was bright enough in itself. Triple beams and money machines were what Whip was about. Side by side with a team of bosses that included Pedro, Black, Fat Tee, Mel, Mutt, Reek, and a few others, they comprised a vicious crew and made hella money and spent it well. Still, Whip wasn't too fancy. He opted to drive a black Nissan Pathfinder and would hit the strip in crispy Guess denim, Timberland boots, a Coogi sweater, and swag for days. Whip was both the problem and the problem solver.

Growing up in the 'hood among Naughty and legendary street hustlers like Whip, most of the younger homies from my generation moved with a chip on our shoulders, yet still had a quiet but pronounced confidence and the highest of expectations when it came to getting money. It was pick your poison: become a rapper like Naughty or a baller like Whip. It was either tearing down sold-out stadiums and arenas or castrating the corner, hard-balling on the back blocks. Either was monumental and held the same weight in the 'hood. As youngsters, those we looked up to admired and respected both. Both represented power. And as young boys we all wanted to be powerful.

I know after I tucked away my football gear, I wanted to be a different type of baller—a kingpin, king of the city, something like Whip. Though Whip was never seen indulging in undisciplined conduct, the majority of us GRatz were under the impression the more we participated in brash activity, we were being made rougher and tougher. Subconsciously, I guess we were preparing ourselves for the deadly games to come with following in the footsteps of 'hood stars like Whip.

I remember GRatz banded together in alleyways peering out into the intersections of the Ave and salivating over the thousands of dollars exchanged for pure product. A large portion of the cash flow was headed straight to Whip's pockets. This dude was the boss. There were times when we were so fed up watching all the money change hands we jacked a customer or two. Sometimes Whip would run us off the block and chase us off porches, from the corners, and down alleyways to prevent us from disrupting his flow. Other times, he would get a laugh out of us. Everybody always came with the extra trying to impress Whip.

I remember Whip taking time out to school us to the game and make sure we knew we had a choice. Everybody didn't have to become a hustler. Nothing was wrong with going to school and hitting the books, he would say. By the same token he made it clear—if you chose the streets then you best be thorough, take no shit, and keep money on your mind. Many may disagree with Whip being the example, but in the 'hood we didn't look up to doctors, lawyers, cops, and teachers. We looked up to those we knew who made gains, accumulated wealth, and achieved success in their own right.

By this time Naughty returned from tour. They heard our demos and still told us to "keep writing." However, when Naughty returned that summer of Nineteen Naughty Three they came back with two new pieces to the puzzle—The Road Dawgz.

The Road Dawgz was a rap group from Inglewood, California. One member of the Road Dawgz was True G who stood about 6 feet 3 inches, light skinned, with a slim build. The other was Luv Child aka G-Luv. Luv was a poster child gangbanger with long braids, sagging Dickies, Chuck Taylors, and a Cali drawl: "What's hannin' Blood?" They, like us in the East, were writing rhymes trying to make it out the ghetto and luck struck for them on Naughty's tour.

The connection between Naughty and the Road Dawgz was strictly business, and not any of the hoopla spread by the media over the years. The plan was to bring the Road Dawgz to the East to produce an album. This connection also birthed the Double ii, minus Blood. Double ii was a musical alliance similar in nature to Snoop's Dogg Pound, BIG's Junior Mafia, or today's YMBCMB. The alliance was groundbreaking and epic. Previously, most alliances were based on neighborhood or region. The ii connection spanned the nation and symbolized the coming together of individuals from Inglewood, California, and Illtown (East Orange), New Jersey.

When Luv and True came to the 'hood from Inglewood, they didn't throw Blood into our faces. It was simply who and what they were. The decision was all our own, and that made them all the more respectable. It wasn't a situation where they were looking for anything to gain, or searching for ways to make another's life anything other than better. It was simple, though we grew up thousands of miles apart and experienced different things, we were one and the same. Just like us, or us just like them, I remember watching True blend in among our own playing basketball in The Oval daily, dunking on homies like Tracy McGrady. I remember how Luv took to the Block knee-deep in ciphers of all kinds guzzling 40 ounces, mad as hell to be smoking East Coast weed. No disrespect to the Rastas who mostly controlled the weed trade in the East at the time, but we all know that Cali bud was Cali love. Luv was on the East Coast spitting lyrics like "straight through the alleys and the valleys of Centinela, now I'm hella tight when I rip and grip mics. I kick the type of shit that Damus and Crips like."

Luv and True loved how life Down the Hill in Illtown was frontline. All day, everyday each corner of the 'hood was crowded with homies on the hang out and hustle, which was much different than what they were used to back in the West. By this time in the early 90s corner hanging was a thing of the past in Cali thanks to the notorious drive by shootings and killings of the 80s. Things were different in the East, but True and Luv came to the 'hood and jumped right in like it was exactly where they belonged—with the family.

The summer of '93 was the first summer of a united Inglewood and Illtown, the bi-coastal alliance formed to change the rap game. Naughty by Nature already had hits like "OPP" and "Everything's Gonna Be Alright (Ghetto Bastard)" and was turning it up in the industry even further with a second album and the anthem *Hip Hop Hooray*. However, the summer of '93 was also the first of many summers where the GRatz and Road Dawgz would hear "keep writing" from Naughty.

Luv and True's trip to the East to solidify their names in the music industry eventually resulted in a couple features on Naughty albums and just kicking it in the 'hood with homies on the daily with nothing more to do. I can't speak on the actions of others, or the lack thereof, but it turned out the long conversation between Naughty and Luv's big brother Squeek Ru from California's Neighborhood Piru back in '92 turned out to be nothing more than a long conversation. Day after day as the Road Dawgz chopped it up in the East you could see the frustration on their faces as their trip amounted to nothing. Then again, I can't say "nothing" because if this trip was never made I wouldn't be who I am today. As a result of that summer, I not only gained two big brothers but also a horde of brothers from the other side of the map.

True and Luv became 'hood legends. Illtown, Down the Hill owes much to them. Part of our identity belongs to them. Our East Coast attitudes and West Coast demeanor was born when they arrived. They were not stereotypical gang-bangers but men; men who cared and opened their lives and hearts to total strangers. We were a bunch of kids who they saw traveling the same direction. They embraced us and we embraced them. Time brought about physical separation and communication died down as they were forced to travel back to California.

Back in California, the Road Dawgz later linked up with Inglewood's own Mack 10 to release an album on his Hoo Banging Records.

I never got the chance to express my appreciation, my gratitude, my love, my honor, and my respect to the comrades in the West on behalf of the 'hood. I thank True and Luv and those who enlightened them *and each and every member from the Q.*

I must admit the summer of '93 changed not only my life but the pulse of my entire neighborhood forever. It marked the transition from one stage to the next. While I was out hustling and chasing a million, I and other members of the GRatz, along with many others from the various clicks Down the Hill such as the Ignorant Individuals, the Steel Click, and EOM, picked up none other than our red rags and gracefully tucked them into our back pockets. My rag was my badge of honor for the world to see, to be recognized and respected. When I picked up my red rag, it instantly became my way of life, my culture, my everything. For some, it represented fashion or a fad, while for others, we breathed, ate, and slept Blood.

Not to be mistaken: the Blood I'm speaking of was not in your music videos, on your radio stations, or in your magazines. The Blood I'm talking about was out holding down its turf; doing whatever needed to be done to ensure each day was not the last. It was far from a game. It was life or death, predator and prey. Though it was much deeper, the wrong colors in the wrong neighborhood could get you missing. Failing to embrace the culture in full could make you a memory. In my 'hood, you didn't choose Blood. Blood chose you. It was never what you could gain; rather it was what you had to offer: your life, if necessary, frontline sacrificing, life sentences, you name it.

When I got put on, the law was simple: tolerate disrespect from no one and nothing—and I do mean nothing—comes before Blood. The code of the streets still applied. We did it for our turf and our turf did it for Blood. Double ii Bloods, to be exact. In '93, our roots were planted. It was Inglewood to Illtown.

In the 'hood, we cared about two things: dough stacking and representing that Blood gang. From its origins in California in the late 60s and early 70s, Blood finally made its way into our lives. And our acceptance of the culture gave us the strength to stand on what we believed in and fed us with an undeniable power like never before.

Until then, I fooled myself into believing our 'hood unity was unmatched, but in reality it was only a façade. We would come together when need be and allowed no one to cross one of our own, but everyone seemed all over the place—one book with many chapters that resulted in almost everyone being on a different page.

It was nothing to see homies tripping on homies. Since the Civil Rights Movement, unity ceased to exist. Every man was for himself. That's how we were raised, so when we were introduced to a way of life built on principle, law, and camaraderie, we were instantly attracted. Prior to, nobody was attached to anything of substance—outside of his or her immediate clicks—and even that was questionable. The way I saw it, everybody was trying to get ahead and anybody other than self was in the way.

So here we were, the blind leading the blind. Then came structure, a foundation on which we could build, something to call our own that—no matter how hard they tried—couldn't be taken away. It was our very own something with which we could identify, so when the underlying currents of Blood hit our neighborhood in '93, it represented a returning to the essence. There no longer existed bandits, strays, or outlaws. When that flag flew, it took on the qualities of a banner; an umbrella that sheltered us from division, individualism, and separatist ideals, just as it did with the many gangs in California during their rise. It symbolized oneness within our neighborhood. This wasn't the 60s and 70s, where "Black People United" was the thing; this was the 90s and black-on-black crime was on the rise. So even though the unity I'm talking about was based primarily on our sole neighborhood, it stood for a lot. Nothing was heard when nothing was spoken, but when the truth was voiced, it was followed by action. And in this case, Blood was the truth we needed to support our cause and urge us into action.

To many, Blood was seen as the worst thing to ever happen to New Jersey. But for those of us who picked up our flags for the right reasons, Blood was like a blessing. Blood solidified our family, a brotherhood, the coming together of similarities and differences. If need be, we were to feed, clothe, live, lie, or even die for one another. For us, Blood didn't mean let's run out and kill a bunch of Crips. Blood was more about us than anything. We identified with the culture, so we embraced it full-fledged.

As far as Bloods and Crips were concerned, gang banging was non-existent when Blood initially touched New Jersey. In '93 there were no Crip sets, and there were no other Blood sets. All of our banging took place between us and them—them being different neighborhoods in town we'd already been warring with over turf, girls, money, and just flat out representing. However, when our flags came out and we started representing the B, the very few areas and clicks we didn't have beef with began to join in with the others.

In these times, becoming a Blood was the most unpopular thing you could do and the Double ii Bloods were certainly hated. Nobody—and I do mean nobody—dared to understand the transformation that took place. Not only did we adopt something no one else was doing, we adopted something from the other side of the map—California and the West Coast. And this was the 90s- West Coast rap was in its golden era. Ghetto America on both coasts was claiming its roots. So being on the East Coast and aligning with the homies out of Inglewood and the West, we were viewed as traitors, like we committed treason. But contrary to what anyone chose to believe, we were never part of what anyone else was doing. When asked if we cared, the answer was always, "Hell no!" It was what we called "Mind over matter"—we didn't mind because they didn't matter. We weren't doing it for others; we were doing it for us, our family. We were all we had and we carried it as such. To those on the outside, we may have been a bunch of kids throwing up gang signs and sporting colors, while to us Blood was so much more. We understood each other and that understanding made us exactly what we were willing to shed for one another: BLOOD.

The fact that we were ready and willing to bring it to anyone who opposed us, or anybody who wanted a taste, fueled our drive. We took the approach we felt we needed and did what we thought we were to do, as Bloods. We grew up with the impression that muscle in motion was the way to go, so when we began flying our colors, it was whatever and however. We were confident that no matter how many linked up in an attempt to bring us a move, as long as we stayed together, we would come out on top. And in doing so, our "We don't give a fuck" attitude was enhanced.

We didn't just jump into a world of violence, although we were no strangers to it. The many other neighborhood clicks and their attempts to back us into a corner was what kept us prepped and primed as youngsters. These wars were extremely serious. We hadn't yet reached the extent of using guns, though there were always one or two around. The market for guns hadn't fully opened up, so instead, we improvised by using anything else a person could get their hands on: bats, brass knuckles, chains, hammers, homemade shanks, screwdrivers, steak knives, ninja swords—you name it.

We had our fair share of bad breaks, but it was our ability to bounce right back that added to our credibility as young gangsters. These demonstrations gave us a sense of invincibility. We enjoyed representing, putting it down as Y.G.z and holding it up for the O.G.z and all in between. Whenever something popped off—no matter how close or how far, they knew it was the GRatz.

Our willingness to get it up for the 'hood earned us the respect of the older homies, but at the same time they would get on our case. I was confused at how our "living the life" upset some of the older homies, and I went to kick it with my bigger homie True out of Inglewood, who was now living among us in the East, for a bit of guidance and insight.

Walking William Street from Munn Ave to 6th Ave, I passed through the entire 'hood. Right up the street from Murda Ave, you had New Street. The New Ave Gangstaz (NAG'z) formed shortly after the GRatz on my childhood block—New Street. New Ave Gangstaz for the most part were close in age to the GRatz. Their strength was never in numbers. They made their mark putting it down when it was necessary and other times for recreation. The NAG'z were made up of the homies Bash, Milkman, Bompton, and Devil.

Holding down the top of the hill from the intersection of Grove and William down to the old Stockton School was the almighty 153rd Steel Click. With the likes of Auto, Buckshot, Chip, Dream, Flocko, Gator, Man, Ratman, Soup, Tall Dog, Trigger Slash, and others. The Steel Click was strong in numbers and an army unto themselves with the likes of East Orange Mafia (E.O.M.).

Continuing down William Street you'd go right into 18th Street or the Block, the home of legends. Not just 'hood hustle game legends like Mook Daddy and Lil Steve—true older homies from the Block who took a fall federally for running a major crack operation on 18th Street right around the time Naughty by Nature took off—18th Street was the home to Naughty. Treach and Kay Gee grew up on the block and Treach lived on the Block even after success in the music industry. The Block was nonstop action, a parade of celebrities, groupies, gangsters, hustlers, fiends, you name it. The Block was legendary.

When Naughty by Nature would throw their infamous summer block parties of the 1990s on 18th Street, the Block would be flooded with people from all over the globe and more females than a little bit.

On days when the party speakers were stored away and the outside celebrities went back to their day-to-day, perfect strangers dared not turn onto 18th Street. On any given day, the Block was like Trump Plaza on one porch and Amateur Night at the Apollo on the next.

There sat Vic Tuff, one of the 'hood's most illustrious hustlers. Anything from cards, dice to pitching quarters, you name it, Vic Tuff would play the Block from sun up till sun down looking for somebody, anybody to hustle. Ten- and eleven-year-old ghetto boys were fair game and just as venturous and conniving. Never mind school, young'uns like Quan, G-Reek, Lil Lionel, and Nerve Body (RIP) would be out on the Block at two and three in the morning. The only education they cared for was math. If it totaled 21 Blackjack, three of a kind, or a full house it equaled dollar signs and no mistakes were made.

Next door on another porch or in a driveway sat Big BooYa with a car or a double cassette boom box supplying the beats. Homies like Devious and Trife formed a two-man rap group and a click of their own. Why? Because in the early 90s rapping was the only avenue the young had to freely express themselves. In addition to expressing yourself, one hoped their talent and potential would be recognized, a record deal would follow, and the burdens that came with being a ghetto bastard would vanish.

18th Street had it all, including the Block's young tenders Wop, Hassana, and Sharonda, the love interests of all the young homies who played the Block. All three were light skin, except for Sana who was a pure red bone, with ponytails, feisty attitudes, and pretty smiles.

The RudeBoyz and the LDz (Living Dead) played 16th Street and William. They were a rare breed of soldiers who lived Down the Hill but originally hailed from the West Indies and South America. Most of the homies from 16th Street were Guyanese like Butcha, Peabody, Rude Boy, Saddes, Weasel, among others and were relatives of some of the old head dreads from the hood like Dex, Shaka, and Wraga.

Fifteenth Street was home to the Ignorant Individualz in the likes of Beemo, Big Clay, Ern, Evo, Krutty, Nate, Streetz, and others who played 15th Street like their predecessors Big Hak, DyDy, Gut, Tech, and others. During my youth, the Ignorant Individualz ranged in age from seventeen to twenty-five. The Ignorant Individualz and the Steel Click took no shorts. These two clicks produced some of the 'hood's most notorious. Everything about the way they settled their beefs was grown man. Also on 15th Street was rude boy Texi and a few other dreads.

Fourteenth Street was where William Street turned into 6th Avenue or the Ave and East Orange became Newark. The Ave was where the hustlers dwelled. Sixth Ave was one of the top strips in Newark when it came to the circulation of drug money. It ran neck and neck with spots like Prince Street, Hayes Homes, Bradley Court, and Little Bricks. Over the years, the Ave went through names like "Pill Hill," "Baby New York," and "Little L.A." because of the non-stop traffic that flowed. It didn't matter what time of day or night; the strip was always live.

The list of young black ghetto entrepreneurs who played the Ave went on and on, from the likes of Original Gangsters, such as "Magnetic," "Beeb," "Harold," "Whip" and "Alkabir" to families like the Spencers and the Tripletts. Now I had the opportunity to be thrust upon that list, and I had no plans of spoiling it by thinking small. The risks and consequences that came with the game were becoming more apparent but so were its short-term returns, in large sums. I felt if we were going to risk prison terms or death out here on these corners, the rewards had to be worthwhile. The only thing I saw that made any sense was money, money, and mo' money—lots of it.

The 'hood's Middle Bar was on the Ave between 14th and 13th Street. Homies like Squeak and Lil Man (Sidewalk Soldiers) played the townhouses on 13th Street.

Twelfth Street held another group of rude boys, mostly Jamaican. Homies like Bigga, Mermaid, Monarch, Peanut, Rooney, and Teach. The 'hood's rude boys went hard with the hustle and were equally as vicious and in some instances even more wicked when it came to holding down the 'hood and keeping the D.T.H. MOB in a class by itself.

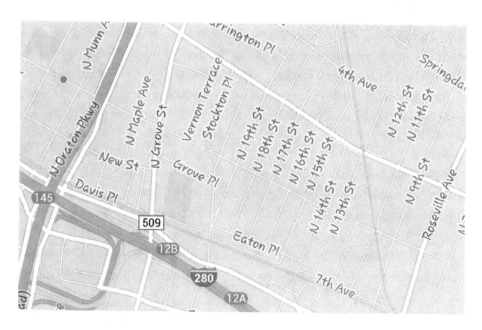

In total, the D.T.H. MOB formed like Voltron and numbered in hundreds. Let alone all those on the outside willing to do whatever it took for a chance to become a part of the family. Each block segued into the other. Each click segued into the next.

The natural structure in the 'hood was indicative of age, geography, and the torch passing from one generation to the next. We all shared the duty and responsibility to maintain respect for the neighborhood.

When I pulled up on True, it was as if he knew what I wanted. As we sat and got faded, he went in:

"Check it out young homie. It ain't all about running the streets and putting in work. Don't get me wrong—if you have to eat, eat. I can't knock you for that, but know that when it comes to this flag, it must be respected first and foremost. We have homeboys who have died for this Blood gang; homies who will never see the streets again behind what we're repping. Without question, young homie, protect, defend, and rep the 'hood by all means, but know that for every action there's a reaction. So when you're out committing or indulging in senseless acts, know that the tables will turn."

"This life we live was never about a color, because both sides want the same thing: a way out," he said. "It was the means that created the problems. When one's means to an end interrupted another's, things got violent. And once the guns started busting, it was hard for them to stop. As time went on, our color took on a meaning of its own. RED: it represented the color of blood, for all our fallen homies, just as it represents the ultimate sacrifice—what we must be ready to shed for one another."

I told him how we were getting it up with these other neighborhoods and how nobody seemed to understand Blood or its purpose. What he explained to me next made all the sense in the world:

"Dig this young homie. If you're a person who knows struggle when you see struggle, it's only right that you embrace it. If you're one who truly desires camara-derie, when you see it, you embrace it. Why? Because you identify. It's not about the hardships, trials, or tribulations getting there. It's about the deep-rooted understand-ing of what the next homie is going through and possessing a want and need to see each other out. Contrary to what anyone believes, there are unseen footprints in the sand and a guiding force carrying us through life. What is meant to be will be, life is not a lie."

"Have you ever looked at the similarities between Jersey and Cali?" he asked.

"No, why?" I answered.

"Well," he replied, "just as Cali had its many different street gangs, like The Businessmen, The Gladiators, Brims, and Green Jackets, y'all have just as many: The GRatz, Ignorant Individualz, Steel Click, Ruff Necks, Zoo Crew, etc. The gang culture in both states existed before the Red and Blue. On another note, both states rose to the occasion with the riots in the 60s because both experienced the same struggles. And though headquarters was in the West, both sides took to the militancy, structure, and discipline of the Black Panther Party, just as both the brothers and sisters of that movement experienced the evil hands of the government with their divide-and-conquer tactics dealt out through the CoIntelPro."

He continued. "See, young homie, we have been identifying and fighting with each other since way back when, so it seems only right that this wave [Blood] brushed ashore. It was only a matter of time. But I say all that to say this: When you're out rocking that red flag, rock it with pride and understand all that comes with it."

I took it all in stride and saw things a lot differently after that day. The way I would push it as a Blood would be in accordance with the only way. In the meantime, when I wasn't out banging, I was hustling. I knew that to be successful at it, I had to stay off the police's radar—but once something jumped off, all that went right out of the window.

The school year was right around the corner and I was set to begin my freshman year at East Orange High School, the same high school my father had attended. As GRatz, there was no way we could enter anyone's school without being dressed to impress. The Dickie suits and Naughty Gear were cool, but as freshmen in high school, we were walking into a world where everyone sported the latest, which at the time was Guess, Polo, Girbaud, Champion hoodies, black college (HBCU) sweatshirts, and Timberland boots.

We didn't lose sight of our roots and where we came from, but when it came to fashion, some things were hot and others were not. Still, the problem wasn't putting the mix in motion; it was the fashion and the effort we would have to put in to secure the funds we needed to keep it looking good, especially in school. I had my parents and grandparents to rely on, but since my grades started slipping during the previous school year, my father's idea of discipline was to make sure I didn't receive any luxuries—until my grades were better—other than one or two outfits and a pair of sneakers.

High school also meant beef. Generation after generation, school year after school year—it was now our turn to pick up where those before us had left off. I don't think anybody knew the underlying reason for the Up the Hill/Down the Hill beef, which existed in East Orange since we all could remember. That's just the way it was. Up the Hill versus Down the Hill and the north side versus the south side represented decades of hatred that preceded our parents' era. Nevertheless, ready for whatever, to school we went.

When school finally started my freshman year, I was thirteen years old. High school was like a fashion show, and in order to "grace the runway," you had to have on the latest. After giving it little to no thought, I knew what needed to be done. It was a no-brainer—go hard in the streets!

In the short time I had taken to the streets, I accumulated enough dough to floss when I felt it necessary, which was just about every day. The problem was I couldn't bring any of my clothes home, so I would have to leave things at different homies' houses. I'd leave out for school an hour early and return home an hour late, swapping out and keeping my indiscretions under wraps. Lord knew if my parents found out what was going on, there would've been hell to pay. So I did my best to keep things discreet. The only thing I had to do to keep my parents off my back was to find a way to secure passing grades and keep advancing in school. I no longer cared about As, Bs, or Cs. Now, as long as I passed, I was cool.

For the first few months, for all the wrong reasons, high school was definitely the place to be. But passing grades seemed a whole lot harder to attain than I thought. Socially, things were so live and so much was going on I didn't want to miss a beat. If it wasn't homeroom, I refused to enter a classroom. A few homies and I would meet up and head straight to the train tracks.

The train tracks were a spot where just about anybody in the school who smoked weed would dip off. After a few blunts, all signs led back to the school cafeteria, where you could post up, chill, and check out each and every girl who attended the school. High and feeling myself, I would do just that.

My freshman year at East Orange High the dropout rate was through the roof. School totally lost its appeal. Sad to say but school ranked at the bottom of one's list of priorities. I already knew it was only a matter of time before I was added to the list of youths who chose another route.

Citywide, the youth saw struggle and the answers needed to overcome couldn't be provided in a classroom—or so we thought. Chemistry classes were given in the kitchen and mathematical geniuses were groomed in the streets. Young ones knew there were twenty-eight grams in an ounce, just over thirty-five ounces in a kilo. These were the equations that would feed our existence and fuel a thirst for more.

Schools were no longer a place to learn; they had been converted into play-grounds and battlefields—places where you picked up girls and showcased your willingness to be as ruthless as need be. There was always a guarantee at school you would run into the type of action that could build or break your reputation. Schools became hosts of a full-time gangster party.

The security guards and teachers alike seemed fearful to even direct kids to class so the hallways were packed from eight in the morning until the last bell sounded at 3 PM. In the hallways you could distinguish the various neighborhood clicks by where they posted up. By one garbage can you could find Little City clicked up. Down the upstairs ramp, which hid students like a side block, were the Kerri Hilson look alikes—pretty girls like Asia, Malika, Shakia, Deema, and others. Down the Hill posted up across the hall from the gym. It would be me and Big BooYa aka Face, my high school running-mate, who happened to be the younger brother of Naughty by Nature's Kay Gee. Face was a known class clown-type and due to his relation to KayGee he was a celebrity in his own right. Also there were Tall Barry, Nakosi, and others.

I also met Devil aka Red Dev my freshman year in East Orange High School in the basement's arts and crafts class. I never lost my passion for art since my pre-teen days when my parents paid for me to attend art school, looking for anything to keep me from falling victim to the streets. I wasn't interested in the formalities of art, I just wanted to draw, and I kind of discounted the course. Years later I still had the itch and so did Dev. With more than one way to be artistic, me and Dev we went at it in a friendly rap battle. By this time I had emerged from my rap shell and had no issue with dropping a bar or two. Dev's abnormal voice and unique style won me over. In attempt to steal a deal, we would cut school and camp out in the backyard of the rap group the Fugee's studio, the Booger Basement, which sat on the corner of Clinton Street and Central Avenue in East Orange amid goats, sheep, and an assortment of other farm animals. The deal with the Fugees never happened, and I decided to holler at Gangsta and Newz in regard to Dev being the missing link to an amazing puzzle. And it wasn't long before Red Dev became the fourth member of the GRatz rap group. Now it was me, Stickman Gangsta, Bad Newz, and Red Devil.

The GRatz, as a whole, would hit the high school like twenty to thirty deep and get into it with whomever. One minute, everyone would be at school laughing and joking and the next, punches were being thrown, chairs were flying, and blood was spilled. Once that happened, there was no chance of letting up. I'm sure if we could've gotten our hands on a few guns that lives would have been lost. Once the lunch periods ended, everyone headed to Main Street, raiding Charlie's Restaurant and Roberto's Pizzeria—the two hangout spots. We would fight until the police came and shut the block down. As soon as the law showed up, we would walk off like it was nothing and head down to the same corners where the homies got money.

Some of the uniformed cops we called Cherry Tops, for the sirens atop their cars, would follow us as we walked off. They wouldn't dare touch us because we were so deep and seemed scared to death. Instead they would park, sit, and stare. We would cross over 14th Street where William Street turned to 6th Avenue and East Orange turned into Newark and sort of dare them to come and get us. Once they stepped out of their jurisdiction everything was fair game. We would throw rocks and bottles from rooftops and alleyways, sending the police right back on their way. But just as fast as they'd take off, they'd return even faster, with what seemed like the entire force hopping out and looking for trouble. Best believe if you were caught, you had it coming, so the chase would be on. Everybody would take off running, scattering like roaches looking for their great escape. We would hit the cuts (alleyways) that led to the many abandoned homes we as GRatz called "Rat Holes."

Rat Holes were places we would put little furniture in and treat like our own. This was where we would go to get high, drunk, and take girls. For the homies with nowhere to go at night, the Rat Hole was shelter. Most people couldn't relate to us posting up in abandoned homes, but we didn't mind. Our privacy was well respected. At least until the police found out and started raiding them, resulting in arrests and juvenile bids for many of the homies.

After the brawls, we still had to attend the same school and lived in the city, so it would be hard to avoid drama on the streets and even harder in school. It was nothing to bump into a gang of dudes from opposing crews such as Munnhattan Posse, Harrison Hustlers, North Side Killer Gangsters, and the Little City Ruff Necks on the way to class or on your way home from school. And if you did, you best had been ready for whatever.

When the school bell rang we would post up on Main Street with bottles, bats, chains, and knives. It didn't matter if we were outnumbered or not—and the majority of the time, we were. What mattered was that it became clear if you touched one of ours, we touched two of yours.

Our beef with Little City proved to be the worst of them all. For me, since was I partially raised there and had family there, the Little City beef was more personal. It certainly taught me to put emotions to the side. When the beef was on, nobody saw family and friends. I once traded video games and slept over the houses of most of the kids we were fighting with from Little City. Our parents were like brothers and sisters. My family, the Butlers, was known around these projects since the 60s. All meaningless, as they gunned, I gunned back.

One day I left the Ave around 3 in the afternoon, in attempt to fool my parents into believing I was in school all day. On my way home I ran into about four or five kids from the Little City Projects crossing the bridge near Oraton Parkway and Freeway Drive. It was Lay G, Darrell (Esko), and a few others whose names I forget. I knew they spotted me, but I kept it moving in hope they found it in their hearts to give me this one pass. My stride grew faster, and so did theirs. I looked back to see them pointing, I could hear them debate who would rush me and set it off. I contemplated running for the house, but I knew chances were I wouldn't make it. Fuck it, I gave it a try. I took off running. One whose face I would never forget was fast on my trail. He was gaining. Think fast, Mass! Think fast! I slowed my pace and allowed him to catch up. His momentum propelled him right into my arms, as I turned around. I grabbed hold of his shirt and flung him to the ground. There was not a second to waste, I had to get mine in quick. The rest of the crew was rushing in. By the time they made it to where we were, I was already putting a pounding on their homie. However, this didn't last too long. They began to use their feet as weapons to kick me and hit me over the head with bottles. It was something like a bar fight, except there was no bar. We were smack dab in the middle of the street. Pedestrians and passing cars wanted nothing to do with the situation and sped by. After a few minutes, I was on my way home with a busted head from the broken bottles. My face was still cool, so I didn't need to hide much from my parents. It was just another day in the life and exactly what I signed up for. That day they caught me. The next day would be our turn. And when your time came, you had two options: run or take what you had coming—and hope it would not be long before you could get revenge. For us, it never took long; if one of ours was violated there was no hesitation or delay.

All sides refused to throw in the towel, and these high school showdowns carried on for most of the year. That's until the school itself grew tired of its hallways being trashed, its teachers caught in the middle of the mayhem, and the merchants on Main Street blaming the school's inability to control its students for poor business. In effect, our education was cut short as East Orange High School forwarded notification its doors were no longer open to our kind. I can't say I blame them, but there were some among the bunch, or bunches, who were forced to fight their way to and from school every day in pursuit of an education, only to be expelled for their association. With the school's "if you weren't a part of the solution, you were part of the problem" attitude and policies, they failed to understand the hardships and struggles certain kids went through just to attend school. And in doing so, they thrust more kids into the streets that they should've been fighting to keep them out of.

As for myself, my expulsion catapulted me headfirst into the streets. With school no longer there to consume my time, I spent those hours on the corner. Hustling became my bread and butter, and little did I know I was becoming addicted to fast money.

Just as I was about to give up hope, a big break occurred. One day while me and the homies were shooting hoops and bumping our demo in the backyard of 20 North 18th Street, Pookie Gist (Kay Gee's older brother and Naughty's manager) made his way into the back, claiming the weed smoke was too heavy and the music was too loud.

Pook reminded me of Russell Simmons—you know, the peace and quiet, yoga type. See, Pook was well known in the music industry and had established himself as Naughty's manager in the early 90s. After lecturing us on where we were (*his* house), he began his 'hood-famous head nod. He focused his ears in on our demo a bit longer, and then asked who was rapping on the tape. Stickman Gangsta, being the leader of the group, stepped up and responded, "It's us, the GRatz."

Pook replied, "I know who it is, but *who* is it?"

"Me, Newz, Mass, and Devil," Gangsta answered.

"Well, I want the four of you to be here tomorrow at 12. We going to the studio."

And just like that, after a few minutes of listening to our demo, Pook put us on.

Pook put us on legally, a rare but true fact. If it had been the streets you could say Pook handed us a hammer (gun), and a pack (drugs), and provided us with a block, and told us to eat. But this was not the street and Pook was not dishing out any of the above. Instead, we were given a microphone, beats, and a state-of-the-art studio and commanded to cook crack, make hits. We had the recipe and now we were given the opportunity to move beyond the "keep writing" and "not right now" that Naughty was feeding us.

Pook showed to be far from out of touch with the youth of our times. Just like everyone else, Pook knew about our turf wars and about how the GRatz had a reputation for being a crew of delinquents. But to Pook none of that mattered. One could not deny we were hungry and if provided with an avenue, an outlet, and not a block (street corner) we would do big things.

Be it opportunity or genuine concern, Pook believed.

For the rest of the day and night, we partied like never before, getting all types of high and all sorts of drunk. I didn't want it to go to my head so I kept my cool; it was only a studio session—something we did on a constant basis. But in the back of our minds, we had made it. The next day when we arrived at Pook's house, we hopped in his 430 Benz and headed to the studio. Not the musty basement studios we were used to; I'm talking about a top-notch studio.

When I entered the studio I played it cool, but the beauty of the place blew me away. I was amazed by the equipment, the size of the mixing board, speakers taller than me, a soundproof booth, not the blanket-insulated closets we were used to, state of the art microphones. The works.

We didn't record that first day; we just sat back, got acquainted, set up our schedule, and listened to a few beats. Before dropping us off that night, Pook made it clear if he was to invest his time and money into our project, it meant no standing on corners and absolutely NO HUSTLING. We were to stay away from anything that could land us in Juvenile Hall. It sounded easy, but our neighborhood was riddled with all types of situations that could land you in the Youth House. Outside of the studio, the corners seemed like the only place to be, and if I wasn't hustling then how was I to eat?

Pook kept us pretty busy. If we weren't in the studio, we were at a video shoot. If we weren't at a video shoot or in studio sessions, we were at shows getting a feel for what was ahead. We were in the game, living like rock stars, teenagers living a life many only dream of. We didn't mind partying all night in the studio; we were doing what we loved. But having become accustomed to the 'hood and lacking the mindset of a true businessman, I couldn't stay away from the block. There were times my unwillingness to leave the strip alone caused some friction among the group. By continuing to cub the block for dough, it was said I was jeopardizing the whole, which I guess was understandable. However, my whole thing was I needed money in my pockets *today*, not tomorrow. And sitting broke in the studio all day made it hard to see the big payday.

During one of our early months of recording, one of the local old heads snatched me up and introduced me to a whole different lane, a lane in which only the big boys were allowed to swerve—the coke game. He put me on the ins and outs and kept me fresh. And, just like that, I stepped up my hustle to keep the money rolling in. I was what you'd call a runner, paying like I weighed. You had to earn your keep and that meant busting your ass to fatten the next man's pockets. Never did it get me rich, but its lessons were priceless. I learned the differences between a weed hustle and a coke hustle. I knew immediately the coke game would put me on as a bonafide hustler.

My day came. The Ave was hot; police were patrolling like crazy. They walked the beat, posted up on the corners, and were harassing everyone in sight. Somebody had been shot and whoever it was had to be damn special. Normally a shooting was an in-and-out process for the police. But the heat that was on today called for the shop to be shut down. I hit a few cuts (backyards, alleyways), snatched up my stash, and trooped up the hill to kick it with my homie Mad Dog, who stayed on the corner of Munn Avenue and William Street in a two-story building, which held the homie M.D's mom's cleaners and yet another bodega on its corner.

The apartment on Munn was the spot, a cool place to get money, but not in the least bit cozy. At all times there were at least two to three and sometimes four big-headed, stocky, bow-legged pit bulls stomping around the apartment like they were one of the homies. The apartment reeked of weed smoke, alcohol, Eukanuba dog food, and feces. The spot was a one-bedroom, and everyone would be piled in the one bedroom doing whatever—playing video games, smoking, drinking, bagging up, and sleeping. The spot was unlike anything I had ever experienced, and ever have since, but it was the SPOT.

When I got there, we rolled up a few blunts and did what we did. After a minute, my homie stated he didn't have much time, and was on his way to New York to replenish his supply. He asked if I had any work, because his spot was on "E" all morning, and he hated turning away clientele. I still had about $400 of the $500 worth of product I'd been hit with by the old head. In learning this, he instantly went to the window and yelled something out to someone. Within the next ten minutes, I sat in his bedroom counting out $400 in full, no shorts. I was amazed how fast I had just sold out. I thought about how I had been busting my ass all day on the Ave—barely bringing in $100—and in a matter of ten minutes, a fifty pack was done.

My homie was his own boss. He did things the way he wanted. As for me, I was only a runner who still had to deal with the ins and outs of traffic on a strip where it was "Ball till you fall." After we finished the weed, the homie asked if I wanted to head uptown to New York, New York, big city of dreams to re-up and maybe do a little shopping for a party jumping off later that night at Club Big Shields in downtown Newark. I had never been to New York before, and I figured I could make a quick flip, do some shopping, and still manage to have the money right in time for my old head to come through. I couldn't turn it down. He and his shorty and I caught the PATH train to 33rd Street in New York, then the A and C Express uptown to hit 145th Street and St. Nicholas Avenue.

Once we came up the steps and exited the subway station, the sight was unbelievable. On one corner sat a flurry of rude boys pushing low-grade stress weed (junga) dressed in red, yellow, and green Rasta caps that concealed their dreads, sporting a mix of Bob Marley and Haile Selassie T-shirts. Ladies offered braids and lock-jobs. On the next corner sat young black entrepreneurs peddling mix-tapes by Ron G and DJ Clue, along with bootleg VCR tapes—the kind where mid-movie you'd have another movie-goer walk in front of the lens of someone they didn't know was behind them trying to make a dollar out of fifteen cents by taping the movie with a hand-held recorder.

And there I was, just a kid who had been chasing his dreams since as far back as I could remember, stepping into the city of big ones. The reality of the situation dawned on me—we were in New York to do a deal. However, I refused to let the butterflies get the best of me. In somewhat of a daze, I just sort of floated through the moment. I made sure to memorize the street signs so I could share my journey with the homies whom had never been. And worst-case scenario, if the deal went bad and police arrived, the way I came was the way I would go.

The negative thoughts of police interference were quickly dismissed as we continued to walk by more and more uniformed police who stood within an earshot of the many Latinos posted up and down Broadway yelling, "Fish scale, Papi. I got what you need."

This shit was crazy. It was like the police didn't even care. I guessed not. With the dangers police faced in the Big Apple and on the salaries they received, turning a blind eye was probably one of the ways they kept food on their tables.

I must've looked a little nervous, because before we entered the spot, my homie told me to breathe easy and let him do all the talking. In these times, grams were going for $19, $20 apiece, so the math was already done. I knew exactly what I would be copping. I handed my homie the money and let him run the show.

When we got inside the apartment, the only furniture in sight was a couch, a table with a digital, and triple-beam scale, and a refrigerator. There were three Latinos, but only one moved and did all the talking. This was a scene straight out of a *Scarface* flick. I watched and listened. Then all of a sudden, to my surprise, my homie stuck a finger inside the pile of cocaine spread out before us and put it to his tongue and around his gums. I was at a complete loss and filled with anger and disappointment. My heart sank as I looked at my homie and thought my brother was getting high off his own supply. After the dealings were done, I continued to say nothing, but while on the train ride back to Jersey, I guess he sensed the change in my mood and asked me what's poppin'. I couldn't hold it back any longer. I stressed the importance of never becoming weak to the point of violating our 'hood laws. He just looked at me and laughed. I found nothing funny. In fact, I knew such a violation would get you written off. He continued laughing and then said, "Nah, homie. I was just testing the product to see if it was that raw or not. If you put coke on your tongue and it doesn't get numb, it's garbage."

Up until that point, I knew nothing about any of that, but reading the sincerity in his eyes, along with his nonchalant attitude, I began to laugh. I wanted to say I knew, but I already gave myself away. I was slightly embarrassed and took it in stride and chalked it up as one of the many lessons the game gave. We made it back to Newark Penn Station safe and sound and caught a cab back to the homie's spot.

When we got there, the homie taught me how to bag up. Customers must have seen us as we arrived. They were already knocking at the door, while we bagged up.

This spot was flowing. We split the sales, taking turns maneuvering through the pit bulls that crowded our every step. It was still early, and we didn't get to do any shopping in New York, so the homie suggested we swing downtown Newark to pick up something to wear for the party. On the way back from clothes shopping, we hit up Buy Rite, a used-car dealership, to see if we could cop some wheels.

Buy Rite sold cars ranging from $1,000 to $10,000, and as long as you had the cash, the deal was done. Personally speaking, none of the cars were worth anything, but at our age, it didn't matter what you were driving; four wheels boosted your 'hood notoriety.

With the $400 I took uptown, after bagging up, I had a little over $1,200 in product. I still owed the big man $400, so that left me with $800 to play with—and that's what I did: I played! We got on with the day's adventures. A few hours later, we had shopping bags in the backseat of our newly purchased used 1985 station wagon. It was nowhere near much, but it had four wheels and it would definitely be better than pulling up to the club in a cab. In New York that may have gone over but in Jersey showing up to the club in a cab was a no go.

The remainder of the day went smooth. After showering at the homie's house, I was fresh and ready to rock. Customers were still banging the door down. Even though I never drove a car a day in my life, I was part owner of the G-ride sitting out front. After a while, a few more homies slid though and we all got high and drunk waiting for it to get a little later. You never wanted to be the first ones to the club.

Before we hit the club, we made a pit stop at the Exxon gas station on Central Avenue and Munn. When we pulled in, for some strange reason, my antennas went up when I saw a man standing near the phone booth at the gas station's entrance. I ignored it and we filled up at the gas pump. Right before the homie handed the attendant the money, we were boxed in. What looked like the entire police force had us surrounded, guns drawn with each cop yelling something different. "HANDS UP! DON'T MOVE! CAR OFF!"

It was crazy. We were dragged out of the car in a hurry, slammed to the ground, kicked, punched, and then cuffed. We kept quiet and dealt with the BS. We already knew there was no need to ask what was going on. The way we were treated, you would've thought we killed somebody. It wasn't until we reached the police precinct we learned what we had been arrested for: *carjacking*.

The basement of East Orange's precinct held about six dimly lit cells with sticky floors that reeked of feces, vomit, urine, stale coffee, cigarettes, and anxiety. One side held three cells facing the back end of the East Orange Post Office, and the other side allowed you to see the street and the driveway where the police vans would drop off more coming in to join you in cuffs.

I knew for a fact we purchased the car earlier in the day and had its title in the glove compartment, so for the life of me, I couldn't understand how they came up with this scenario. Come to find out, instead of using the temporary plates from Buy Rite, the homie had used stolen license plates from another car; a car that just so happened to have been carjacked. What luck! But in our 'hood it was like that. After being trapped in the precinct for hours, the police realized the mix-up and released us. It was certainly a crazy night.

When I arrived home the day after, my mother and father said they needed to speak with me. Somehow, while I was on the ground at the gas station, a family friend was driving by and spotted me. Though he didn't feel the need to stop and see what was going on, he decided to give my parents a call as to my whereabouts. My conversation with my parents was actually no conversation at all—just them yelling and screaming about how I had no business being near Central and Munn Avenues —let alone arrested—and how my behavior was beginning to change and I was becoming downright uncontrollable. They'd also made it clear I was to enroll in Clifford J. Scott High School the next school year.

I knew I had no win in this debate. I said nothing and headed to my bedroom, a place where I began secluding myself whenever I was home. I knew what the deal was, but I wasn't trying to hear it. From where I stood and the way I saw it, I found my way in the streets. And at what most considered a tender age of fourteen, I was out providing for myself. I didn't have to though. Still, nothing gave me the satisfaction like doing for self, even if the means clashed with what others believed to be just. When in Rome you do as the Romans.

My parents loved and wanted the best for me; however I didn't know what I wanted for myself. I literally lost control. My weed habit turned to popping pills, smoking wet (PCP), and drinking regularly. I was all over the place, just like my priorities. I felt I was right and exact, as long as I kept money in my pockets and my gear was up. I could hear my parents yelling, "Slow down!" but all I saw was green and everything was a go.

4

JUVENILE JUSTICE

THINGS WERE CHANGING in '94 and '95. Gangsta, Newz, and Devil were barely around anymore. Their studio hours tripled. I was still part of the group, but somewhere in between, and I noticed songs being recorded without me. I was in the studio less and less because I could not leave the block alone —but I didn't trip. We were all out to live our dreams. I was stuck with a nothing-comes-before-Blood mentality, so I brushed it off and figured they wouldn't move too far along without me.

I kind of felt in my heart of hearts something wasn't being said, so I gave up on everything. I questioned my life's purpose and myself. Truth in the light does little to guarantee understanding in the night. I knew it would be only a matter of time before I was out of the group, so to ease the pain I traded the mic for a flag and a pack. Besides, gang-banging wasn't a part-time job. I stepped "off the porch" for a reason: to eat! So with no time to sit around, I hit the streets ever so hard.

For the average kid, a summer job might have been cool, but I wasn't your average kid. And since I traded in my worker mitts with the old head, the only time I wanted to hear the word *job* was when I was handing one out. Minimum wage? I couldn't see it. Why flip burgers when I could flip bricks? My little weed hustle was still floating around the halls of the high school, but Munn Avenue and William Street became my second home. Enough was never enough. The more money I touched, the more I wanted. Who cared if the police station was right down the street? The way I saw it, the law had a job to do and so did I. A game of cat and mouse—and I had to be smart enough to beat the trap.

For the most part, the police knew what was going on, but figured us to be petty nuisances. If the homies posted up on the corners outside the building, there would be foot chases here and there. But I understood this was a game of chess, not checkers, so I rarely ran into situations where I was forced to take the chase. Too many homies were sitting in the Essex County Youth House in Newark waiting on program acceptance or already down old dusty road at Jamesburg, New Jersey's juvenile prison, for me to not take their experiences as lessons.

Overnight, it seemed, homies began to fall victim to the system. Prisons of all kinds, juvenile and adult, were black holes where once one had fallen the recovery rate was slim to none. My road dawg Troub got caught up. He still had dreams of making it big like the rest of us, but while pursuing them, he and the homie Rockin' Roc got trapped by the mayor of East Orange, Bob Bowser, and his police bodyguards, accused of a string of robberies. It was obvious they would be going down for a while—whether they had done it or not—just because of who had arrested them. During this tough-on-crime era, justice for juveniles meant discipline. Discipline that could only be given behind bars.

When Troub and Rockin' Roc got locked up, it kind of took a toll on me. Although I still had an army of homies I could rely on if things got rough, Troub and I had been hard to separate since that day at football practice.

I managed to keep it moving. But before long, I looked around and found myself damn near alone. In a matter of months, the homies were gone. A few of us still remained, but a large portion had taken a fall. In one way or another, ninety percent of those who got knocked fell trying to make ends meet and put food on the table. Instead, they ended up in the Youth House or Jamesburg.

In the early 90s, Newark and East Orange would beef in the Youth House until they reached the 'Burg and there, they would come together under Essex County. Troub and other homies earned their respect on the inside. He would call me from the Youth House and tell me how he would rather be anywhere but there. Maybe it was the luck of the draw or simply God looking over me, I hit the precinct for minor incidents, but I had yet to hit the Youth House. I knew it wouldn't be a good look, considering the line of business I pursued. But a part of me wanted to hit the Youth House out of curiosity.

One day Oop, Na Bills, and Muta, my childhood friends from Carnegie, picked me up after school in Oop's four-door gray 1987 Dodge Omni. Next thing you know, Oop backed into an unmarked task force car paying more attention to a dice game on the side of the street than his rear view mirror. The police hopped out with their weapons drawn. We immediately yelled for Oop to pull off and the chase was on. It started on Munn Avenue across from Building 67, where most of the action took place on South Munn. We weaved in and out of traffic, ran red lights, and sideswiped cars until we were boxed in, in front of Irvington High School. After a light pounding, we were escorted back to East Orange's police headquarters.

Police knew the car wasn't stolen, and there wasn't much they could do, other than to arrest the driver. When asked for my parents' phone number, so I could be picked up, I responded by requesting to go to the Youth House with Oop. After we all requested, the call was made, but we were denied and released due to lack of space.

Growing up, we saw the big homies go in and out of jail and prison like it was nothing, so we thought it was natural—you know, the thing to do. When it came to earning stripes, hitting the inside was on the list. It added to your credibility as a gangster. The old heads carried it like they were built for the pen, with job titles ranging from robber, hustler, murderer, and kidnapper. They'd take the law into their own hands and even when caught, it only seemed to result in what they called "a little vacation." I admired their sense of humor about such serious situations. That was when I learned what it meant to smile in the face of adversity.

Prison stories made their way to the streets like *The Daily News*—and from what I heard, jail definitely wasn't a laughing matter. But if it meant laughing to stop from crying, then that was what was done. It was never about the struggle itself, but how you carried yourself in the midst of the struggle that mattered. Some saw it as a sign of weakness if you could throw it and couldn't catch it in the same stride, likely causing you to become the next target.

The game I walked into was no joke. I saw myself as a hustler, but to the streets, I was one of them (for lack of a better term). The game is one big melting pot—everybody mingled, everybody knew everybody and, just the same, anybody could get it. Age was nothing but a number. Young and old, women and kids—a target was a target. If you had what another wanted and weren't willing to go the distance to keep it, you were as good as got. I was nobody's victim. I was a hustler but by all means I had to be ready and willing to weather the storm if it came rolling through.

I remembered the jewels the big homie dropped on me about senseless acts, but the truth was, characterizing yourself as just one thing—like just a hustler—was a big mistake. I couldn't imagine my mom dressed in black because her son gambled away his life not prepared to dance with the devil. I knew what I had to do and just like that it all but fell from the sky.

I was sitting in the building on Munn Avenue and William Street around one o'clock in the morning when one of my regulars walked in with no money, but something just as good, something I had been looking for—a gun. It was a six-shot .38 Special to be exact. Before I even grabbed hold of it, my adrenaline was pumping. I wasn't concerned with how much; my only question was, "Where's the bullets?" He had a whole box. We hit the roof for a test drive to see if it worked. I loaded it and emptied all six shots into the air. I felt satisfied and, in exchange, I gave him a clip (ten vials of cocaine) and sent him on his way. I reloaded the .38, stashed the box of bullets, and hit the hallway on a new high. I'd just purchased my first hammer for one hundred dollars.

That night, I sat in the hallway thinking back on all the old gangster flicks I grew up watching with my dad. I was now living in one. I couldn't wait to get home the next day to show off the gun to my little brother. He, more than anyone, knew how much I had taken to the streets. On my many curfew-imposed nights home, we would sit in the room and I would tell him all the stories about the 'hood, how I turned Blood, and how much money I was stacking. Now I was going home to show him my first gun.

My role-modeling was anything but positive. But what did I know? The generation before mine was big on "Each one, teach one" and what I was taught was the game. My brother's future was doomed. I was the reaper stealing his life before he had a chance to live.

The game I stepped into was life or death. Now, in my hands, I held the power of both. More so for my defense than anything, the hammer went with me wherever I went: Munn, The Oval, the Ave, even when I made my trips up to Scott High School.

From where I stood, things were going good, money was rolling in, and everyone was eating. The 'hood was on the same page. And throughout all the ups and downs, hard work paid off and the GRatz inked a deal with Quest Records. The legendary Quincy Jones owned Quest Records. This was major. Mr. Jones had rocketed many artists to the top and we wanted to be next. The deal with Quest Records led us to New York to mix an album in Chung King Studio with the likes of Warren Riker. The GRatz were in the studio working on their album and in the room next to them would be the likes of Mary J. Blige and other 90s music superstars working on their albums. You could literally run into your favorite artist on a bathroom break, or have someone from their entourage come in looking for an extra blunt only to result in one big smoke out. No one in the GRatz was over sixteen years old. We went from sleeping in abandoned buildings and cars, posted up on corners, and running from cops to watching the ink dry on a recording contract with Quest Records. This moment gave hope to the hungry homies in the 'hood. I didn't sign on the dotted line. I was already more consumed by the streets. But I was somehow still rewarded with my five minutes of fame.

After taking it in early one night, I remember sitting in the kitchen with my Moms, Pops, and little brother when the phone rang. It was my relative Mally GoGo who at the time lived out in the Amboys in central Jersey. When I answered, he was screaming and going crazy. The first thing that came to my mind was something happened with him, but after a minute I could hear music blasting into the earpiece. It didn't really register at first, but then it caught me. A GRatz song was playing in the background. I asked how he managed to get his hands on the song. It was a song we recorded in the studio with Pook back when we first started our sessions. There had to be a catch because Pook didn't even allow us to have copies of the album for fear of it being leaked. Come to find out, my cousin just got it off the radio. I couldn't believe it! Hot 97's Funkmaster Flex had played the single. At that moment, you couldn't have told me dreams don't come true.

I ran out of the house and went straight to 15th Street and William. By the time I arrived, things were already live. It was like a movie. Anybody who had four wheels had their hatches open, doors open, and radios blasting. All you heard was "Yeah, straight from Jersey, the GRatz"—my leadoff line being scratched back and forth by the one and only Funkmaster Flex.

In almost an instant, the Ave lit up and everybody was outside. Things had turned into a party and we were the guests of honor. It was definitely a joyous moment for everyone. Not only had one of ours made it, we all did. Dating back to the days when the homies paid for studio time, throughout the journey, a little bit of everybody had contributed. There was no stopping now; from here, the only place to go was up. The sky was the limit and we all had plans of flying high. Next to come would be the videos, tours, selling out stadiums, and making platinum hits.

We grew up talking about doing it big; well that night was a big first step. Maybe we didn't need to rely on a life of crime to get by. Here it was we had three homies (Dev, News, and Gangsta) who came through the trenches and, after applying some self-discipline and staying focused, things were coming to fruition.

We already cleared the air regarding my signing. I was to collect royalties, tour, and be included in all the other aspects of the deal. I was cool with what it was. I couldn't shoot for the moon while gazing at the stars. At this point I was happy to still be along for the ride. My thirst for more limited my ability to drink up now that the bar was open. Still in all, I had my whole life ahead of me. But at that moment, I was the happiest I'd ever been. The GRatz: Let the world tell it, "wouldn't amount to anything" and "Only bad things happened to our kind." Exactly what *our kind* was, I still didn't know. The way I saw it, we were a bunch of kids who didn't let yesterday determine our today.

Opio, a soldier in the struggle, advised, "Adversity is nourishing food for those strong enough to digest it."

I could imagine the looks on the naysayers' faces when they heard us on the radio. Only thing to do now was to go through the motions, be a little patient, and allow nature to take its course, for a forced hand is no hand at all.

I thought back on when we first started hitting the studio. My parents didn't agree. In their eyes, music was a coin toss, luck of the draw, and besides, they didn't like that the studio hours cut into my schooling. They were unaware I was already dipping in and out of school at will. So even though the radio play died down after that night, once was enough to last a lifetime and show my parents the sacrifice had been well worth it. I still wasn't convinced they shared in my happiness. I knew they remained persistent about me getting an education. To me, school only seemed to be in the way of things I wanted. Out of respect, I didn't voice this, but my parents and I stayed at odds. Especially following the night I happened to walk out of my bedroom on the way to the bathroom and saw my father and his friend attempting to sneak in the house—each carrying a garbage bag. There was no way he was sneaking into the house with a garbage bag full of trash.

It didn't take a rocket scientist to figure out they were up to something. After using the bathroom, I stumbled back to my room like I was too sleepy to pay attention to what was going on. I knew my father's reputation in the streets, just like I knew the one his friend had. His partner creeping into the house with him was a reputable 'hood figure out of Little City Projects who would later become my godfather—Jeff Crew.

Jeff was a true money-getter and this night showed just that. Not sure if dark-skin was in at the time, but one thing for certain, green never went out of style and that made Jeff a player throughout his tenure as a hustler. Jeff now sat in my kitchen, whispering back and forth with my Pops. It was nothing major. It couldn't be. Pops gave up the streets way back when. He was now a hard-working man, one who always lectured me on right from wrong. Pops was Mayweather smooth, in and out, cunning. One hell of a businessman, because until that moment, he sure had me sold. I never doubted his word, but what one said and what one did was now in complete contrast.

I waited a little longer before I peeked out of my room to see exactly what was inside of those bags. Tiptoeing out, the sight before me stopped me dead in my tracks. Stacks and stacks of money were piled on top of and around the kitchen table. I had never in my life seen that much money. Not hundreds, not thousands—who knows how much sat there. It was unbelievable. I would have never in a million years thought Pops would be counting stacks of dead presidents in that capacity like it was nothing.

In their world, I was still young, but I was nobody's fool. I was out playing the same game. Anger rushed over me as I replayed all the times my Pops went off on me. "I don't want you in this area," "I don't want you around that person," "I want you home at this time," he'd say. He came up with a new set of rules on the regular to protect me and my brother from the streets. And there he was knee deep. When I would tell him I wasn't out doing anything wrong, he'd counter with, "If the people around you are, then you're guilty by association." I guess we both were.

I couldn't sleep that night. I thought about how I believed I was out in the streets seeing some type of real dough, but after witnessing my dad and his homie Jeff, I realized I had been doing nothing but playing; throwing rocks at the precinct for pennies. It was definitely time to get serious. The only man to discipline me was no longer in a position to tell me anything. The gloves were off. No doubt, I still respected my Pops but the days of "do this" and "don't do that" were over. The rebel in me was now up and running.

While I sat awake in my room, I assessed the way I had been doing things. No matter what profession I pursued, there could be no half-assing. After that night, I went and busted it up with Gangsta, Newz, and Devil. I made it known even though I was to collect royalties, the reality of my situation was—even though they vowed to make sure I'd always be good and want for nothing—I wanted to be better and secure my own needs. And the only way to do that was by taking the bull by the horns. In the eyes of everyone else—including the other members of the group—everything would seem perfect, but I would always feel as if I was riding another's coattails. I would support the movement and do whatever was needed of me, but by the same token, I wanted to—no, I *had to* do for me. As a classical writer once noted: A man anticipating another man to reign over his kingdom (self) shall be nothing more than a jest.

I had no hang-ups about how I earned my living. What mattered to me was whatever I had, I earned. Wasn't providing for you and yours what being a man was all about? That's not to say there's anything wrong with a little help along the way, but just like the old saying goes, "Nobody is responsible for you but you."

I continued to take matters into my own hands. It wasn't broke, so why try to fix it? So right back to the spot on Munn and William Street I went. Every dollar I made, I saved. I didn't want the cars or the jewelry. Those days were over. I even switched up my attire to save money on clothes. It was also a tribute to another 'hood legend, Kyame—may he rest in peace. Seven days a week, you could find me in army fatigues, white tees, Timberland boots, and a red fitted hat. What you saw was what you got. But what you didn't know was I was filling up shoebox after shoebox with more and more money. I was hyped about my hustle. This was the era of Raekwon's classic album, *The Purple Tape*. I would listen to that whole cassette tape, front and back, before I hit the spot, while I sat in the spot, and when I left the spot. It put me in that project-hallway-top-of-the-staircase-strapped-up-with-a-pack kind of mood. I was constantly on my grind.

Then one night, I sat in the staircases smoking, drinking, and waiting for the next sale with a few homies, and we heard gunshots ring out. Those who were packing immediately drew and rushed outside to see what was up. Exiting the building, we could hear tires screeching and smell the scent of gun smoke and burned rubber. When our feet finally hit the pavement, we didn't see anything. Then we spotted it; down toward the YMCA on the corner of Arlington and William, somebody was laid out. We ran like track stars to make sure it wasn't one of the homies. As we got close enough, we noticed it wasn't a homie; it was an old head stick-up kid.

The stick-up boys of the 90s weren't so much the experienced extortionists and robbers like those in the 80s. Now, stick-up boys mostly were junkies with a disregard for everything but getting high. He wasn't dead, but we could see he'd been hit a few times. Trying his luck, he came through thinking his shit was sweet and almost got murdered. Word through the grapevine was he lived. And though nobody ever found out who did the actual shooting, William Street between Arlington and Munn was dubbed "Murda Ave."

Just like after any other shooting, the neighborhood got hot, but with the precinct not even a football field away, E.O.P.D. turned the heat all the way up. I figured since I had nothing to do with anything, I would wake up the next day and hit the spot as usual. When I got there beat-walkers were on the corners, the YMCA was taped off, and a marked police vehicle sat parked in front of the building. I knew what time it was. I continued walking by, as if it wasn't my destination. Out of my peripheral, I noticed the cop car window rolling down. The cop yelled, "This spot has been officially shut down!" I wanted to say something slick to remind him the game didn't stop, but feeling the pack bulging in my pocket, I thought twice and just shook my head and kept it moving to the only other place I seemed to know—the corner of North 15th Street and William.

The neighborhood and its dysfunctional bits, regardless of the hang-ups, made us all family. I remember some of the most unashamed individuals who would do just about anything for a hit of that rock or a bag of that blow. Whether it was the girl next door who pranced through the 'hood all pretty but would lie on her back for whoever came through on the late night with a bag of bud, or one of the turf's known and respected *uncles*, like Uncle Tack.

Tack maybe weighed a hundred pounds soaking wet, and he stayed high all day off a mixture of many different narcotics. He kept a shopping cart overflowing with soda and beer cans, aluminum siding from someone's house he destroyed, and anything else he could cash in at the scrap metal yard. A week's worth of filth stained his skin. Even Uncle Tack sagged his pants to show off his Naughty by Nature boxers. Uncle Tack rolled with an Uptown Anthem ditty-bop. Tack got way high but was also a pimp, and he kept a trick on his side hanging on to his empty pocket until they earned a few dollars for a treat.

"Who got jumbos?" "Who got jumbos?" You couldn't help but get a good laugh out of Uncle Tack.

"Right here Tack. Stop playing. You know I got you."

"I only got seven dollars nephew but I got you when I get back from seeing my connect." Tack swore he was a real live hustler. It didn't matter if his connect was the scrap metal yard.

"Whatever, Tack. But look, before you go, let us know the lady's name you all hugged up wit."

"Never knew her name you know. I'm down with O.P.P."

We all busted out laughing. Uncle Tack was family. The streets eventually caught up with Tack and we lost him.

Next was Uncle Plucky. Uncle Plucky was my homegirl Nee Nee's blood relative but he was the 'hood's family. Plucky's habit seemed unbreakable. He had a nod like a rocking chair. It still didn't diminish his skills or lessen his ability to drop a Chevy engine inside a Cadillac coupe or a sound system that could be heard for miles. A bag of that boy would get Plucky's motor running. Plucky sported greasy attire and looked like he sweat oil. He stayed with a snapback cap that looked like it was soaked in anti-freeze, with a fix-all toolbox and a mean sniff game. Nobody really cared how much he indulged as long as the work got done and the price was right. Plucky wasn't the only one in the 'hood getting high. For the most part the streets came with pushers and users. A mechanic who was also a heroin addict was a 'hood bonus, wasting thousands at an auto body shop was absurd. Why get Maaco when you could go to Plucky and get your entire ride "pimped out?" A skag bag bought you a tune up, upgraded transmission, and tinted windows.

Plucky's own 80s Thunderbird was dusty gray with oil brown guts (interior) and went from zero to sixty in the drop of a dime. It wasn't the prettiest car in town but its NASCAR dash was a sight to be seen and remembered. That was until the homie Kwasi, high on PCP, kicked Plucky's entire front windshield out and took off running up William Street like Smokey in *Friday*.

Last but not least were the neighborhood Aunties. These were the female users whom the drugs got the best of. Some were pretty, others worked over. Some had jobs. Some had tricks. For a high, they had all the sense. Broke and disgusted, preying on young hustlers—trap spot temptresses. There was nothing they wouldn't do. While the hustlers sold white, they bartered their bodies. You could catch one leaning, bent over narcotic numb, taking backing shots or dirtying their knees, head bobbing and weaving in broad daylight. There were no secrets in their faces, not an ounce of embarrassment.

"Ay Wanda, what was you over there doing?" A question for laughs.

"None your got-damn-bizniz. Y'all just mad cause I ain't giving yall none! I don't know why y'all knocking my mothafing hustle no way. Aint nobody questioning yours," she went off.

"Yea, you right Wanda, but look we gotta extra bag if you hit the lil homie off," we replied as her attitude vanished.

"Where at?" Wanda asked anxiously.

"Wanda, get ya ass outta here!"

And with a spin worthy of a Paris runway, Wanda turned around, smacked her ass, and said, "Kiss my ass!" before walking off.

Down the Hill was daytime drama, no soap opera the young and the restless but hopeful, nonetheless. And the things we hoped for did damage to our dreams.

My life had become so consumed with my hustle in the building on Murda Ave, I'd seen less and less of 6th Ave. Not that it was a bad thing. However, in an instant, I noticed the difference between coming through to kick it and hustling on 6th Ave, working the cuts, dipping from the cops, and creeping on the come up. The last time I was on 6th Ave in full blast, I was pumping a little weed. This time around, I was out to make my debut as one of the big boys with cocaine as my product. We were Bloods, and the way I saw it, Bloods rule, so the days of going along to get along were over.

A lot of things changed during the time I spent on Murda Ave. As Bloods, we were out representing and putting it down around the town. The days of running around like chickens with our heads cut off were over. Homies were paying their dues and getting a little money. When it was time for work, it was all about the cause. No longer could the big homies exclude us as just a bunch of knuckleheads who did nothing but stay in something. We were growing up right before their eyes. The young homies, mostly GRatz, were taking over 15th Street. That was definitely a good look. But I knew homie love was one thing and cutting into the way somebody put food on their table was another. I respected the protocol. A few homies had 6th Ave laid out, so overall it was theirs to claim.

Personally, I wasn't trying to swing through and scrape up a few dollars, taking out of another's mouth. If anything, my intent was to bleed the block and continue stacking my shoeboxes, all while contributing to the block's growth. And whatever came out of that, I was all for it. It never became a problem though—I was welcomed with open arms. And once again, it was on.

I knew that to start things on the right foot, I had to pull out a few tricks with my next flip. I was sort of like the new kid on the block with the customers and—although we all knew product sold itself—the thing was to get the customers to trust you enough to give your product a taste. I scoped out the scene and observed what was moving. That night, when I put my work together, I went a size bigger with the packaging than the norm—my favorite red tops, SS-45 Illusions, ten dollars a pop. When these hit the strip, my name was known in no time and my product was sought after. I turned down nothing—I took shorts, change, food stamps, and every once in a while I gave out credit. I did whatever it took to keep them coming back. In return, they loved me and with that love came their money.

Did I mention that once again it was on?

Everything I stepped "off the porch" for appeared to be within reach. Not only was I getting money, we were putting Bloods on the map. Once you came Down the Hill, it was clear this was Blood turf. It was red everywhere you went in the 'hood—from the Orange Street Bridge, across Roseville Ave over past Park Ave, all the way up to Murda Ave. Flags draped the light poles, walls were tagged, and on every corner you were sure to find a gang of Bloods, dressed in red and getting their daily grind on.

Homies who caught earlier juvenile bids like Damu, Rockin' Roc, Al-Snatch, and others were touching down and ready to get active. Now, they were home; making up for lost time seemed to be their only concern.

It was the mid-90s and the media spawned an East Coast/West Coast *Rap War* marked by battles between Bad Boy and Death Row Records, Puff Daddy and Suge Knight, and the deaths of Biggie Smalls and Tupac Shakur.

Not long after Pac was shot in New York, B.I.G asked "Who Shot Ya," and Pac fired back with the songs "Against All Odds" and "Hit 'em Up." It was like with the release of each song from either camp, the media continually referenced an East Coast versus

West Coast Rap War and repeatedly pointed to Suge Knight's gang affiliation to a California Blood set. Rumors began to circulate that B.I.G. was affiliated with Crips.

In stirring up an East Coast/West Coast Rap War and alleging gang affiliations the media in turn played into gang notoriety and created aspirations for many in the East. This cast us, Double ii, in the East riding a West Coast line into the forefront and further into somewhat of a no-man's land.

Up until that point we represented Blood and were focused on money. We didn't do too much banging outside of pre-existing neighborhood beefs because there were no Crips around. However, during this time blue rags and taggings began to pop up in NSKG 'hood around the high school and surrounding area. Word was NSKG converted into Third World Crips. We didn't know if it was being done as a sign of their opposition to our 'hood and what we stood for or if they really got put on as Crips. Nevertheless, beef was everywhere—North and South, East and West. There was no doubt that us being out East and holding up a West Coast 'hood only contributed to the hate. Shots were thrown from all over the land. Other crews were thirsty, so when NSKG began going out of their way to catch anyone from Down the Hill slipping, regardless of their affiliation, it was time to see if these fools were really bout it, bout it—similar to the new wave of music coming out of the South—Calliope Projects, 3rd Ward, New Orleans to be exact.

Not long after Pac was shot at Quad Studios in Times Square in New York City, he was killed as he sat in the passenger seat of Suge Knight's BMW on the Las Vegas strip. In similar fashion on a road trip to California, "I'm going back to Cali" the Notorious B.I.G was murdered in a vehicle. Both murders, though a time apart, touched me personally. Their music had a way of traveling no matter if you were in the East or West. In some ways their music helped mold me and was definitely a big part of the soundtrack of my adolescence and my coming of age in the streets. I could listen to their music and feel they were speaking to me directly. Something many of today's artists lack.

After the deaths of Pac and BIG it was open sesame in the music industry and that's when artists from the South started to break out. Master P's movement had us all the way up North, still in our trademark army fatigues and Dickie suits, on the block bouncing to their new sound, peddling crack rock like the ice cream man, and head-busting just to make 'em say unngghh! There truly was no limit.

The many beefs we had with others still existed but died down somewhat as everyone found themselves on a paper chase. NSKG was attempting to make its mark. They took over Walnut, Park Ave, Arlington, and the surrounding area. So for the young homies who still attended school, it was hard to get around them. The only way we knew to get back was to take things to another level. In '93, the Bloods hit Jersey, but in '95 and '96, the Bloods got active!

When the choice was made to up the "B," all was understood. Opposition would arise and when it did, one needed to be prepared. There was no turning back. You either got active or got gone. Money was always the motive, but now—with Crips popping up—banging was my primary focus. With a war going on, everything else stopped. We were taught nothing comes before Blood, so even with money being my first love—and ticket out of the ghetto—it had to be put to on the backburner.

We didn't turn Blood to war with Crips, but we knew it came with the territory. Dating back to the Up the Hill and Down the Hill beef, both sides already had a genuine dislike for one another, so when the colors came into play, it didn't start the problems, it intensified them. Prior to, we had our run-ins but found ways to co-exist. Now, there were no passes, no neutral zones. For the next year, things were back and forth: gunshots, beatdowns, stabbings, and colors flying like never before. During that year, it became clear both sides refused to let up. Whether people believed what was taking place or not, one thing was for certain: the war between the Bloods and Crips was now raging on the East Coast.

I don't think anyone cared, as long as the war stayed within the confines of little old East Orange. Although the number of bodies dropping due to gang violence was low at this time, the impact of what was occurring between those involved was dangerous. Psychologically, one took on the attitude that "If society respected violence, that's what I would become." There were teenage kids whose days revolved around survival, even if it meant destroying the life of another. The more the affluent and upper echelons of society ignored the gang epidemic, the more lives it touched—some positively, some negatively. By 1996, almost the entire north side of East Orange was Crip, just as almost the entire Down the Hill East Orange was Blood.

That same year ('96), Troub finished his Youth House bid and the homie "O.C.O.D." touched down from Jamesburg. My road dawg Troub was home. And though I never met O.D. prior to his juvenile bid, I instantly gravitated toward his strength after his release. I got a boost of energy with their arrival. The GRatz partied in The Oval to welcome them home with more than enough liquor and weed to go around.

O.D was stocky with a nappy afro and a temper that kicked off in no time. For those who got on his bad side he was treacherous. O.D. was a no-hesitation, act-first-ask-questions-later kind of guy. The last time he was on the streets, I was running up and down football fields, trying to make it to the NFL. Only a year or two older than me, he was one of the kids who didn't make it to practice and was out demanding the respect of men twice our age. With the arrival of Troub and O.D., I knew things were about to get turned up even more.

Troub told me all he thought about while locked up was our dreams of getting rich. As for me, that's all I'd been doing—searching for a way, determined to make true on the plans I constructed and the goals I set way back when I first realized the struggles and limitations of my community. In doing so, the innocence of my intent vanished. It became all about me and my homeboys. If you weren't with us, you were against us. With all the guns and drugs that made their way to the 'hood, my attitude was to feed it back to them. If moving work and toting guns was what it took, you could consider it done. That happy-go-lucky, "we are the world" mentality did nothing to put food on the table.

I watched both my parents bust their asses, day in and day out, just to make ends meet. They never complained and for that they had all my respect. But at sixteen years old, I saw things two ways: bread and water versus steak and champagne. If the latter led to three hots and a cot, I respected that too.

While out chasing the dream, Troub got locked up again. This time it was a drug beef. You may wonder when getting locked up trying to make ends meet will stop. NEVER! Man will continue to sacrifice all he has until he finds himself and his beloved people no longer removed from equal opportunity. Sound farfetched? So do the consequences.

Do we expect individuals to die a slow and quiet death with no hope? Like Pac said, "There will never be peace until we get a piece." This time around, the judge had no tolerance and sentenced Troub to yet another stretch. On the other hand, I still managed to duck the law. That was until one night when money seemed to slow down—all the way down.

I had been out on 6th Ave for hours and still hadn't made a single dollar. I didn't move one dime out of a fifty pack. I had never experienced a dry spell like this. I decided to call it a night. As I headed back to the bodega on the corner of 6th Ave and 14th Street to purchase my goodies, a red vehicle pulled up and damn near ran me over. Inside was a white female, who rolled down her window and asked me for two dimes. Under other circumstances I might have let the sale pass, but since I had not made a dollar that night, I told her to back up and follow me to 15th Street, then pull over and hit her lights.

As I ran up the street, I heard a homie call out for the sell. Honoring his plea, I continued on to my stash. Greed! Greed had made me a marked man. I pulled out my brown paper bag filled with jumbo red tops and grabbed two dimes and casually jogged back out, looking in both directions to make sure no police were creeping down the block. Immediately following the transaction, a funny feeling came over me. But I brushed it off and made my way back to the store. As I exited the store, goodies in hand, I was swarmed by a flock of unmarked police vehicles. Undercover cops rushed me, threw me on the ground, and placed me in cuffs. Since I had no drugs or weapons on me, I figured I would be searched and released (the norm in the 'hood, unless somebody's stash was found and they were made to wear it). After I was placed in the backseat of the Crown Vic, I could hear a female voice over the police radio, repeatedly yelling, "North on 15th Street." That's when it hit me; the lady I just served in the red car was a cop.

I couldn't believe I just sold drugs to an undercover cop. There was no doubt in my mind I was going to the Youth House. The buy and bust was enough, but I didn't need them to find that brown paper bag stashed in the alley on 15th Street. In a hurry, they drove directly in front of the house where my pack was stashed. The female undercover I served sat somewhere hidden, but I could hear her direct the remaining officers to where she saw me travel just minutes ago. From the backseat of a police cruiser, I could see the police, basically standing on top of my stash, though they couldn't find it. As each minute passed, my hopes grew higher as I figured they would soon give up. That's when I heard, "Bingo! We got it!" They'd found forty-eight vials of cocaine, stashed in a brown paper bag. Of the fifty-pack, the only two dimes I sold that night were to an undercover. I was more than certain I was going to jail, but I took it on the chin and casually went through the motions.

After being booked and processed, I was transported to Essex County Juvenile Detention Center. Not too long before, me and a few of the homies were outside, hollering up at the windows of the Youth House to Troub, Rockin' Roc, Lil BJ, O Broadway, and a couple other homeboys who were doing stints. Now, with my can't-wait-to-hit-the-inside-ignorance-filled mentality, the Youth House became my reality. As soon as I hit intake, I got a taste of the everyday struggles those on the outside who thought catching a case was cool knew nothing about.

The Essex County Youth House stayed full, and most times overcrowded, leaving juveniles of all ages with plastic cots that we called "blue boats" for beds. Age segregation didn't exist. You could have seventeen-year-olds sleeping next to twelve- and thirteen-year-olds. Break the law as a juvenile and Essex County had a place for you, young and old.

Mandatory haircuts were the policy when the infamous Joe Clark ran the Youth House—the same Joe Clark played by Morgan Freeman in the 90s movie *Lean On Me*. I refused to undo my braids. As a result I was placed in a hogtie, with my feet and hands shackled together behind me, while a corrections officer ran clippers up and down my head, not caring how it came out as long as the hair came off.

Following the hogtie and haircut, I was forced to remain in restraints for a few hours, then taken up to the nurse to begin my physical before heading to a unit. When finished, it was a little after midnight and the units were already asleep. I was handed a blue boat and told to find myself a spot on the floor of the day room. That night, I lay in my blue boat and thought I'd finally gotten what I wished for and, now that I did, I wished I never had. Greed had been my downfall. My inability to see all money wasn't good money had me sitting in cuffs. I hadn't even done a day on the inside and already I knew jail was for the birds.

All this time I was so caught up with what I thought it meant to be a gangster I hadn't realized I was playing to lose just for a rep; all that was over now. If I was in it to win it, I had to act like it. All I had to do was get out and things would be completely different. Before I knew it I dozed off and when I woke, the first voice I heard was Troub's. Of all the units in the Youth House, we ended up in the same one (3-C).

Troub was surprised to see me. He got on my case for a minute then spent the rest of the day catching up on things in the 'hood. He gave me the ins and outs—all card games were open but entry would cost no less than a morning muffin, which was the currency in the Youth House. The TV was to stay on music videos. Nobody seemed to care about worldly events. The only news that mattered was who had been shot or killed and that didn't take the television news to find out. Black-on-black crime didn't get CNN coverage, or even the five o'clock news. In the 'hood and in prison, news traveled by word of mouth.

In the Youth House, if someone stared at you too long, it was a test and called for a trip to the bathroom for a blocked-door boxing match. You took shorts under no circumstances. With the beef between various cities in Essex County—East Orange, Newark, and Irvington—nobody wanted to be seen as soft or a sucker. It would have been a reflection on their side, their city. Troub also had some good news to offer when he told me that I should be released after I went to court—given my criminal history was little to none.

For the next few days, Troub and I reminisced and talked about how we still planned on doing it big. To us, doing it big meant being in a position to enjoy life; being able to provide self and loved ones with not only life's essentials but the finer things as well. Most of all, we wanted room to breathe. The 'hood makes you feel smothered. You feel trapped, boxed in by invisible barriers. At times, it can seem there is no escape from the 'hood. Subconsciously, we will things into existence. Everything is said to first begin with the thought, and my misconstrued thought process as it related to making it out of the ghetto and getting ahead in life was what led me to this point. I guess you could call it juvenile justice in that I got what I wanted.

I forgot all about the video shoot Gangsta, Newz, and Dev were supposed to do that upcoming weekend for the song "Let's Get it Started," which appeared on the *Sprung* movie soundtrack that also featured Jay-Z and other notable artists. Flyers were posted all around about the GRatz video shoot at the Peppermint Lounge on Central Ave in Orange. While Gangsta, Newz, and Dev lived out their dreams, I was in the Youth House. It was the life I chose.

A few days passed and I was called for court. I was happy to finally see the judge, but nervous about his decision. I was shackled up on the chain gang and loaded on a van to Essex County's old juvenile courthouse on Market Street in Newark. After what felt like an all-day process of bullpen therapy, a practice used in the system to make you anxious and keep your mind racing, I saw the judge. I was labeled Class B and released to an outpatient drug program.

After court, I was returned to the Youth House to be signed out. I knew I was leaving, and I didn't mind going back. Besides, it gave me another opportunity to get at my road dawg Troub before being cut loose. Later that afternoon, I was informed that I would not be leaving until the next day. That night, Troub and I broke day with him feeding me more insight on the game's dos and don'ts.

The next day I sat back in the day room and waited for my name to be called as Troub played Spades for muffins. I looked around and couldn't help but grit. Not at anyone in particular, rather at the predicament of not only myself but that of hundreds of inner-city youth. What I saw was only a small piece of the puzzle spread about nationally. Scores of inner-city children lured into the juvenile justice system by drug money and a seemingly better life. Once in the juvenile justice system kids were treated as adults, often times inhumanely and written off by a system that did little to set a positive example.

What I also saw standing there was rebellion and the cause and effect of a down-trodden society and an uncompassionate justice system. For mere children—kids and young adults—there existed no median, no middle ground, and no gray area. And this came from the difficulty of simplicity and painting all with the same brush in one broad stroke. Break the law and be imprisoned. But little attention seemed to be paid to the rebelliousness and resistance this form of punishment created.

As I stood there I became a statistic tallied into the effect. The initial "cause" that led to the arrested development of the youth was ignored. Juvenile justice as the only answer spawned a more deviant behavior. In just a few days I got a feel for the hardness that lived within the walls of the Youth Authority. There were gang beatings, strong arm robberies, vicious assaults, and advantage was taken far beyond what today has come to be described as bullying.

While some had parents and family members on the outside who cared, most did not. So the pain of feeling and being alone was played out by some who shared and distributed their pain to others.

Socrates stated, "When you desire wisdom with the same desire you have to breathe then you will attain it." The problem with that philosophy in the hardened ghetto streets is that its juveniles fear the road less traveled and the path to acquire wisdom doesn't come with a GPS.

Incarceration does little to rehabilitate grown men and women, so why are people dismissing claims that imprisoning minors is more harmful than helpful? Call it as you may but the entire process breeds hatred. When you think of acts of revolution, rebellion, and social uprising, know that ninety percent of its perpetrators are youth and those who have experienced some degree of imprisonment and had been a victim of the not-so-cute face of their beloved "system."

When lil boy kool is locked up he isn't educated on how to get out and stay out. He's taught how to survive on the inside, how to adjust to the coldness around him by hardening his heart. Sometimes these tools for survival are given to them by the COs themselves. Cries for mommy and daddy? Well daddy was most likely doing a bid himself. Mail call was most often an imprisoned son receiving mail from an imprisoned father. The imprisoned father quietly sits inside his cell miles away hoping his letter got through. Instead the imprisoned son only cares about the envelope and the picture of Pops puffed up on weights posing in his B-boy stance.

Conversations among kids:

"My daddy's down Rahway."

"Who cares? Rahway pussy. My Pops down Trenton where the killers at."

"Both of y'all lil niggas shut up! Y'all don't even know who your Pops is."

That cold dose of reality simmered the imprisoned boys more than the medication they were being force-fed, drugs such as Depidol, Risperdal, Thorazine and Ritalin that sedated these young children and made their weak minds even weaker.

At that age I knew nothing about politics and, truthfully, I didn't care. The only politicians who resembled my complexion at that time were Jesse Jackson and a handful of local politicians along with your self-appointed politicians—you know, the Al Sharpton types. Periodically, I'd see them parade up to a podium and hear them rant about racial tensions, hate crimes, injustice, and so on. I don't say this to downplay any of those issues, because they're all extremely important. However, I couldn't help but to boil inside as I wondered if those same voices cared what happened to kids in this part of town. From where I sat, blue jumpers and shower shoes seemed to be the latest fashion—with sizes small enough to fit even the youngest of the young, ten, nine, even eight-year-old kids. Kids were dying in the streets. Others without a parent's nurturing were warehoused in a center based solely on discipline.

> YOUTH: the period of life between childhood and maturity.
> AUTHORITY: power to influence thought or behavior.
> DISCIPLINARY: of or relating to discipline; corrective, penal, punitive.
> CENTER: a central area.

So we have a central area with the power to influence thought or behavior in a penal or punitive fashion, during a period of life between childhood and maturity. In Essex County's Youth House, Joe Clark and his staff most definitely influenced behavior each time they left a kid shackled in a room with nothing on but his underwear. Those tactics never should have been acceptable under any circumstance. It's understood some kids deserved some form of discipline. But to punish children without showing them a better way was totally unfair and unjust. But I guess, as the old saying goes, "Life isn't fair; deal with it." In cases where parents obviously failed to instill discipline in their children, should the system be responsible for discipline? And if you think so, shouldn't their mode of corrections be just?

Kids were growing up in neighborhoods you couldn't imagine. Some barely able to read or write, let alone be fully capable of comprehending the full effect of their actions. But they were stuck serving grown-man sentences. When your childhood is snatched from you, you're forced to make decisions that will either make or break you. When kids were witnessing actual death, or for that matter, dead men walking—the answer to every question posed sounds the same: SURVIVAL!

In a detention center, a part of you slowly dies until the date of your release. Upon release, you hit the free world with three things on your mind:

1. Make up for lost time.

2. Get some get back, and

3. Exact your revenge on the very system that deprived you of life.

How does one do that? Rebel against any and all forms of authority.

I was snapped out of my pensive daze when my name was called for release. It was a bittersweet moment. I was leaving, but Troub was still trapped. As I left the unit, I looked back at Troub and he looked at me. The only words he spoke were, "Do it big." As I was being processed, sitting outside awaiting my release was the one woman who accepted and respected me for who I was—good or bad—my mother. That wasn't to say she condoned any of my wrongdoings, because she didn't, but I guess a mother's love for her child was too powerful for her to abandon her seed.

On the drive home, I could see the disappointment in my mother's eyes, yet she said nothing. At that moment, I knew what it meant to feel another's pain.

Emotionally I was hurt, because I knew she was. I disregarded her feelings, concerned with nothing but my own, which were none. In the streets, you're taught not to deal with feelings and emotions. Despite her pain, I knew I meant well and my intentions were good. If I made it in this game, I would gladly reward her with a million smiles for each second of pain and sorrow I'd caused.

When we arrived home, I called around to see if, in fact, the GRatz shot their video and made it one step closer to fame. During my calls, I learned—for some unknown reason—the video shoot was cancelled and, as of yet, there was no new date. For me, this only confirmed I couldn't give up now. I had to remain determined with my eyes on the prize. Besides, to throw my hand in after getting knocked was like admitting I was never built to last from the beginning. I was already in knee-deep.

My days in the Youth House were nothing compared with the months and years of others. Yet it was a wake-up call. It wasn't like I was scared straight, but it did open my eyes to the things I had been doing wrong. I aimed to be big while carrying it like an Average Joe; spending long days and even longer nights on the corner, hand-to-handing, chasing sales up and down the street, and making myself an easy target for the law. Now after I witnessed my Pops and Jeff Crew counting stacks in the kitchen on the late night and after I got knocked for selling two dimes to an undercover and earned a trip to the Youth House, like Troub said, it was time to "do it big."

5

ANYBODY COULD GET IT

My time in the Youth House offered me insight on what was needed to take my hustle to the next level. Seeing my Pops with garbage bags full of cash motivated me to go even harder. To do so, I would have to apply not only my street smarts, but my book smarts as well.

My first course of action was to find some hungry workers who were willing to put in the hours and bring in the paper, just as I did in my early days as a runner.

Second, I had to up the quantity and quality of what I was supplying so my flips came back quick and revenues would cover expenses. I knew from my days as a runner that the split off a pack was usually 80/20, no matter how much work you were pushing. So, to beat the odds, I began offering 70/30 to whomever wanted to make a dollar—and I meant *whomever.*

If you came out for the day in need of a few dollars and didn't know where or how you would get it—I was the man to see. Everyone was treated fairly and equally. For those who stuck around and decided to become permanent pushers, they were rewarded with shopping sprees and other little incentives.

Before I knew it, I had more people looking to do business than I had room for. Every man was his own. Questionable acts were corrected through physical force. It was cut and dried. I refused to deny anyone the chance to put food on their table—or whatever else they wanted to do with their earnings. Who was I to judge?

I always found a way to put those to work who wanted it. It didn't necessarily have to be a job directly serving customers, if that was your choice. If you didn't want to grind, we had other jobs: drivers, lookouts, and baggers, those who ran errands, you name it.

Recently out of the Youth House, and I was coming up. Most would say I was a young boy doing it big, but in reality, I was nowhere near the dream I envisioned. I was still a "pup" in the game, and my life already doubled in responsibility. As a hustler, a peaceful environment was mostly what I hoped for—less drama and fewer cops. Whether you wanted it or not, in a moment's notice, your life was susceptible to chaos and confusion in the streets. Though the two didn't coincide, it was the life I chose. Pac said it best: "You can't go to war if you ain't got your money right." But as a gang-banger, everyday life *is* war. So with an everyday war came an all-day grind.

I attempted to handle my business in both fields. Banging or not, my homies and I loved money. We didn't just sit around plotting hits and wilding out 24/7. We understood it took green faces (dollar bills) to get where we were trying to go. By the same token, it was clear that when you got put on the set—twenty-four hours a day, seven days a week, and twelve months a year, you'd better be ready for war. When duty called, nobody wanted to hear about anything taking precedence over Blood, not even money. Putting money before the set could make you "late." Neither I nor anybody else was an exception to the rule.

To a hustler's benefit, our day-after-day drama between the Crips on the North Side simmered down. Though things were still on sight, the chase lessened. The hatred remained the same, if not worse. But over the previous year to year and a half, a mutual respect had been born for the way both sides put it down. Once hanging out around the school went away, so did the beefs with the other neighborhoods. So in actuality removing us from school also removed some of the sources of drama in our lives. If we didn't cross paths at a club or party, it was pretty much out of sight, out of mind.

With the outside tensions easing up, it became a lot easier to juggle my hustle, and therefore the conflict that existed over war and money worked itself out on its own. But like most inner-city youths in America who grew up watching the finer things in life pass them by, I wanted the lifestyle of the rich and famous. Actually, I didn't care about being famous, as long as I attained the riches. We had a saying in the 'hood: "For the right amount of riches, we'll make you famous."

Now, with the paper rolling in I was very much in a position to do for self. There was no more hiding anything from anyone, even my parents. Hell, I had already been sent to the Youth House for selling drugs, so although they didn't approve, it was no longer a mystery. I began coming home with new outfits, sneakers, jewelry—the whole bit. When I learned how to drive, I took the liberty of pulling up in front of the crib.

My parents noticed I had become too far gone. One day after I entered the house, my father pulled me to the side and gave me an earful. He screamed on me about my behavior and the things he would not tolerate under his roof. He still had no idea I witnessed him at the kitchen table counting money with his partner Jeff Crew. After soaking it all in, I decided it was time for me to man up and step out on my own. As soon as the disagreement was over, I packed up a few belongings and the shoeboxes of money I accumulated and informed my mother that I was leaving and wouldn't be coming back. At the time, she had no clue what was going on. All she knew was that her oldest son—no matter how far gone—told her the words she never wanted to hear under such terms, "I'm moving out."

Trust it hurt like hell to witness my mother cry, but I had to go. I questioned whether the tears were a mother's instinctive reaction to my sudden departure, or out of fear that she had lost her son to the streets and I would be gone for good. No matter how much I tried to put it off as something else, my mother was losing a son. Our smiles would no longer be up close and personal but from a distance. My mother's love would now be in the form of nonstop questions, such as "Are you alright?" "Is everything fine?" and "When are you coming home?"

From my point of view, if I was doing for self, then my rules were the only ones that mattered. As long as I was in my parents' house, their rules would apply. My mother felt it was her duty to nurture her seed until she had no more of herself to give. Still mentally immature, I didn't realize that whether at the age of twelve or twenty-two, there was a script one must stick to. Structure, discipline and guidance are needed in a child's life. If all the rules are your own, there is no right or wrong, so how does one learn from mistakes?

A few years before, I had stepped off the porch and entered the game. On this day, I was stepping out of the house to enter the world. The comforts of home, sweet home were over and done with. It was go hard or go home. I just terminated option number two.

They say you don't recognize a good thing until it's gone. Well, I would just have to see. How would my life with no rules play out? I had no idea, but I was willing to chance it. It couldn't be that bad. I grew up with homies for whom a single dollar was hard to come by. They had nowhere to go at night and still managed to hold on.

Shortly after stepping out on my own, while playing the block, I spotted one of the local girls from the neighborhood strolling down William Street, on her way home in a nurse's outfit. Something about a hard-working woman turned me on. I loved the get-up-and-get-it attitude. To me, those were the qualities of a rider. It wasn't all that likely to see young females in the 'hood headed to and from work. Some were already taking on the responsibility of raising a child. Some struggled to find work. And some felt as a female they should not only be protected, but provided for as well—the sit-on-their-ass types. Then you had the diamonds in the rough, those who had grabbed hold of opportunity and refused to let it go.

The young lady—from what I saw—definitely had potential and she wasn't sitting around waiting for anything or anyone. I knew her from around the way as Saleema. Saleema was a pretty female; a mix between thick and chubby, caramel complexion, about five feet six inches tall with shoulder length hair. With all respect, she had that sophisticated 'hood persona. You know the "I want to do right, but I'll always love the 'hood" thing. She was the sister of one of my homies, Streets. She was also cousin and niece to some of the most notorious Triplett's, who were all kin to Whip, our 'hood's kingpin in the 90s. Their father was none other than Big Saleem, a reputable old head in his own right and from an older generation of

Tripletts who pioneered our streets. Saleem's brother, Papa Gangsta, was Whip's father, and Saleema's uncle. It was trouble, trouble, and more trouble if you get my drift. Everything that ran through 6th Ave prior to the uprising of the Bloods street gang was Triplett.

With nothing to lose, I tried my hand and hit Saleema with the "let me take you out" line. She politely declined, figuring me to be another joker from the 'hood. Rejection is always a tough pill to swallow, but I let it ride and continued on my grind. The next day—same time, same approach. This time she smiled and accepted. We exchanged phone numbers, and I told her to look out for my call.

After a long day of Blood, sweat, and dollar signs, reality set in—if not a hotel, my car, or just staying out till daybreak—I had nowhere to go. It was times like this I wished I had never left home, but my pride wouldn't let me return, at least not that soon. So I gave Saleema a call and asked if I could swing through. She let me know that it was cool. Without hesitation, I made my way up to her spot. She, her mother, her younger sister Shaheera, and younger brother Lil Leem aka Hip Hop had just moved from 12th Street to the corner of 15th and William Street.

That night, Saleema and I stayed up all night, just kicking it about the things we both wanted out of life. Just like the rest of us, it was her dream to make it out of the ghetto. Having that in common solidified our bond. A silent pact was made as we set out to join forces and make it out. Though she wasn't hands-on in the streets, she knew just as much as I did. She was the easy-going rider type, a Bonnie to my Clyde.

Before I knew it, I had a new place of residence—17 William Street, second floor—smack dab on the corner of all the action. My new honeycomb was definitely no hideout. But the move opened up new doors for me in more ways than one. Living on the strip was extremely dangerous. "Never shit where you eat"—but as a dog I was Doing Only Gangster Shit. While the location was a risk, it provided me with 24/7 access to every dollar that made its way through one of Newark's most profitable strips. Long after everyone grew tired and faded to black, you could find me playing the gate—posted up, pack in pocket, gun on waist—building a clientele that would years later thrust my name among the list of elite.

During the day I would head upstairs for a quick nap, while my team of hungry young hustlers bled the block. It was around-the-clock action. Instead of chasing the money, the money came knocking. Four, five, even six o'clock in the morning, lines of customers were looking for that pick-me-up. This was the fast life, you know, C.R.E.A.M.—Cash Rules Everything Around Me.

Though I can't honestly say that my life, in its earlier stages, was one overwhelmed by struggle, I knew what it meant to be down. The wear and tear of these soiled streets affected us all. That's why I never had an understanding of a "gray area," the middle ground. Just trying to stay afloat was a sure way to find yourself drowning, especially once the waters started rising. For most of us hustling was our lifejacket, the most apparent chance of survival, and we hustled to make a dollar out of fifteen cents. Still, once that dollar was made, the struggle continued, so the process repeated itself until those dollars stacked up.

It became evident that money was not the cure to social suffering. Money was like hands over opened eyes that still could not obstruct the burdens of inequality and the limitations that came with life in the ghetto. It was "Mo' Money, Mo' Problems."

Was the illegal success fair? Many thought not and it wasn't. It was selfish, to say the least. Even though our corners fed well, the heavy flow of drug money through such an obviously poor community was symbolic of the addiction and disease that penetrated deeply into the homes and families of the pushers and customers who roamed the streets at all hours of the day and night looking for their next sale or their next blast.

While I played 6th Ave faithfully, miles away from the 'hood and just minutes away from the New Jersey/New York border, a band of our 'hood's superstars weaved in and out of traffic, finger tapping the throttles of their custom-made motorcycles when suddenly the sounds of screeching tires overcame the air waves. BOOM! In an instant a 'hood legend was gone. It was Whip, killed in a motorcycle accident.

The news hit the streets of Down the Hill like a tsunami. Within minutes, 6th Ave was flooded with people from all over. I have no idea how the news spread so fast but, then again, Whip always had mass appeal and wide notoriety. Sorrow and disbelief were written all over the faces of everybody on 6th Ave. Everyone from children and residents who weren't active in the streets but knew Whip, on down to the gangsters and hustlers, were out shedding tears and sobbing. The 'hood was emotionally crushed. It was so unexpected. Everyone appeared to ask, in silence, how could this have happened?

Vehicles were lined up and down the strip blasting Puffy's "We'll Always Love Big Poppa" on repeat all night. It was a tribute to our fallen. It seemed as though each time the song came on more and more people arrived and more and more tears fell. Together we mourned, pouring out liquor as we witnessed a graffiti artist bless the wall outside of our Middle Bar with a mural of Whip and his bike. Whip's loss was heart-wrenching. Who said the streets don't feel? The 'hood's hero and main bread-winner had fallen.

With the motorcycle death of our 'hood's finest, Malik "Whip Wop" Triplett, man among men, and the hustle game's Michael Jordan; it was like everyone Down the Hill went into a frenzy as they silently contemplated the void left by Whip's loss. Surely, all paid their respect, but behind the scenes many were plotting to become the next Batman in a neighborhood full of Robins. This statement isn't to belittle anyone from my team, or to make any other look inferior to Whip. But as truth has it, in my eyes, Whip Wop was the epitome of a purebred hustler.

Whip's death left a lot of one-time ballers with ribs touching and backed-up bills. It was like The Lox said, "When the big dog dies who's gonna feed the pups?" And after Whip's death what we had was a litter full of hungry pit bulls foaming at the mouth, one plate, too close and SNAP! It is money and hunger that sends nations to war and the 'hood was not above the internal strife spawned by hunger. Bob Marley said it best, "A hungry man is an angry man."

Growing up watching Whip and others, and even when we started to acquire a little flash of our own, there was no doubt in our minds how well our corners fed. Not one of us wanted to be low-level anything. We didn't know the phrase "Can't beat 'em, join 'em," so the division became clear and even intentional. There was deliberate drama. No matter the group, the pressure was on and cooking.

In the streets competition represents a threat, so it is through relentless acts of aggression that men play to win. This led those small groups of three and four within the click to become opposing forces. Certain parts of the strip began being marked by different clicks within the set, who vied for control of the lucrative drug trade along 6th Ave and William Street.

Outside the 'hood it was war over red and blue and inside the 'hood it was a struggle over green. We tried to keep the internal drama quiet. However, at times, things spilled over. A dispute between homies would lead to backing out, guns drawn, and loud rumbles. How easy it was to forget.

Hustling is like every other trade. You will find some who are good at it and others who are not. Only a select few will master the art. Money created hissing among peers. The bickering escalated into tension and stare-downs. The fiends were caught in between whatever erupted. You could see the fear in the eyes of customers who came to the 'hood to get their fix. I guess they could see the hostility in the pupils of the pushers' eyes. Find one who knows what it means to be treated like nothing because they have less and they will attest to the fact that the fight for something is well worth the sacrifice. As we all progressed in our own right, there would be many more episodes, including near-death and death. No matter how you dress dissension, its causes and effects are never pretty.

With Whip gone and no agreement in sight as to who would control the strip or how the block would be divided, the smell of dirty money filled the air, and long-term friendships weren't powerful enough to overcome its luring aroma. It was a dollar and a dream, a pistol and no conscience. At this stage in the game, none of us had the heart to fold. The product and the people would determine winners. There was never a need for our 'hood dilemmas to end with one bowing down but there was always a winner and a loser. It was only more animosity thrown into the gumbo.

There was now no one to appoint or be appointed "that nigga," and a jockeying for power in the 'hood was on. Some took to the paper chase collectively and formed teams and others went about it on their own accord. At the end of the day, money was the motive, and the cunning ways of crooks took to the forefront. Handshakes were no longer accompanied with smiles and embrace. It was clear anybody could get it.

And everybody was eager to get it. It was like the block slammed the door shut on friendships and money now trumped the camaraderie that once defined our 'hood. Our 'hood's mainstay of "let no man separate what we create" was converted into mantras such as "No Use For Friends," "Fuck Everybody," and "Born alone, die alone." In the blink of an eye, enemies were born. Or did they always exist?

Though we remained one set, division eased its way into the 'hood in the name of the almighty dollar. With each corner so close, there was no way to avoid anyone. You could be in plain view but out of each other's sight. What was once love was in full transition into hate. The yellow lines in the center of the street became un-passable. The divider between 15th Street and 14th Street was as clear as day. Speak to another's sale, entice another's customer and it was back to the same old shit once more, backing out with guns drawn. There was no order. Things heated up and got so intense that shootouts would ensue from one corner to the next, one side of the block to the other. Fools dodging in and out of cuts, dressed in all black, pistols still smoking, the Ave turned into a shooting gallery. Even when the drama wasn't loud there was still tension.

The Ave got to a point where bulletproof vests and fully loaded hammers had best be a part of your daily wardrobe. Once a strip as live as 145th and Broadway in New York City, 6th Ave had become as quiet as a country road in the South. Nobody dared risk being a spot-on target. There would literally not be a soul in sight until the sun went down. That's when the sounds from Down the Hill erupted. Hustlers hollering, "I got you right here," as customers weaved in and out of traffic looking for their pusher of choice. The echoes of gunshots and the loud cries of the fallen could be heard a mile away, as Gore-Tex and Timberland boots pressed the pavement. As for me, I can't say I was all for it, but at the same time, I wasn't much against it.

When our in-house beef kicked off, it wasn't long after I had been disciplined by the homies for some shit I didn't even do. My discipline was the result of a homeboy who failed to squeeze during an altercation with some fools from the other side of town. He was undoubtedly afraid of the consequences and before I made it to the 'hood the following day, he already gave an alibi for himself that pointed to me as the frozen gunman. Other homies, with little to no reason, decided to ask questions later. Almost immediately after I stepped foot on the Ave, I was approached by a line of the homies demanding fades. I was too gangster to explain my side of the story. When told to step in the backyard, I wasted no time. I was thoroughly served. The end result was two black eyes and a lip full of stitches. That day, I learned valuable lesson: ANYBODY could get it!

Not until that day did I realize how slow I had been to the way the streets worked. In the streets, and in the game, regardless of how many times you hear how much love another has for you, boundaries can and will be crossed.

Since that day I witnessed more men than I can count fall victim. Many back-stabbed, betrayed, abandoned, sold out, and double-crossed. Rule One: there are no rules. If it was done to me it could be done to anyone. So while I had been headstrong on the "We are brothers; we shouldn't fight one another," the mentality of others was the complete opposite.

For the next two weeks, every time I glanced in the mirror, I wanted to kill the world. But I had to accept the lay of the land. When it came to disciplining others, I didn't mind, so now that the shoe was on the other foot, I had to wear it. Truth be told, I wore it well. There wasn't any hiding the bumps and bruises.

People must have thought I was crazy the way I hit the block the next day, early morning, like nothing ever happened. One thing I did realize was that in this world, you get back what you put out. Karma is a motherfucker. You do dirt, you get dirt. Funny thing is it's your street credibility. He who laughs last, laughs the longest. It's all one big set-up and once the plot thickens, oftentimes it's already too late. Today's pleasures were tomorrow's pains. But while everybody bounced back and forth, in and out of alleyways trying to make a dollar without becoming a casualty, the 'hood, the set was losing the very thing we all vowed to always hold above anything else: UNITY!

Money and drugs consumed us to a point where we no longer recognized or cared to recognize one another. One pull of the "Wet" (PCP) and people disappeared. All you saw were roadblocks and barriers and interference to your way out, or so you thought. Friendship was inhaled like a shotgun blast and swallowed whole, only to be spit out and stepped on like it never existed.

If Whip could have seen what the 'hood had come to or found out what all the division was about, I know he would have been rolling around in his grave. Whip taught us many things, but betrayal and separation were never among them.

Since the very first day I entered Oval Park for football practice, I couldn't help but notice the brotherly love that flowed throughout. Now, I stared into the eyes of some of these same men and all I saw was blood—not Blood, but blood.

At this time, though we were getting money, believe it or not, we were strung out on drugs. We had this belief, as long as it wasn't coke, crack, or heroin it was OK. Our drug consumption only created a more volatile atmosphere. I mean, it was nothing to catch a homie gone off some Jersey City Wet, Macavoy pills (Xanax, Codeines), Sussex Ave alcohol, and Weequahic section weed, all before the night fell. Talk about mixing it up with the medicine! Now walk with me:

What we have is a neighborhood full of miseducated men caught in a quandary of life and death being pulled closer to self-destruction as thousands of guns mysteriously and non-coincidentally make their way into the same urban neighborhoods where, feeding on their state of confusion, young men are hypnotized into accepting a pistol and a pack of drugs as their escape. They are angry and they are frustrated. What is the result? Just what the doctor ordered: the good dying young! This isn't just my 'hood, it's a problem all over the world. And the cause isn't just guns and drugs. The slow death begins the instant a child enters a school and isn't provided with a proper education because of his zip code, the colors he wears, and the style of his hair or the complexion of his skin. No child left behind? Step outside your comfort zone, and tell me how true that is.

I could go on and on about the many who lost their lives long before their time, and for many different reasons, but when it comes to the turf, it's one death that always leaves me with the chills.

It all happened so fast. I ran upstairs to re-up and got caught in a conversation with Saleema. While digging in the back of the closet, I heard the sounds of gunshots, which over the years had become all too familiar. Out of instinct, I reached for my hammer and rushed downstairs ready to bust on whoever had the heart to disrespect.

As soon as I hit the porch, gun in hand, I saw a few of my homeboys—Nas, Troub, Loonatic, and Snoop—crowded around a body sprawled out on the ground. As I crossed the street, my body began to tense up, as I couldn't believe my eyes. There was O.D., staring up into the heavens, as if he knew what awaited him. Still, I could see the rebel in him fighting for a cause. The Grim Reaper calling; O.D. refusing to answer. O.D.'s life always appeared to be a fight to the death. Could he come out on top once more or would he gracefully bow out? Suddenly something tugged at my heart and without yet knowing the outcome I found myself asking God why.

O.D. was rushed to University Hospital in Newark—a busy urban public hospital with doctors, nurses, and hospital staff posted outside the emergency room in fluorescent colored scrubs steaming cigarettes, chatting about the many victims of violence who were rushed through their doors daily.

This was University Hospital: The overwhelming amount of young females who entered with no insurance looking for abortions because they had failed to practice safe sex (the AIDS rate in Newark was close to 25 percent of the population, damn near that of sub-Saharan Africa); the victims of the many domestic-abuse cases. Because the hospital was the main trauma center for New Jersey, oftentimes adversaries who were there to support one of their own would encounter those who more than likely were responsible for the assault. Both parties tight lipped, though they remained heated about the situation. With the authorities present the beef would be postponed. Family and friends hollering at nurses as their children screamed in pain and vice versa.

As O.D. was rolled into surgery, we all sat around wishing, even praying for his survival. While we sat in the waiting room, other homies began to show up. But when O.D.'s mother, Ms. Allen, returned from upstairs with a look of earth-shattering pain in her eyes, all we could do was turn to one another and promise to never take our mothers through an experience like that. In the end, we lost our beloved brother. Marcus "O.D." Allen, I love you brother—your life means more to me than you'll ever know.

Rumor was something came up missing from Skrap's house and O.D. was responsible. Skrap and his brothers Damu and Evol supposedly confronted O.D. about the situation and things got hella heated. Some ran with the story O.D. pulled a strap to back his way out of a corner and pointed the strap at Skrap, and that led to retaliation. None of us believed it. The actual truth could only be told by those involved, which I seriously doubt will ever be spoken.

We were just kids, sixteen and seventeen years old, when O.D. was murdered. A reality of this magnitude shook us all. Death was nothing new, yet as GRatz, 80s babies and so on; this was our 'hood's first time experiencing a homie killing another homie. The fades, the disciplines, and other forms of act right had never gone this far, at least at this stage of our upbringing.

Gassed off the gun smoke and bravado of busting his gun, years of brotherly love had been trashed in a split second. Those of us belonging to the same everything (gang, 'hood, struggle) were now torn by not only death but also murder. There I had it, seventeen years old, two homies carried off by force—one to the grave and the other waived up as an adult and sent off on a long stretch to prison. Our awakening came that night.

Youth our age should have been heading off to college, preparing for freshman orientation, and just getting used to driving without a licensed driver in the passenger seat. And here we were stuck in the 'hood preparing to bury one of our own. During this period the "average" kid didn't have a thought in their mind of such tragedy. Imagine swapping the good times of college life for the sorrow of funeral parlors, closed caskets, cemeteries, prison, and a lifetime of emotional damage.

Envision your son or daughter murdering your neighbor's child in cold blood and each family having to stare the other in the face on damn near a daily basis thereafter. Imagine walking over the very spot where your brother was murdered by the hands of your other brother.

The turning point from fistfights to hitting homies the ski-mask way happened overnight. Even with my earlier discipline, I knew anybody could get it, but this unfortunate episode made it loud and clear. Nothing about this incident is looked at as entertainment, yet every time I hear the lyrics to Jay-Z's record "Where I'm

From,"—"where you can't put your vest away, and say you'll wear it tomorrow/
'Cause the day after we'll be saying damn I was just with him yesterday" takes me
back to the day O.D. was murdered.

After that night, my love for my remaining homeboys tripled in size, while,
for anyone outside of my neighborhood, my heart was as cold as ice. While the
set had begun a tremendous turnaround for the better, I was mentally and emotionally uneasy. I remember days when I would sit in the hallway of my house
on William Street, empty out my .357 revolver, slam a slug into its cylinder,
spin it around and watch it twirl. At such a solemn moment, almost as if my
thoughts could be read, suicide is what I envisioned. In a far distance I could
hear B.I.G.'s:

> "I swear to God I just want to slit my wrists and end this shit
> Throw the magnum to my head, threaten to pull shit
> And squeeze,"

The stress built up and it felt like death was calling me. In the secluded stairwell,
palms sweating profusely, a mixture of panic and relief. Maybe the world was better
off without me. The roar of lawlessness that normally overwhelmed every inch of the
neighborhood was mute. Clutching the pistol, finger tap dancing against the trigger,
I thought about death again, contemplating a coward's end right before putting it to
my own head and squeezing the trigger.

Did I want to die? Honestly, then, I didn't know. Now, I believe that was a part
of what was driving me crazy. I had given up—my parents, my family, even a part
of myself—all for the love of the streets. Now that I was off the porch and in the
streets there was no turning back. Whenever I wasn't high, drunk, or riding around
in the matrix—gun in lap, looking for some work to put in—I realized the streets
loved no one in return, and the choice I was making wouldn't make anything better
for anyone.

I didn't really know how to cope. I stayed high as an eagle; numb to the realities of "this" life and ignorant to the truth stated by Nietzsche, "only where there are
tombs (graves) is there resurrection." *Despair didn't have to be all, end all.*

My eighteenth birthday was fast approaching and with statistics showing a large portion of young black males meeting their maker before the age of twenty-one, I began wondering how much longer I had before my world was overcome by darkness (death). It's scary, but what could I do? Kids dying in the streets had become a daily ritual. Sometimes, circumstances dictate the outcome. I thought, "Fuck it, one death is better than a thousand." If I were going out, it wouldn't be on my knees or tiptoeing around town.

Every day thereafter, I approached the next twenty-four hours as if it were my last. Sad to say, but all my legal troubles began when I adopted this mentality. For most of my juvenile life, I was able to escape the clutches of the system. With exception to the buy and bust, I barely had a run-in with the law—something that was extremely rare, coming from my neighborhood. However, all that began to change.

They say everything happens for a reason, so I always search for meaning in the many bad things I've experienced and endured over the years. Back then, I would hear none of it. How could there be something good in losing my loved ones O.D. or Skrap G? But now, as I look back and have a more proper understanding of life, I see where O.D.'s untimely death opened our eyes to the extent of the division we inflicted upon our 'hood and those in it for money and respect.

Just as times were changing, so were the laws of the ghetto. The fades only bred us to become more violent over the years and, in the end, only caused us to conceal more animosity for one another. Nobody loved to take a loss, so when one did, plots and schemes of revenge were set in the minds of many. Brothers owned ill will for one another since the days of Cain and Abel. The effects were mild to us until O.D. died. After, it seemed every incident ignited more serious drama and encouraged more dissension.

With this particular incident some felt betrayed by the rules. Do they side with the fallen O.D. or do they look at the rules of the game, even though this time the rules were not in their favor? No name or face was to be put on anything other than a t-shirt after an altercation, yet we never expected it to happen like this. Some homies, even Skrap's brother, gave up information on the incident, and many others wanted revenge. Both led to more drama. This issue unearthed the disbanding of the GRatz and led to strained relationships between brothers (literally), and raised family feuds.

I'll say by the time we turned seventeen or eighteen, the GRatz were basically completely over and done with. Quest Records shelved the album the homies recorded, mastered, and mixed down. When Quest heard the final product, they felt it was too gangsta and not in line with the company's image. Through it all, we were near grown men, at least in our minds, with different goals, which brought about distance. Distance brought on doubt and dissension. It was a bomb on the brink of detonation. The hanging out rapping, drinking, and non-stop chain smoking was done. For most, it all amounted to large-scale paper. It was either paper chasing or gun busting.

Just a year prior the GRatz shared everything from socks and sneakers to food and shelter and now we couldn't share something as big as a corner. Breaking down a block was impossible when every penny counted. It was considered stealing to have another's hands in your cookie jar, no matter how big the jar. Stealing was a punishable offense that came with no exemptions. If we weren't seated at the same table at the end of a long day paper chasing, you were considered competition.

Shortly after turning eighteen, out of boredom, I rented a car from one of the local customers in the 'hood—a normal occurrence. Those who were strung out on drugs rented out their cars for hours, sometimes days, in exchange for that great white hype (cocaine). To my luck, on this particular go-round, the guy who I rented the car from ended up having a falling out with his people, who, in return, reported the car stolen. With no clue, me, Nas, and Jungle cruised the town with the factory radio blaring. With our high fading, we decided to swing through Fairmount Ave in Newark to see what that exotic weed from the townhouses was hitting on.

While driving on our way to Fairmount, I damn near hit a pedestrian as I drove up 16th Avenue. Luckily, I swerved just in the nick of time. I thought everything was cool. I failed to notice Newark Police's Auto Squad (team to track down stolen cars) was trailing us. As I pulled over to run in the corner store on 16th Avenue—almost as if it were a repeat of the gas station episode a few years back—we were boxed in and swarmed by undercover cops in cabs, trucks, and vans. I was inches away from being rammed when they jumped out, guns drawn and ready for resistance. No questions asked, we were dragged from the vehicle and sped away.

It didn't take a genius to figure out we were headed to jail, but we still had no idea why. We were young, reckless, and terrorizing the town, so there was no telling what the charge was. They sure didn't see the need to tell us at the moment. It was typical for a lot of officers I crossed paths with over the years to assume you already knew what you were being arrested for. In their eyes, if they were called to a scene, all parties were guilty until proved innocent. More often than not, there were no Miranda Rights read to you and you had to prove your innocence as opposed to the government having to prove your guilt.

When we arrived at Newark's police station on 17th Avenue and MLK, known as the Wild Wild West, it was said that we were being booked on carjacking charges. There had to be a mistake, as I knew damn well that we hadn't carjacked a soul. In my 'hood, we barely robbed. Since the generation before us, stickups took a back seat as more and more guns flooded the street making robberies more risky, and more people opted for the drug trade. With no way to explain this to the police, we were pretty much assed-out. And there we sat in the Wild Wild West precinct, which was much like every other in the city- rundown, full of corruption, filth, biased officers, steel-cage bullpens, police issue 9-millimeter handguns, pepper spray, and wanted posters. There was a mixture of both black and white officers straddling the fence between cop and street thug. The only real difference between the city's precincts was the degree of unwarranted ass whippings they religiously handed out.

I got the alleged carjack victim's info on my arrest sheet, and I decided with my one phone call I would have my people go and make it perfectly clear there had been a misunderstanding. After the call, it was simply a waiting game. They were scared to death when my people showed up at their door demanding they head down to the station to set the record straight. And in pajamas and all, they rushed to it. The desk lieutenant at the Wild Wild West precinct sat, somewhat puzzled by the alleged victim's family walking in ranting and raving that we be released. As a compromise, the carjacking charges were dropped. However, we were booked on RSP (receiving stolen property). A quota still had to be made.

The conviction rate didn't really matter to street cops. All they cared for was the arrest total. Years later I would read a newspaper article with a headline something to the effect of "if you want to commit a crime and get away, do it in Essex County." I thought back to that day in the Wild Wild West and a few other instances where it was evident we were innocent but still charged, and enjoyed a rare smile. The truth of this column was sadly overlooked. It wasn't necessarily true that individuals were getting away with crimes. The truth was our lower-level crime fighters did little when it came to investigating crime. It was all about arrest totals.

One can't say it was all honest and aggressive crime fighting. A 2011 Department of Justice investigation, stemming from allegations made by the ACLU, brought to light the corrupt practices of crooked cops looking to enrich themselves. In a racially divided Newark Police Department, these cops used the same criminal means they were supposed to combat—and those means were rampant. The real assailant could go free as long as the police department had "someone" to answer for the crime and quell public outrage.

Even without the corruption, which at the time was way more perverse than reported, you still had a bunch of hungry officers looking to rack up arrest totals, and there lies the conflict of interest between police departments and prosecutors' offices nationwide. Cops want arrests, and prosecutors need convictions. In many of America's crime-ridden cities, aggressive yet lackluster police work is overwhelming superior courts, burdening taxpayers and crippling the American legal and criminal justice systems.

That night, I got my first taste of Green Street aka The Green Monster, a holding area beneath Newark's municipal courts for those arrested all around Newark. As soon as you entered Green Street, the pungent smells of mildew, piss, and any other unpleasant odor you could imagine hit you directly in the face. After processing, you're thrown into a bullpen for hours with a wooden park bench, a toilet you wouldn't dare touch, and a cellmate—or cellmates—who just might be "rocking and rolling" from being forced to kick their drug habit cold turkey, a painful sight to see.

The bullpens at Green Street were decorated in graffiti: so and so was here, NWK, the Brick City, and "Blasé" headed downstate. There were about six ranges, in two sides of three. The farther back you were, the less attention you received, prepping and priming you for where you were headed: the Essex County Jail. Luckily for us, our stay at Green Street lasted only two days.

Dirty and smelly after hours of sitting in the basement's bullpen, we were all smiles when we were loaded up to be transferred. We weren't headed home, at least not yet, but getting out of Green Street was a beautiful feeling.

We were taken to Essex County Jail and were led up to the second floor intake, where we were stripped down and given our dirty green two-piece uniform. One could taste the stress and disappointment of lost freedom in the air with every breath. Second floor intake at the County began the journey.

"When your name is called, step up to the gate," the CO yelled out.

Sitting in the back of the bullpen, I noticed the voice, but had yet to see a face as inmate after inmate crowded the gate, trying their hand on coming up with something to smoke from one of the orderlies.

"Butler!" I heard my name called and casually strolled up to the front. I was in no hurry, until I saw an all too familiar face of a family friend who was like an uncle. He knew exactly who I was. Not aware of the drastic turn my life had taken, he asked me what I was doing in jail. Then, not wanting his nephew to take a walk on the wild side, the Essex County Jail, he jumped into action.

Without my knowledge, my bail had been reduced from fifty thousand dollars to five hundred dollars. After he punched it in to make sure I hadn't been arrested for any unacceptable charges, he returned and asked if I had the money to post. I slid him a phone number to call and, within hours, I walked out.

While out on bail, I knew things would be different. I couldn't allow charges to pile up or I would definitely be on my way to one of the many correctional facilities that lined New Jersey—Annandale, Yardville, and Bordentown. Also, while out on bail, I immediately sprang into action to make sure the bails of those I was arrested with, Nas and Jungle, were paid. Nas was released the following day, while Jungle had to sit on a detainer.

I contemplated hiring a lawyer but, since this was my first adult charge and I made bail I figured things would be OK. Considering the list of troubles I could've been in, getting caught for receiving stolen property was the least of my worries. The only difficulty I might have would be convincing the judge I wasn't one of the many car thieves who mashed the gas up and down the streets of New Jersey's cities. Gang-banging in Jersey hadn't been considered a problem, but ever since the movie *New Jersey Drive* you had a hard time getting anybody to think we in New Jersey did anything other than steal cars. Little did the world know that the stereotype of New Jersey being filled with nothing but car thieves and stick-up kids was about to change.

Troub was a few months short of being released from Yardville, where he and Itchy Mu spent most of their stay. Itchy-Mu was a twenty-some-odd-year-old out of Little City who got money, took no shorts, had a mean right hand, and was known for his flash. Since our younger years, our time on the streets together was slim thanks to the juvenile justice system. Now we were on the verge of reuniting on the streets where anybody could get it.

6

BLOOD RULE

IN LATE 1997 and early 1998, under the leadership of someone I grew up getting down with who was like an older brother to a few others and me, Little City Projects was gradually making its transition into "The Bity," a full-fledged Blood neighborhood as Gangster Killer Bloods (GKB), an East Coast set that later became known as G-Shine. Now, opposed to a year before, as soon as you'd hit Sussex Avenue, you'd see brick buildings banged out in red tagging "GKB 00120 BLOOD RULES."

When Down the Hill was beefing with Little City a line was drawn, and communication with my family still in the projects had been little to none. Now, with the arrival of Blood, the almighty red rag bridged a gap that existed for years. We buried the beef, and the Double ii Bloods and the Gangsta Killer Bloods of The Bity took to each other like never before. We grew up trading blows. Both sides took respectable wins and honorable losses, so there was no question if there were certified gangsters under the umbrella.

Under no circumstances were busters tolerated. If you picked up that flag and got caught faking, your face got ripped. A buck fifty was the term for slicing someone's face with an ox (razor). Homies who journeyed across the water to New York—most often via the George Washington Bridge—to replenish their supply and got trapped off by the law were sent to Riker's Island. They returned with the treacherous skill of tucking a razor under their tongues, and in almost an instant, they could spit it out and slice your face a million ways.

Not only did they return with such a dangerous talent, they also brought back something unheard of until that point: Lessons! These lessons pertained to the United Blood Nation (UBN). The United Blood Nation originated in New York's prison system among East Coast Bloods and represented the unification of all East Coast Blood sets in New York's prison system. The culture of the UBN differed from the West Coast culture we were raised on. What these lessons consisted of, I can never share. However, I will tell you this: If you got caught rocking that red of any sort—chucking up B's, talking in codes, even slashing C's—and didn't know what that "red was like," you were in for a rude awakening. It was testament to the dedication and loyalty possessed in those days and was meant to weed out those perpetrating and exploiting the culture.

As Bloods, we were committed to a cause greater than self where even if others didn't agree, dishing out death or accepting it in the same was no problem at all. The gang was what we loved, so to see an imposter disrespecting the legacy and the lives of homeboys who paved the way, something had to give.

Other Bloods were popping up around the city and ties among the different sets had yet to be established. I heard about different Blood sets springing up—the Sex Money Murders, The 9 Treys, and The 72 Mob Pirus—but had yet to politic with any of them other than the Gangsta Killer Bloods. You could bump into a gang of Bloods where no one knew the other and questions were raised of who was official or not. For many in the East, Blood originated in the New York prison system. Believe it or not, some were not familiar with the origin and evolution of Blood from its roots in California and had yet to realize Double ii was in its own lane—in the East riding a West Coast line. Nevertheless, the homies of the UBN in the East were serious about riding in what they believed in and it would only be a matter of time before things came to a head.

Every set was on a mission to make its mark. No gang stuck to its turf. Gangsters were all over, painting the town red—parks, high schools, you name it. A wave had taken over. Either you stepped in line or got stepped on. While the agenda had become to make everything in sight red—Bloody red, Crips were silently coming together. We were clueless about their connection and still under the impression the only Crips in existence were the North Side Killer Gangstas. We continued mobbing.

That is until a night when boredom got the best of me. I wasn't one to party much and stayed away from the club scene, knowing the odds were in favor of nights ending with teardrops and closed caskets. I was out on bail and didn't know what the future held, so when the homies decided to G-stroll Up the Hill to a little club named Gregory's at the top of Central Avenue, I figured why not? I knew this wasn't our turf and had a gut feeling something was bound to jump off, but it was what it was. All work and no play was good for no one. I was dressed to impress—fresh kicks, jeans, crispy white T-shirt, flamed fitted cap, and of course my favorite, twin .357 snub-nose revolvers. We loaded up and mobbed to the party.

When we arrived, it was as if the bouncers knew we were from a different part of town. They took us through all sorts of hoops before they finally agreed to let us in. They laid out certain rules made specifically for us, like the first sign of gang-banging, throwing up signs, or things like that and we had to go. Everybody knew about the Double ii Bloods from Down the Hill. We had been to war with the large majority of others. Since way back when, when I first cut school to meet Gangsta, Mad Dog, and others at Hart Middle School to throw blows with the opposition, it seemed the beef was never ending. I don't think we even realized how much noise we were making in the streets.

Once inside the club, which was a little hole in the wall, I scoped out the spot for a position with an easy exit. I headed to the back by the pool tables. From that angle, I was able to see the door and nobody could get behind me as I threw back shots of Hennessy and clutched a Corona.

There was a dance floor in the next room with small dinner tables, a DJ booth, and mirrors lining the walls. I stayed in pocket and shot a few games of pool—a skill I acquired trading bank shots in our 'hood's Middle Bar with Ms. Kat and C.C., the Middle Bar's owner and bartender.

As the music blasted, time flew by, drinks were devoured, and all seemed smooth. That's when I noticed a group step through the door dressed in red from head to toe. Instantly, I knew they were Bloods. If you weren't on gang time, walking around dressed in that fashion was a big mistake. I wasn't the only one in the club who noticed. You could see the fear build in the eyes of other club-goers, as though they figured it only a matter of time before things got ugly. Since nobody wanted to be that somebody, the dance floor slowly began to empty and people started to play the wall. The DJ put on DMX's "Where My Dogs At." Things got crazy. Red flags waved everywhere. Bloods rushed the floor B-hopping and G-stacking, busting their guns. "Blatt, Blatt" echoed throughout the club as if actual gunshots. I was a true gang-banger at heart, so I knew it was time to squad up.

Just as I whispered to two homeboys to get a head count and make sure everyone knew the quickest way to their straps (guns), I noticed a commotion near the front of the club. There was no doubt in my mind what had taken place and who was involved. When I made my way through the crowd, I spotted my homeboy Streets ready to fire on one of the Damuettes, a female Blood, from 72 MOB Piru. She saw Streets on the dance floor chucking up the 'hood and approached him, razor in hand, and said the all-too-familiar phrase at the time, "What that red be like?"

Being asked "What that red be like?" was a slap in the face. It questioned who you were and your dedication to the movement. Any true Blood in the East knew when asked "What that red be like," you responded with an aggression of your own for the apparent disrespect. The question alone was enough to send things up in a blaze and caused many disputes between Blood sets.

Growing up in Double ii 'hood, we were raised to answer to no one. There were no big I's and little yous. If you weren't a big homeboy from the set, you had nothing coming. So when G-checked on what that red be like, the homie Streets banged the 'hood on the female and figured it to be what it was going to be. It might sound harsh, but if a homegirl jumped out of line with a homeboy, there were no exemptions. Act like a man and get treated like a man. In certain 'hoods there was no gender bias. Some homegirls were shot callers in their own right. Some homegirls bled the block. Some homegirls busted their guns. And some homegirls got their asses beat if they jumped stupid.

The homegirl from Piru quickly realized Streets wasn't having it and slowed up. This gave other Damus the opportunity to intervene. Set tripping (Blood on Blood violence) was supposed to be a no-go, but fades were most definitely official. Given the homegirl upped the razor on Streets, there was nothing I could say or do other than prepare for whatever move he wanted to make.

In the midst of the chaos, the Damuette explicitly questioned whether or not we were official Bloods and claimed she never heard of Double ii before. In my mind, that was cool, because when the club closed, the real party was going to begin.

With no more to discuss, we made it clear we were to get it up at closing. While the crowd parted ways, their big homie, a Damu by the name of Holiday, mashed in and screamed on his pups about the disrespect directed our way. Without hesitation, he made it known he knew the Double ii Bloods and what we stood for. He sensed we still wanted to pop things off, so he put it on the "B" that ol' girl would be thoroughly disciplined. It wasn't my call. I looked to Streets to see if he wanted to go with it or not. Streets didn't really want to trip with other Bloods, so he opted to let it ride. I had no firsthand knowledge of how the Pirus we clashed with functioned. I knew Pirus were known for putting in work in the West, so to squash that beef prevented plenty of bloodshed.

When the party was over and the tension simmered, the Pirus stood in the street and at the top of their lungs in unison, they chanted things like, "It's time to eat food. It's time to represent and kick in the door waving the .44, all you heard was Blood don't hurt 'em no more." We were more laid back with ours and preferred to stay off the radar, while we strived to make millions. The roll-calling in public and other front street demonstrations wasn't our M.O. At the time we had no clue what they were saying or doing. It was evidence of the differences in culture between us and Bloods on the East Coast. We were never taught such things coming under a West Coast line.

It was our lack of knowledge of East Coast gang culture that kept us in run-ins during the early stages of Bloods' rise to dominance in the East. We understood our roots and the lineage of our set and it was without doubt Inglewood for life. However, I had to brush up on these "lessons" coming across the water from New York to function in the same streets as the United Blood Nation and the many East Coast Bloods who had begun to fill the streets of New Jersey, predominantly Essex County.

I also knew all knowledge was good knowledge. As a Blood, I wanted to know every piece of history attached to our journey from the Van Nesses to the Brims, the Slausons to the Gladiators, the Figueroa Boys down to the 5-Line Bounty Hunters. In my eyes, Crip history was equally as important. I read up on Tookie Williams, Raymond Washington, the Eastside and the Westside Crips. To run around gang-banging and putting in work and not know the cause, your cause, meant you were nothing more than a wannabe who could never be recognized in the eyes of real Damus and Locs. To expand my knowledge on the East Coast perspective, mainly the UBN, such as codes, sets, colors, and more, I went to go see one of the first Bloods to come out of The Bity.

He understood my hunger and blessed me with all I needed to know and informed me to learn it like my last name. Though my 'hood was out of California and we did things differently, he gave me thirty-one days to put it all on cap. I was honored. I ate, slept, and shitted with those lessons on my mind. I wanted to know it all, not only for myself, but so I could pass it along to every other Blood in my neighborhood who took our way of life as serious as I did.

During this same period, Down the Hill started to heat up with more and more police. As red rags began popping up in neighborhoods you wouldn't imagine, the law most likely decided to focus on what they knew to be the epicenter of gang activity—Down the Hill. Things hadn't even peaked. Honestly, it was just taking off and gained momentum each time a Damu stepped foot on a new block. In my 'hood, Blood was nothing new and whether they shared this with the public or not, the police knew this.

As far back as the early 90s I remember police parked down the street surveying us as kids. They observed us rocking red rags and representing Blood. Now, with what they considered to be a germ spreading like an epidemic, the Double ii Bloods naturally became the law's first target.

Initially, the law concentrated on the Block's big dogs, respected names like Hammer, Finsta, Diesel, and Fam. They seemed intent to make the connection between us all, including Treach, Kay Gee, and Vinnie of Naughty by Nature. All in all, early on, they sat back and watched. It's possible there were a heap of "hold offs" coming from their superiors. Maybe there was a lack of manpower, or perhaps it was a casual approach to a movement that was clearly growing day by day.

Sista Soulja's *Coldest Winter Ever* was gone. The summer of '98 was the world's hottest summer and not because of rays emanating from the sun. Gang-bangers on both sides were heating up the 'hood with sizzling hot ones. It seemed prison or an early death was inevitable.

In addition to being Bloods, we were serious hustlers. This made the law's job to cart us away to jail a lot easier. One of their strikes came just days before I was to head to court after pleading guilty to my earlier receiving stolen property charge because of the car situation with the fiend.

It was August 11, 1998, a little more than a month before my nineteenth birthday. There wasn't too much East Orange Task Force didn't know about the green house on the corner of North 15th and William Streets. After a long night of scrambling, I decided to sleep late, only to be awakened by the loud screams of our neighbors who informed Saleema her father was being arrested.

I got up and was on my way to the window to see what was happening when Too Gee (Omar Broadway), strolled in, blunt in hand, not wanting to be the next in cuffs. Saleema left to go see what was up with her Pops.

I told Too Gee to light the weed. What was going on outside with Saleema's Pops had no bearing on us behind closed doors, or so we thought. We passed the blunt back and forth. With the high kicking in, I lost track of time and the fact Saleema even left the house. Somebody getting arrested was an everyday thing, so this was nothing new.

Me and Too Gee were still smoking when interrupted by a thundering kick to the door. I snapped out of my daze just in time to catch the door as East Orange's Task Force tried to push through. No warrant, no probable cause other than they claimed to have found drugs on Saleema's father and they knew this was his place of residence. Later, I would find out the real reason for the raid was phone calls and complaints from neighbors, which confirmed I was bringing in a lot more money than people believed.

Task Force heard the barks as my pit bull rushed the door in defense of his throne, and they quickly yanked the door back shut and began yelling, "Put the fucking dog in the bathroom!"

No way in the world. I kept my weight pressed against the door and whispered to Too Gee to flush the stash before they bum-rushed the apartment and took us all to jail. The yelling continued, "Put the fucking dog in the bathroom. E.O.P.D!"

Too Gee stood in the doorway of my bedroom with a look of shock on his face as he looked for an escape route. There was nowhere to go. Police were lined up outside the back of the house. Saleema's younger brother Lil Leem was scared and began to drag the dog into the bathroom. Unable to yell, I pled with my eyes for Lil Leem to let the dog go. Still, he continued dragging the dog away. Police noticed the growing distance of the barks and tried their hand. They slammed through the door and over-powered me straight to the ground. They dragged Too Gee and me face down into the hallway. In seconds, they were picking apart every inch of 17 North William Street.

After a few minutes, they picked us up off the ground and positioned us on the couch in the living room. We sat on the couch and watched them deliberately destroy the apartment. They sliced furniture with knives. They emptied drawers, closets, and cabinets and threw clothes and dishes all over.

"Where's it at? We will find it. Where is it at?" cop after cop yelled.

Hear no evil; speak no evil. "I don't know what you're talking about," was my only reply.

"Ok, when we find it everyone's going to jail and the little boy is going to DYFS [Division of Youth and Family Services]."

I knew nothing. They thought they came up on something when they stumbled across a Timberland shoebox filled with all sorts of paraphernalia (crack vials, razors, rubber bands, and my trademark red tops), but they became angry when they realized it wasn't enough to keep me locked away. I had to stop myself from laughing when one cop kicked the contents all over the floor, but I knew it was only a matter of time before they found what they were looking for.

"Bingo! We got your ass now, Mr. Kingpin!"

Out came an officer with a lunch pack filled with 127 bottles and a little over an ounce of raw cocaine. As I sat there, I heard B.I.G.'s "10 Crack Commandments": "Never sell crack where you rest at, I don't care if they want an ounce tell 'em bounce." Now here I was caught up, after ignoring one of the many jewels dropped on me over the years, cuffed and on my way to the County Jail.

When led down the stairs of the apartment I saw Saleema in one police car, her father in another, and—of all people—my mother standing to the side. She must've just pulled up and looked as if her heart was ripped from her chest as she watched her oldest son led away by the law. There was definitely no denying it any longer: The streets had her boy.

Once we arrived at the precinct, I was forced to watch the law's big show. They crowded around a table directly in front of the bullpen, high-fiving one another as if they just came up on the world's biggest bust. In total, they seized around six to seven thousand dollars in product. But for them, it wasn't about the bust, it was about finally getting their hands on the young kid they heard was promoting gang activity and pushing work in and out of the back blocks of Newark and East Orange.

They made it evident they had their man—me. Police from as far down the totem pole as beat-walkers to those as high as sergeants and lieutenants hit the gate each with a slick remark of their own. "Let me see you get everybody out of this, Mr. Kingpin" and things like, "What's up, Gangster?"

This was the infamous East Orange Task Force and their antics. These were the same police I grew up watching tear apart families in my community as far back as my days of living on Carnegie Ave. Now, older and in a predicament of my own, I saw firsthand exactly what happened when the older homeboys on my block got carted away.

After being processed—fingerprinted, record-checked, and photographed—a procedure I was now familiar with, I was led to the lieutenant's desk where my charges were read. Then I was given my one phone call. Bail hadn't been set and there wasn't too much I could do, so I skipped the call and headed to the basement of the East Orange precinct.

I briefly spoke with Saleema's father while we waited in the precinct to go to the County Jail. I assured him I would undoubtedly accept my weight. I already planned to do so to cut his daughter loose. It was the right thing to do because what they found was mine. I just hoped he would do the same and all would work itself out.

I had to figure out a way to post bail before my sentencing day for the receiving stolen property charge, then only three days away, or prepare myself to walk in front of the judge already donning my county greens and be sent downstate. I sat in the precinct's basement and listened to the many stories of others who were also arrested. Even in the precinct there were killers and drug dealers. Everybody was somebody. The story that bothered me most was one told by a guy who said there was no way we would be jail dropped and arraigned in three days. I truly needed a stroke of luck, but with the cards life was dealing, I wasn't willing to bet on it.

I paced back and forth within the confines of a six-by-eight-foot cell. My stress and aggravation must have been giving off silent signals. Almost out of the sky, the man in the cell next to mine began to quote verses from the Bible. The Book of Proverbs 16:9: *We can make our own plans, but the Lord determines our steps.* Proverbs 16:33: *We may throw the dice but the Lord determines how they fall*; And Proverbs 19:21: *You can make many plans but the Lord's purpose will prevail.*

Much of my family on my mother's side was strong in their faith and true believers in religion. On the other hand, I strayed from the church and there I sat in the basement of East Orange's precinct desperately in need of a prayer. It is said God looks out for sinners too. How true. After listening to my neighbor's sermon, I dozed off and was awakened by an officer yelling my name, insisting I get ready. I was to be on the next wave out of the precinct to the County Jail.

I could not have been happier. Part of my mission was to get to the courts on time. Once at the County Jail, I would see the judge and be granted bail within twenty-four hours. I had just left there a few months earlier, so I pretty much knew how it went with processing.

I hoped to see the same person who helped reduce my bail on my earlier trip, my uncle/family friend in receiving and discharge (R&D). I figured he could pull a few strings one last time. But when I ran into him, he brushed me off like I didn't exist. He wasn't a fan of my running in and out of the County Jail like it was the thing to do. When he finally decided to acknowledge my presence, he asked, "How does it feel to be ignored?"

I had no clue what he was referring to and at the time I honestly didn't care. All I wanted to hear was he was going to make things happen. In return, I questioned him.

"What are you talking about? Who am I ignoring?" I said, trying to keep my cool and not explode.

"First off, you're ignoring and disrespecting your mother and father who just so happen to be like a brother and sister to me. Second, you're disrespecting yourself. I grew up with your parents and watched them both sacrifice day in and day out to make ends meet for you and your brother—and you repay them by leaving home to chase these so-called street dreams that will do nothing but lead you exactly where you are right now or to a much-sooner death. You're so caught up, you don't even realize the negative effect you're having on your brother. Whether you want them to or not, the things you're doing are subconsciously embedded in him. But of course, you know it all, that's why you're here, right?"

It was most definitely not the time for his spiel. I had already had enough on my mind with court, bail. I wasn't trying to catch what he was throwing. However, it was righteous. I entered the game with a positive agenda—to lift not only myself, but also my homies out of our struggles and remove us all from the list of Have-Nots and land ourselves a respectable spot with the Haves and Have-Mores. I truly wanted to brighten all the darkened days we had come to know. In the process, though it may sound clichéd, I became a product of my environment. Attracted to the rapid pace life twisted and turned; fascinated by a life where my nights were everlasting and my weekends were never-ending; duped by the illusions of power I believed lay in the drug money that flooded my neighborhood. Overnight, all I wanted was what I needed and what I needed, I no longer wanted. Easy to do wrong, hella hard to do right, and I was a living example. When asked what that Inglewood was like, I wasted no time and responded, "Banging and Balling."

I became selfish, concerned with nothing other than my gang and money. This I knew and I felt the pain, yet I continued. Was I a fool, stupid, or just didn't give a fuck? It was none of the above. I was addicted, sick, and diseased. A homeboy of mine once told me, "It's not only the user who is addicted, but also the pusher. As hustlers we become just as hooked on the hustle and lifestyle as the fiend is on the drugs." He was talking about the 'hood fame, the ghetto celeb, the boom, boom, boom of my heart pounding each and every time I woke in the morning prepared to venture out on another paper chase. All of it had me in a coma-like state, going through the motions of life, unaware of my unconsciousness. Something I see daily now that my eyes are open.

After the conversation with my uncle in the County, and him denying me assistance, I ended up in R&D for hours. I fought myself for what seemed like forever. This was where I was mistaken. It was not my uncle who abandoned me. It was my better self who let me down. But there I was playing the good old-fashioned blame game. It was everyone else's fault but mine. Later that afternoon, I was given my bedroll and sent to the second floor.

Picture the second floor of the Essex County's Jail as one big dormitory filled with bunks and the filth of every man who believed he had what it took to outsmart the system and found himself trapped. The second floor was without question a place where you had better watch your step. It was nothing to run into an enemy, someone you robbed, shot, shot at, or stabbed. There was nothing but air and opportunity separating you and your potential death.

Maybe it was the stress of men who were forced to chalk up a loss in a game we all played to win. Whether you wanted to see the inside in an attempt to gain false stripes, recognition, or notoriety, jail was ugly. It was Remy without the rocks, no chaser, raw reality. A hard shot when swallowed that burned like hell.

The County was uncompassionate and callous. Jail usually offered heightened safety but the County was nearly as dangerous as the streets. Confrontations spilled their fair share of blood and guts. In the County the best of the best got served. Nearly every day something went down. Inmates got high, drunk, robbed, stabbed, beat down, raped, you name it. Some inmates with more game than a little bit hit on female COs and were given free passes into restricted areas of the jail to indulge in intimate exchanges. The average person would most definitely dread the place, Bloods included.

With the impact gangs were having on the cities of Essex County, most of the men who entered the County Jail were either gang members or affiliated in some fashion. Some who were affiliated and happened to have names for themselves were considered bulletproof, or not to be fucked with. Others were left for the wolves. Men would enter the jail with the latest sneakers and attend their bail hearing in slippers. I wasn't tripping off of any of that. Honestly, I was trying to get to sleep so I could hurry up and see the judge.

After a long night of tossing and turning, one eye open in case someone I hadn't spotted me, I was on my way to arraignment. Once before the judge, things went according to plans. She had no information about my sentencing date for the receiving stolen property charge, which was then twenty-four hours away. My bail was set. My people were seated in the courtroom, and I had no worries about posting bail.

On my way back through the underground tunnel from the courthouse to the jail, I ran across Saleema on the chain gang. She was on her way up to see the judge. I could tell by the look in her eyes this was foreign land, but I also noticed something that made me smile. It was a look that said, "I'm going to hold it down." When she spotted me, I yelled for her not to worry, as we both would have our feet on solid ground by the end of the night.

Back on the second floor, still a nervous wreck, hoping no detainers or warrants fell from the sky, I tried to relax and played a few games of Spades on the bottom of garbage cans we used as tables. I more or less did this until I heard my name called to pack up. The clock was winding down, and I just made it. At 10 PM I walked out of the gates of Essex County Jail. My only dilemma was whether or not I would appear at sentencing the next day for the receiving stolen property charge or get low.

I did not want to turn myself in because when I was released I learned Saleema wasn't. If anything I owed that much to her. Our relationship had its ups and downs, but in my times of need and uncertainty she never betrayed me. I believe loyalty to be one of the strongest qualities a man or a woman could possess. I decided after I was certain Saleema's bail was paid and she was released: I would face the courts and deal with whatever they had in store. Her freedom would surely make the decision easier. Having a strong woman by my side while I did my bid would help make my time fly by.

The next morning Saleema's bail was paid, and she was due to be released. My mind was racing so fast I didn't sleep a lick. With the new drug charge, I was surely looking at least ten years. One thing I knew for certain was every minute spent behind bars made the system richer and me poorer. My "I want to see what jail is like" attitude was long gone.

When morning came I watched the clock and every tick of its hand. I was scheduled to appear at 9 AM and receive probation unless it was figured out I had been arrested again. Nore's "Niggas on the Run Eating" flooded my brain. I couldn't see handing myself over to the law for them to take away my best years. Funny, none of that mattered until that moment.

We walk through life and question nothing, accepting what stands before us as though it has to be. Then the time comes for us to reap the spoils of the life we chose. Suddenly we are overtaken by deep sorrow and regret. Not to discredit the awakening lifted from remorse, but the choices we make trying to escape must not be made with our eyes wide shut. Part of the reason for this is our struggles and wanting thoroughly to make it out. Having experienced the lowest of the lows, one adapts to their reality and develops a false perception of success and what has to be done to achieve it.

Where I'm from, the fast cars, big jewels, pretty ladies, and a pocket full of dough defined success. What one didn't know was that with failing schools and scarce employment much evil would need to be done to climb that ladder. In hindsight, it was a pure case of ignorance influencing decision-making. Many of us came from families where no one made it to college, so obvious pathways weren't so obvious at the time. The majority were never taught or even considered success as a state of mind, a state of being, and not based on what you have but who you are. Most never thought to look at life in the long run and consider the consequences of their actions now and in the future. Without much fundamental knowledge and long-term vision, kids lacked direction and chased and determined their own success—which in most cases led to barbaric behavior. Each man preyed on the next, scoped for weakness, and discovered ways to exploit others for personal benefit. Drug dealers, murderers, robbers, you name it, all blinded by the beauty of empty treasures that cure the need for a quick fix yet are never long lived.

All of this ran through my mind that morning. Had it not been for my mother's signature on the bail slip, there was no way I was going to show up to court. But as a man I had to own up and not allow my mother and father to be punished in my place.

I entered the courtroom with my mother and father at 9 AM with the appearance of the perfect family. We were met by a public defender who eagerly gave us the rundown on what to expect and suggested everything would be OK. I hoped so. After pacing the hallway for almost an hour, my time came. I took my place behind the defendant's table. Out walked one of the few African-American judges to preside in Essex County, the Honorable Michael Giles. After the first few minutes I could tell he didn't know about my new drug case. That eased my nerves. However, the lecture he gave raised my antennas.

Judge Giles stated he had no problem sending me to prison if my behavior did not change: "You're going to have to keep that job, because if you don't, it is going to constitute a violation of your probation. Then you'll be brought back before me and we'll be talking about finding work making license plates. You do know who makes license plates?"

After I replied yes, he went on a little longer, handing out my fines, probationary term, and other restrictions. Had Judge Giles discovered that my "job" was nonexistent I'm sure he would have buried me underneath the jail. Then he closed with this:

"All right Mr. Butler, I hope that this has brought you into the realm of reality and we'll see if what you say is so by your conduct for the next four years while you're on probation."

And there you had it, I was given four years' probation for receiving stolen property, my first adult case. Not stressing the sentence, actually, I could not have been more pleased as I darted for the door.

Outside the courthouse, there was my Cosby-cool Pops dressed to the nines in linen slacks, an Italian sweater with square-tip gator hard bottoms, and Moms looking every bit of Claire Huxtable (Felicia Rashad), always classy. Then, there was me. I was far from Theo and too cool for my own good. After a collective sigh of relief my "perfect family" parted ways. My father headed back to work and my mother went home on her day off. Me, I fell face first into the temptations that would create a cycle of "All rise before the honorable judge."

I did not want to end up counting reps and maximizing sets in a prison yard, so I took the advice of my older homeboys and shot down Neck to the Ironbound section of Newark to pay a visit to one of the top criminal defense lawyers in New Jersey at that time, Paul Bergin. Paul represented actors, rappers, and a list of other high-profile clients in high profile cases. I knew he was the guy to see.

Paul's office was graced with an assortment of plaques, pictures, and other accolades. It didn't take long to detect his confidence, maybe even an air of arrogance. It was as if no case was too big for him to handle. I liked what I saw, and I liked what I heard. I posed one last question, "How much will it cost me to beat it?"

Paul took in my appearance—I was a slim, baby-faced eighteen-year-old—and began to arrange payments. I figured he saw me as nothing more than a low-level hustler/gang-banger who would probably need forever to fulfill my obligations. He said he'd cut me a deal and take the case on a $5,000 retainer. I got a kick from the look on his face when I reached into my pocket, peeled back $5,000 cash, and placed the rest of my stack back into my jeans.

I felt a lot better when I left his office. But I felt somewhat foolish and bothered. Here I was hustling and stacking only to get arrested and have to post bail and pay lawyers. It was a tax in its own right. Was it worth it? Whether it was or wasn't, truth was the game had me in its web. The weight of the world was so heavy it would test just how heavy of a load I could bear.

With my newly retained attorney and a fresh probation term, my legal woes were on the back burner and street life reclaimed its spot at the forefront. I had to pay lawyers. And I was right back on my grind.

It was 1999. Things were still crazy in the streets and gangs had the land in an uproar. Thinking back to the chaotic times, infighting and the destructive state of the Bloods in the late 90s, one night remains fresh on my mind. All week, word circulated Club Zhane's on Eastern Parkway, near the Irvington bus terminal, was hosting a Blood Bash and the featured performer was a then-hot new rapper and chart-topper from Murder Inc., Ja Rule.

We were unsure of what the word was in Ja Rule's hometown of Queens, New York, but in Jersey we firmly believed Ja Rule was Blood. There was nothing anyone could say or do to change that. We had to be there! Not to party. Not for women. We needed to be there to represent for the Blood. Nobody wanted to miss out. It wasn't just a party, it was an opportunity to send word back across the water to New York about just how serious Blood was in New Jersey—especially since East Coast sets were founded in New York's prison system. All other East Coast sets were considered a branch of the one parent, the United Blood Nation in New York. Most East Coast Riders I knew in Jersey didn't mind, thus not too many will admit that every child craves the attention of his parents.

For me and other homies from the set—Uncle Rat, Flock, Tall Dog, Chip, Auto, and Dream, all members of the 'hood's Steel Click—things started out all wrong. The ominous beginning to this night was clear indication it would end ugly.

We were parked side by side, blocking the street and screaming from one car to the next, discussing where we were going and checking to make sure everyone was strapped. One homie whose name we won't reveal upped his pistol and stated in a drunken slur, "I got me."

"All right cool, let's roll."

Before we got a chance to pull off, BOOM! The homie sent a hot one straight through his leg while tucking the gun in his waistband with no safety.

"A-YO, what the fuck?"

The single shot was the only sign it wasn't the enemy. The homie was already faded on pills and Wet. Cool, calm, and collected he confirmed what we all knew.

"I'm hit," he stated.

Damn, hospital attention was not an option. With the angle of the wound there would have been no mistaking what happened. Then, not only would the homie be in the hospital hit, he would have been on his way to jail. The homie was hyped up on the night ahead and voiced, "I'm cool, don't trip. Let it drip dry. I'm going to see the homie Ja Rule."

Not one of us with common sense of our own put up a fight. The club was waiting.

When we arrived the club was packed with gangsters from all over. Everybody was in attendance and it was red everything. Everywhere was flamed up. Gangsters were getting their boogie on. The party was pumping when Tall Dog and I slid over to the bar. We grabbed a few drinks to take with us and then spot on, in my sight, was "Fu." I had been looking for Fu for the past year.

Fu reminded me of Craig Mack, minus the afro, facial features and all. He stood around five feet ten inches and weighed 180 pounds with a low cut. Back when, I had employed Fu illegally, giving him work to flood the Teen Streets courtesy of his relative who was like an older homeboy to me. Our business dealings were smooth. That was until Fu, thirsty for change, saw a couple of grams of raw cocaine and a few dollars and decided it was worth more than his life. Fu ran off and was in hiding since.

Fu quickly realized he was spotted and had no escape. Instantly, he went into damage control. He pleaded his case. All the while, he spoke in Blood codes in an attempt to make me aware of the fact, while in hiding, another homie put him on a different set with no clue he was an outlaw. During Fu's charade, a childhood friend of mine, Mustafa, whom I hadn't seen or spoken to since my days back on Carnegie

Avenue approached. Come to find out it was Mustafa who put Fu on the set Gangster Killer Bloods (GKB).

At the time none of that mattered. What was mine was mine and no East Coast law, which punished set tripping, was going to stop me. With all due respect, this was Jersey and the work we put in was on the East, but we were Double ii Bloods, a West Coast set by nature. If push came to shove, we didn't have to adhere to any rules or laws other than those handed down from the Q (Inglewood's Queen Street, the foundation of our set).

With murder on my mind, I was pissed I wasn't able to sneak my pistol inside the club. Certainly, Tall Dog and I could have served him right then and there. However, this violation called for much more than a thirty-one-second beat down, a common form of discipline within the UBN.

"What's poppin', Mass?" Mustafa hollered over the loud music, oblivious to what was going on.

My temper was already past boiling, and I shouted, "His Top!" and pointed in the direction of his supposed pup or lil homie Fu.

Hollers of "Hold, Hold!" broke up the heated discussion.

Both sides sensed something was brewing. Out of nowhere everyone began to crowd around. It was too much of an inconvenience to explain why this bandit's head was on a platter. I already resigned to the fact there must be trouble, and I was ready to eat food. Out of universal respect for the "B," Mustafa, and the set he was pushing, I listened as Mustafa repeatedly gave his word that Fu would pay me back every cent with interest or be personally served by the very 'hood he ran with.

Just as things started to ease up a Damu whom I had never seen before came rushing into the crowd yelling orders, "Sha Blood said he want all of y'all in the club now!"

I thought to myself, who was Sha Blood? Was my situation unimportant? Lastly, who was he giving orders to when he said "all of y'all"? I looked at Tall Dog and Tall Dog looked back to me. We must've thought the same thing because at once we screamed, "Man, FUCK SHA BLOOD!"

Eyes went wide and all seemed to stop. You would have thought we said fuck The Most High. At that moment it seemed his people didn't know what to do—get it popping with us for disrespecting their big homie Sha Blood or get into the club per their big homie's order. They entered the club. By the time we entered, Ja Rule was minutes away from taking the stage. All the hype was downplayed shortly thereafter when Ja Rule took the stage to perform. Not even a complete song into his set, Bloods rushed the stage in an attempt to basically muscle Ja Rule into sporting a red rag. Ja Rule refused to do so and things grew out of hand. A fight broke out and sent things into an uproar.

I guess things got a little too serious for Ja Rule. He, like plenty others, didn't realize how serious the life was until it was too late. The too-late sign for Ja Rule came when a dozen or so bloodthirsty Damus, draped in red with do or die looks in their eyes all but tied the rag around his head. The homies on stage weren't playing by a long shot, and I honestly believe Ja Rule was afraid to put that rag on for fear of not knowing what would come next. It was entertainment meeting reality and the line was clear.

The show was cut short due to mayhem in the club. We made sure all of us who came together were safe and made a quick dash to our vehicles, strapped up, and returned in a hurry. By this time the front of the club was jam-packed. Still, I had no problem spotting Mustafa.

"Where Fu at, Blood?" I questioned.

This night was ending one way—RETRIBUTION! Mustafa was well aware where my mental was and with a look of deception, replied, "He already left, homie."

I knew Mustafa hurried Fu away to prevent an inevitable outcome. Before I could voice my anger, I realized we were surrounded.

"What's poppin', Blood?" a short, dark-skin homie from Piru questioned. "What that red be like?"

His G-check wasn't a result of him believing we weren't official or even about my situation with Fu. Instead, it was in relation to the "Fuck Sha Blood!" remark made earlier. This was the ugly we saw in the beginning of the night coming to a head.

Uncle Rat, not known as a talker, took off, punching the person closest to him.

...Gunshots rang out!

Before you knew it bullets were flying from all directions. Others who were unsure of who was shooting or who was being shot at, drew their pistols and began letting loose. In the midst of shots ringing I found myself crouched down beside Uncle Rat, who had been shot in the mix. My eyes were moving every which way. I could see cars burning rubber trying to get away and unmasked gunmen picking off targets with reckless abandon, flashing lights, and stumbling civilians. Payback was heavy on my mind. Police sirens ripped through the mayhem and, like scattering roaches when the lights come on, everyone began to flee.

Not too long after that night Fu went back into hiding and both sides, the Double ii Bloods and MOB Piru, got together and resolved all issues from that ugly night. Ironically, it was the same MOB Piru homies we almost got it up with before that at Club Gregory's.

By this time the gang activity was unmistakable. The streets of Essex County were always high-stakes drug money, high-volume violence, and downright deadly. Now with neighborhoods belonging to different sets under the guise of red and blue, the gunshots became even louder and more frequent.

Though I can't deny my contribution to what was taking place, there were still times I rolled through different 'hoods and leaned low behind tinted windows, tripping off the way gangs took over. Even the neutrals began to piece together their wardrobes as to not upset the local gang-bangers who controlled the area or just to show pride in their 'hood. There were plenty who didn't fully embrace the gang life but still loved their 'hood and the people in it. We all shared in the struggle. That's 'hood love.

Little kids—fourth, fifth, and sixth graders—could be seen outside schools chucking up Bs and Cs with no clue of the implications of their actions. The next generation was already staking their claim to a gangster's paradise. However, they were taking to the lifestyle without understanding its history, culture, the commitment, and the severity of its consequences. Many just wanted to be a part of what was going on and emulated what they saw others doing. But each gang was trying to outdo the other, and everyone was hungry for new recruits. At some point quantity was sure to outweigh the quality of new breeds. Whether or not I agreed with what gangs were evolving into, the seeds were planted and I undeniably helped to plant them.

The younger homeboys from my neighborhood were determined not to be left out and formed clicks of their own within set—the AfterDeath'z Adolescents (AD'Z) and the YoungBuk'z (YB'Z). They banged their colors, repped the 'hood, and got down when necessary.

The dangers meant nothing. Actually, danger didn't deter, it attracted. Why did people gravitate toward something so lethal?

The 'hood was an environment where you'd be awakened in the middle of the night by gunshots and ambulance sirens. You would learn in school the next morning that it was the kid who sat next to you who lost his life in the midst of the sounds that interrupted your sleep the night before.

Teachers taught what they knew, but what was the lesson? In our eyes it didn't apply. Not many could relate. The mentality was, nobody cared, so why should I? And with such disregard the streets of New Jersey came falling down harder and faster than the London Bridge.

Death, disaster, destruction, and despair were an everyday occurrence and became normal. All you had to do was look out of the window, step outside the house, or drive down the street. The 'hood makes you feel trapped, and as if there was nowhere to hide. If I run to it, I don't have to run from it. And there lies the birth of yet another banger.

I was in and out of court to see if my lawyer had what it took to clean the slate regarding the raid case. During months of suppression hearings and court appearances, my attorney humiliated the East Orange Task Force, which had blatantly fabricated stories about my arrest in an attempt to shield the fact that they didn't have probable cause or a search warrant to enter the house.

Their deceit was apparent. Ecclesiastes 3:16-18: *Moreover I saw under the sun in the place of judgment wickedness was there and in the place of righteousness iniquity was there. Concerning the condition of the sons of men, a higher power tests them that they may see that they themselves are like animals.*

In the end, as my lawyer put it, "We hit a homerun in the final inning of the World Series."

I started out facing a twenty-year max, ten-year minimum extended term. The suppression hearing exposed the corrupt ways of the East Orange Police Department and I was offered a 200-day sentence. Be it right or wrong, I couldn't chance being judged by twelve, a supposed jury of my peers, so I pled guilty to conspiracy and possession of a controlled dangerous substance. My date for sentencing was scheduled for October 29, 1999.

I began to arrange matters so that while I was away from the street, all would be proper when I returned. Troub had been released from his stretch in Yardville months back and remained focused. Worst-case scenario, I knew I had a good man on the streets who would keep my books tight and things on the up and up.

October 29, 1999, came as fast as anything. I just wanted to get in and get out. I knew I had 200 days in me with my eyes closed. When I walked into court, in a matter of minutes, I was cuffed and led away. After a long day of processing, I was assigned to floors ten and eleven on the north side of the County Jail.

The tenth and eleventh floors were supposed to be for pre-trial detainees arrested in serious cases. I had no clue as to how I ended up on such a floor with a drug charge. I hit the tier ready for whatever. Moments after I arrived, it was headcount time. When the count cleared and the southside of the tier went out to day-room one of the Damu homies who heard I arrived came to the gate and informed me he had something for me. After he wrapped it up, he slid a homemade shank through the divider where I could snatch it up and quickly tuck it away. Almost in the fashion of a military instructor giving commands to one of his cadets, he ordered I keep it on me at all times. There had been a lot of tension brewing between the Bloods and Latin Kings.

This was my first time in jail where there was no bailing out and already I was hit with a whiff of its seriousness. I was in on a skid bid and looking to be in and out in a few months, but if worst came to worst, I would gladly accept a life sentence before I buckled behind bars. That first night it was clearly visible how things were broken up on the tier and in the dayroom. There were neutrals throughout the population; however the jail was largely packed with gang-bangers or those who held gang ties. Thirsty criminals already resigned to the notion, whether innocent or guilty, that it would always be just us while we searched for justice. A couple of days passed and nothing jumped off. Eventually my number was called as I was to be transferred to Caldwell's Jail Annex, a medium facility, where I was to serve the remainder of my sentence.

Caldwell Jail Annex was one of the oldest jails in America and years beyond its fitness to house inmates. It's since been condemned. The jail itself, in one word, was horrendous. Caldwell Jail was made up of scattered trailers and one main building that held thousands. There was chipped paint, rusted-over cell bars, rotted out and moldy ventilation, rodents, and roaches. Caldwell was manned by racist redneck COs whose uniforms barely hid their swastikas and Heil Hitler tattoos. It was all about force, and batons, pepper spray, and cuffs were attached to their belts. Caldwell was not known to be as dangerous as other New Jersey prisons, yet it was just a few notches below. Jail isn't prison. But then again, prison wasn't what made things dangerous, it was the people within it. With shared toilets, showers, bunk beds, and dormitory-style living it was easy for one to end up doing another's time, and things had a tendency of kicking off.

Still, I figured I would breeze through the next few months and that's exactly what I did. I snatched up a commissary job that paid far below minimum wage. I worked out faithfully on the unit's universal machine. I studied, and played the phone when I could. Time flew by. It was as if I dozed off and was awakened by two officers telling me to get ready for my parole hearing. I served just two months and was already up for release. My first date up, I was granted parole, and only had a few weeks before my release. I couldn't wait.

In the meantime, straight out of left field, when everything seemed to be right and exact, a weekend visit rendered me lost, puzzled, and flustered. I was about to lose out on what I grew up taking for granted—a two-parent household. Single-parent homes were more common and old news where I grew up.

Single-parent homes for black households in 1990 were at 54.7 percent and 53.3 percent in 2000, while single-parent homes for all races were 24.7 percent in 1990 and 26.7 percent in 2000, according to *The New York Times Almanac 2011*. For my brother and me, our reality was something different. Both parents were always around and, to be honest, our family somewhat stood out as a result of that. Now, something drastic occurred and caused my parents to separate. That's the news they came to break on the visit.

I remembered my parents handled it with class. One did not leave the other to share the story alone. They showed up together in attempt to assure me there still was love. However, there were differences that could not be overlooked. Although I respected the way they handled it, it didn't change the effect it had on me mentally and emotionally. After twenty-plus years, their union was no longer. I loved them both, but I hated their truth. Maybe it would have been an easier pill to swallow had I been home and not in jail.

So many in prisons hush emotions and handle such expression in solitude. I was no different. What my parents did not know was, regardless of my age, their split left me with no one to confide in but myself. In jail, I was removed from everything but ugly thoughts. Old memories of Moms in her nightgown and hair rollers whipping up Sunday's best and Pops in the living room with his Colt 45 and Jack Daniels screaming at the Dallas Cowboys game. This was family as I remembered. Yet, the way I had been raised was no more. I didn't know to whose benefit the move was, but I played along for the rest of the visit as if it didn't bother me, something I had grown good at. Still, to this day, I don't know what caused their split. I assumed it was too painful for me to inquire. All I knew was my parents split, and I was in jail.

Every night I sat in jail and thought of all I was missing. I felt it was a must to solidify my name in the streets upon release. The gang activity in the world was at an all-time high. While the homies from my 'hood were holding things up and putting in their fair share of work, I felt the need to turn it up another notch. I believed I was outsmarting the system when the entire time it was all part of their strategy to get as many people as cased up as possible.

With the system's "he'll be back" mentality, I went from facing a twenty-year sentence with a ten-year minimum to being paroled in two months. Court and prison became a revolving door, with each case worse than the last.

With the exception of my parents separating, everything else I heard while in Caldwell was music to my ears. The only disturbing information I received besides my parents' split was a deadly mistake that cost my young homeboy BJ and homegirl greatly.

Lil BJ (Bobby Johnson) was a name given to him for his resemblance to the character in the 90s movie *South Central*. BJ was one of the loyal, hungry YG'z from 6th Ave. BJ was certainly a product of the neighborhood since a toddler. He grew up on his grandmother's porch in the early 90s watching the life. Tired of watching from the sidelines and eager to get in the game, at ten or eleven years old, Lil BJ found work as a lookout; shortly thereafter he was holding packs. At no older than twelve years old Lil Bobby Johnson was filling his pockets with the illegal drug money that flowed through Down the Hill. He was basically a baby pulling all-nighters hustling harder than most. Every time I think of BJ, 2Pac's lyrics "Up before the sunrise, First to hit the block, Lil bad mothafucka with a pocket full of rocks" comes to mind.

On a call home to report the good news of my parole date and to make sure word was relayed to BJ, I caught a mixture of different emotions through the phone. I asked,

"What's up?" That's when I was told. Lil BJ slipped. While in his girlfriend's house, gun in hand, hairpin trigger, the gun accidentally went off and killed our homegirl and his girlfriend in an instant. This tragedy happened in the living room in a house before Thanksgiving. The result was the loss of a young homegirl, may she rest in peace, and the loss of a homeboy to the system. Lil BJ was barely old enough to get a driver's license and life as he knew it was over and his girl was dead.

There's a time to laugh and a time to cry. I hung up the phone, laid atop my bed, and questioned if God truly understood. How could one live a life at a respectable distance from evil when our lives were beset with death and disaster? With no answer to my questions, I knew both good and evil awaited me in the streets.

January 7, 2000, I cashed my institution check, which was whatever money was left on my books at the time of discharge, not more than a few hundred dollars, and walked through the doors and out the gates of Caldwell's Jail. I jumped on the NJ Transit bus and took in the view on my silent ride down Bloomfield Avenue through the suburbs and back to the 'hood.

I hopped off the bus at the bottom of Bloomfield Avenue and awaited my transfer. While lost in a daydream, someone called my name. I looked up and saw my big homeboy Mook Daddy one of the 'hood's elder statesmen from The Block (18th Street), the same M.D. who thoroughly served some of his best years in Federal penitentiaries after being trapped off at the height of the crack epidemic. It felt like I hadn't seen a familiar face in decades. When I saw M.D. it confirmed I was back in the mix. I got in his ride and we chopped it up as he and his family dropped me off at my mother's house on Oraton Parkway.

I left this same house years ago to venture into the streets. Now, after the streets delivered me the blow that led to my incarceration, I had returned. It felt good to know I still had a place to call home. Still, I didn't want to acknowledge I was blessed. I guess I embraced the struggle more than my reality. Over time, I came to identify more with poverty's ills, making it easier for me to clear my conscience after I did my dirt.

When I walked into my mom's house, I was shocked to be greeted by Saleema. I forgot she was staying at my mom's during my Caldwell bid. Saleema left the apartment on the corner of 15th and William Streets knowing it would most definitely be raided again. The green house on the corner would later prove safe for no one.

I walked in the crib, laid on the bed, and soaked up the perks of freedom. Saleema headed straight to the closet and began to pull out the jewelry and money I left with her before I went in. No need to count, I trusted every penny was there; I peeled off a stack and gave her the rest to put back. I took a long hot bath, got dressed and called my partner in crime, Troub.

Troub was more than pleased to hear I was out. He knew now some of the burdens he held would be shared. Troub told me to sit tight, and he was on his way to pick me up. First, I had to run a few errands and pick up cash tucked away at other spots. Then Troub and I did a little shopping. Within hours I saw my parole officer, tore down New York City's Broadway and 145th, and now stood on the corner of North 15th and William Streets in the heart of the 'hood.

While in Caldwell, I heard plenty stories about the heavy flow of dope money Down the Hill. Now, I was out to witness for myself and the sight before me was unbelievable. Traffic was backed up, lines were around the corner, and thousands of dollars traded hands in minutes. Doing it big was now an understatement. Young homies were out of breath from the non-stop dashes to and from their stashes as they welcomed me home. My pockets were filled to capacity by the time I finished a blunt of goods, and I hadn't touched any product.

Before I went in to serve my light sentence, coke addicts decorated the strip 24/7. Clear vials and colored tops were how we grinded. We fiddled with heroin, moving a few bricks here and there. But now, in early 2000, it was all about new millennium money—dope (heroin) money. With the way dope was pumping, there was no time to play with cocaine and crack. Among hustlers, big boys now handled that diesel, and dope became the drug of choice of users and hustlers. Fiends wanted that blast that would leave them leaning. Heroin addicts lined up to hand over their last. We had millions in sight. It was like overnight someone unleashed the beast. The jungle stumbled upon a new king. Sniff it or shoot it—"Houston, we have a problem."

What I saw on my first trip back to the Ave after my release from Caldwell was just the beginning. After my first week home, I knew I had to fall back. I did not want to make myself too accessible. But every time I stepped foot on the strip and heard hustlers and customers alike, yelling "Cash Money, Cash Money" like they were the only two words of the English language, it made it extremely difficult for me to stay away. Thing was, as I heard the yells and screams for Cash Money, a rumor was in rapid circulation—the Feds had a secret indictment out on any heroin stamped with the infamous Cash Money logo.

Also attached to rumors was a story of a supposed stash spot found by police months prior.

{*(FBI Document Label Section 124, Title "AN ABANDONED CADILLAC USED BY _____ AS A STASH LOCATION IS FOUND BY POLICE) On February 16, 2000, police searched an abandoned Cadillac near ____ North _____, acting on a tip that _____ had left drugs and a gun in a car at that location. The car was found to contain 1,200 envelopes (or 24 bricks) of heroin, 169 vials of crack cocaine and a Tanita digital scale w/leather case. The car also contained a .45 caliber silver Interarms Firestar, Serial # _____, with a laser site, five live rounds and one lodged in chamber.*}

Some rumors could be taken with a grain of salt, but any concerning the law should never be overlooked. I was clear of the car's contents with enough money stashed away to do just about what I pleased and knew it was time to get out. But the more money I made, the more I spent and in turn, the more invincible I felt.

My relatives Shake and Kay traveled up from down South to encourage me to leave all of it behind. I would picture the house on the hill and say, "Just one more run." I wasn't home for a year, and there was so much more I wanted to do.

In April 2000, circumstances grew awry and added more pressure to already feverish times. After a day of militant mobbing on 6th Ave, that night, a homie of mine pulled up with a female in her '99 SUV looking to share some time over a drink or two. The Patio was a 'hood bar that offered only a hint of safety, but it was safer than where we stood. At the homie's request, the three of us hopped in the ride and headed to the Patio for a couple of drinks and a few games of pool.

As they say, God works in mysterious ways, and it was by the grace of God that not long after we departed the strip the Reaper arrived. 6th Avenue, one of Newark's most dangerous strips, had robbed another of their existence. I was not present. I don't know what occurred. A dead man doesn't talk. And one who does knows better than to speak about it. The streets twist stories like pretzels but here's how it all relates.

First off, death was the norm Down the Hill. It seemed every day you'd run into a crowd of mourners outside one of the many funeral homes in the city. It was normal for a family to bury their young before the age of twenty-one. Rest in peace U-God, Lil Faheem and Shinehead. Can anybody tell me why the good die young? When someone dies in the 'hood it's felt but it's also natural, so life goes on. So while another death was unfortunate, I managed to brush it off and kept it moving. The fallen was not a Blood and as selfish and cold-hearted as I now know it to be, then Blood was all I cared about. Not even a day later, the 'hood was in full swing, as if the yellow tape wasn't there.

In the wake of what death does, me and Lil Quan—the same Lil Quan from 18th Street who back in the early '90s, as a juvenile, knew how to stack card decks, toss loaded dice, and get a quarter to lean on a curb—stood only feet away from the drying blood, pitching powder to fiends—-when a gold, new-model, Crown Vic hopped the curb with an obvious agenda. We found ourselves slammed against the hood of the car. The suits and ties were dead giveaways these were not narcotic cops. With clear knowledge of who I was, the two detectives stepped in the direction of my RX-7, parked directly in front of the Middle Bar, and began to illegally search my vehicle. In my head, I played back Jay-Z's "99 Problems": "I ain't pass the bar but I know a lil bit, enough to know that you illegally searching my shit." They found a single bag of weed. I was placed in cuffs, and my car was left behind. They took me to the robbery/homicide unit on Green Street in Newark for a bag of weed.

Once at robbery and homicide, one of the three detectives, who happened to be a female, wanted there to be no mistaking why I was there. She repeatedly yelled in my face.

"We want to know about the murder!"

"We don't care about the Cash Money."

I knew a body dropped but seriously had no knowledge of who did what. My lack of information upset the detectives. The three then voiced various scenarios in attempt to place Troub as the shooter and me as the driver.

"You're going down!"

Ironically, the one to put me at the Patio at the time of the incident was its owner Larry, who was a retired Newark police officer. The entire station had me thrown. I couldn't tell what I didn't know and, if I did know, I wouldn't have told.

It was at least ten to fifteen minutes before they disposed of the petty bag of weed. They assured me they knew the truth or what they thought to be the truth and released me. Whatever the truth was regarding the unfortunate set of circumstances, I had to warn Troub of their accusations. It wasn't long before Troub did what anyone who knew the brute hands of the law would have done and got low! Me and my road dawg had been united but once again, the law forced us to go our separate ways.

Troub escaped the long arm of the law for quite some time but eventually he lost out like most of us do. It was like the 'hood stopped the day we found out Troub got caught. However, money can make so many things right and he was awarded bail and back on the streets in no time.

With Troub on the low, most of my time was spent with two of my closest home-boys at the time, B-Blood and Country. Country and B-Blood were down for whatever, literally anything under the sun. Forever men in their own right, yet it was nothing if I called to have them press out some of the area's self-proclaimed bad boys. Together, we felt a sense of urgency when it came to securing Blood's reign in the East and in summer of 2000, we went on a mission. First, we needed to get our own house in order.

There were plenty in the 'hood who represented the set. Some felt it was their right to represent based on them being from the 'hood but had little understanding of what they claimed. Others from the 'hood understood the set's origin to be in California but were unfamiliar with the culture of the United Blood Nation. It was clear a line had to be drawn in order to ensure the 'hood was on the same page and we stood as one. It was time to erase the division that seeped in to our 'hood after Whip's death and unify the set.

7

DOMINION

MID-2000, THE BIGGER homies were back in California legally trying to secure success. This left nobody around to literally lay down the law. Somebody, anybody, had to be the example by making examples. I wasn't by myself. Collectively, a group of us sought solidarity. We understood in some cases there was a solid foundation to build on and in other cases the need to tear down to build again. We didn't mind making foes out of friends. The we I'm speaking of —Bash and Dev from the New Ave Gangsters, Auto and Dream from the Steel Click, Beemo and Streets from the Ignorant Individuals, Shorty Thug, Beezo and Krum Buk from the YoungBukz, Bito and Big Ak, and a host of GRatz. We believed the end product would be worth the work.

I began to do what I felt was the right thing. I decided to pick the litter, separating the real from the rest. Tightening all loose ends to make a better way for Double ii to become stronger, more united. Association alone didn't mean one was down to play the game. Representing, spray-painting walls, and singing the song was not enough. When I stepped up it wasn't hard to tell many thought I was overstepping my boundaries, attempting to dictate and make different something that in their eyes was running smooth. I felt otherwise.

The journey to consolidate the set was in no way an easy task. On many occasions I ran into problems with homies from my own 'hood that could have turned ugly. There was so much underlying tension from the many disputes of the past that came to define our generation's quest for riches. However, I knew the streets would never be as prosperous as they could be without 'hood unity.

I knew an outsider's thirst to fit in would cause the strong and those who believed they belonged to step up and the weak to fall off. Of course I walked a thin line, leaving plenty of room for many to misread my intentions, but the move was about chances. It was a hell of a gamble and the 'hood eventually won. Unity was the prize.

In addition to unifying the set, another challenge presented itself. This challenge was probably the most difficult. It was to integrate the Double ii with the newly emerged East Coast sets and the United Blood Nation. Even though we were on the East Coast full-time, the relevance of such a bold decision didn't seem to resonate within the set. Only a small portion saw sense in it. I must admit their grievances held weight, but logic seemed more beneficial.

There were some among us who strongly believed Double ii should remain an authentic West Coast set under strict West Coast law. Others believed it necessary, given our location, to integrate with East Coast sets and the United Blood Nation. Early on there was a mutual ignorance between Double ii and the newly emerged East Coast sets of each other's origins and culture. This ignorance led to many stand-offs with both sides refusing to back down.

The 'hood was the 'hood and the connection to the West was genuine, but the reality was we were in two different time zones. We couldn't rep the West and ask what to do in the East. Maybe it wasn't for me to do, given I wasn't birthed on the strip and all, but that didn't take away from the fact that something needed to be done.

The homies who were opposed let it be known, while those who agreed spoke up as well. It was the same groups of three and four who still secretly held animosity from disputes back when who could be heard the loudest in this debate. Equally, as men, we all held voices. I understood it to be harbored feelings being released and I looked at it as part of the process. I stood my ground and refused to budge. I was viewed as crazy and was criticized. My leadership skills were questioned. Just who did I think I was? Unguarded tongues can be lethal when men get emotional. Regardless, I was in no position to take things personally.

It was asked how I could try to enforce East Coast law within a West Coast set. Ironically, this was never my intent. Clearly, we were to follow the only law, and that was the law of the streets. Yet I felt to function among other Bloods, mainly East Coast Bloods, knowing the way was of utmost importance. Think of it as "when in Rome do as the Romans." I didn't try to force anyone to care. But I participated in wild demonstrations serving fools who didn't know what that Blood Gang was about, and I felt it necessary for the set to understand East Coast doctrine and its relevance to where we laid our heads.

Everyone felt they knew the worth of their gangster and it would never be tested, but that just wasn't reality. Red represented something and rocking red without knowledge of what it represented, whether you agreed or not, was disrespect to those who died in its honor. Nobody was bigger than Blood and that was my punch.

After hours of heated debate order was restored and balanced minds prevailed. I awarded each individual his own copy of anything allied with the "B" on both the East and West Coast. I stood in front of my peers in Oval Park, the same park we terrorized as kids, and demanded they learn East Coast literature or be thoroughly disciplined. There were no exceptions. The eyes in the crowd grew cold. I had anticipated their reaction and was satisfied knowing in the midst of the bunch were hand-picked shooters—men who only I knew—who had been assigned and ready to solve any problems. Just a little insurance.

I must admit the struggles we were forced to endure while structuring the set strengthened our resolve. I loved my set and those of us who made it whole. My love eventually became apparent. In a weird way, the fights and the disagreements helped us to bond. Through it all the 'hood grew tighter. I was elected Superior of the Double ii's East Coast chapter and my leadership skills were never again tested.

After the transition, I was still in love with the dough and stuck on the belief that gang-banging was a must, so me, Country, and B-Blood hit the streets of Essex

County and hopped out on the different new Blood sets to make certain our presence was felt and the nation was strong and united.

We weren't out tripping on Real Rights (official Bloods). We just pushed it the way we were bred to push it. With Blood in our heart we went on one. We approached any noteworthy person, click, 'hood, or set with the sole purpose of cementing the name of our gang—Double ii Bloods! When approached, some accepted our proposal of applying pressure on the weak by way of robbery, extortion, moving work, or simply bangin', others didn't. Either way it didn't matter. It was all business. When the smoke cleared there would be no questions.

We weren't to be outdone on any level. If we saw or heard mention of others, and not Double ii, it undoubtedly meant we needed to take things to more drastic extremes. As crazy as it might seem that's the way things were. It was like a competition, with every 'hood wanting to carry the title.

Everything was about one word, domination. Nothing mattered but newspaper clippings and yellow tape. Call the streets crazy but "lock and load" and "ride with us or collide with us" were what everyone was repping hard for. The attitude in general was nonchalant. If someone violated, put hands on him. They tripping? Let's ride out. You trying to get money? Here, go get rich. It was either Bloodin' or bow down.

It was pumped into one's head that nothing came before Blood. Not even childhood friends, neighbors, relatives, or anyone or anything else. It was widely believed an all-day Damu couldn't be faded. Feelings and emotions only got in the way and interfered with one's unending existence as a Damu Rider. The nearest thing to a companion besides a homie from the set was your significant other. Then again, in those times, a gangster had best keep a watchful eye on them too. You had to be wary of the enemy or an informant trying to infiltrate the set through a relationship with a Bloodette. And for the homeboys a red rag was like a diamond, and many ladies wanted to be in the presence of that shine. Was it love for you or love for what you represented? I knew some who found out too late. "Wifey" already set them up. She laid on him the whole time, sucking and fucking, to find the stash. Fallen weak during late nights and early mornings for the low moans and high screams of a Marsha

Ambrosius, suckers exposed everything. Before they knew it, there was a pistol to their head and they were ordered to give it up. It was either that or die slow.

Everything involving Blood wasn't all about the homeboys. There were plenty females down with the set. And no, females couldn't sex their way into the 'hood. I even felt, in general, sexual relationships of any sort among members of the set would create unnecessary issues. But if that's what it was to be at the end of the day, it was better to have a homegirl laid up with a homie as opposed to sleeping with the enemy. However, on many occasions, I witnessed a homegirl telly-up (go to a hotel) with a homie, leaving him sprung from a shot of her goods. Then, the homegirl would come to me to bring the homie up on charges for dealing with feelings and emotions. In most cases it was all business.

I know indeed there were many 'hoods, furthermore many homies, who used rank, position, and vulnerability to manipulate those who were willing to do anything to be down with the movement. Two, three, four, or maybe the infamous five home-boys misleading a female into believing that sacrificing her pussy would somehow make her a part of something that was to be represented with pride, dignity, and integrity. Gang-banging was not gang-banging. With all due respect to the homegirls who took this route, this is in no way a slight to you. I understand to you it was the ultimate sacrifice. The responsibility for such abuse of power falls strictly on unworthy leaders and faulty leadership. Looking back on this sensitive subject, I remember stepping out of my car one hot afternoon to be greeted by a young homegirl who was a resident in a local group home on 14th Street.

"What's poppin', big homie?"

I was shocked at her approach and didn't see it as a compliment. I quickly shot back, "Don't ever let me hear you say that again."

First and foremost this young girl was in my eyes too young to be getting caught up in the life. I walked out of the store and she approached me again, "Nah, big homie. I don't think you understand, I got put on last night." Now this bit of news I knew to be false. During this time, the only way a person was put on the 'hood was in the Oval Park, witnessed by all the homies and with me oathing them in.

"Sorry, lil lady, but ain't nobody put you on this 'hood."

Instantly, tears filled her eyes. I could tell she had been misled into believing whatever transpired between her and some of the young homies was an initiation. I walked around to my driver seat, rolled down the passenger side window, and yelled for her to get in. While driving through the 'hood, we talked and she opened up to me and explained some of the bad-ass young homies had tricked her into believing that if she gave them some pussy she would be a part of the 'hood, a member of the set, and an actual banger.

I was left to clean up a mess that shouldn't have been. This young girl was home-less, had nothing but a bunch of corner boys who she wanted as family, and here it was she had been betrayed. My first course of action was for her to see each and every homeboy responsible thoroughly disciplined for misleading her and using the laws of the 'hood as a tool to destroy a bond, as opposed to building one. Next, I was left with a heavy decision on what to do with her since she had made such a sacrifice. There was no question the sex-in move was far from official, so that would not go. Her and a few of the homies would have to get in the circle and mix it up.

This move turned out to be a disaster and left a nasty taste in my mouth. Not long after she was jumped in, I began to notice a change in her behavior. She was no longer the humble little quiet chick from around the way. She became loud and even obnoxious. I had the perfect remedy.

A couple of Piru homegirls unexpectedly pulled up to see what was good in the 'hood. My wheels got to turning immediately. I jumped in their backseat and told them to spin around the block a few times. I had somebody I wanted them to see. I pointed out the young homegirl, who was dressed in jeans and a white T-shirt with a red rag around her head. The fix was in. This would make her or break her. Faking could get you killed, and that's what I wanted her to see. These unfamiliar faces hopped out on her. All were female, all were Blood, just a different set. There were no homies around for her to turn to. It was only her. Even when alone, you're supposed to be united with Blood. Your heart is what made the connection.

"What's poppin'?" yelled KiiKii, a short, thick, brown-skin Damuette.

The young homegirl looked stunned. I sat and watched from a distance. Her response would determine if she could continue to be one of us.

"What's, pop, poppin'."The stutters told it all. Kiikii sensed the fear and cocked back and punched the young homegirl in the face. It was on. Sunday-to-Sunday the young homegirl sat on the corners as if she would undoubtedly take on any female who disrespected the 'hood, let alone her personally. So I was in utter disbelief when I saw her turn around looking for some sort of aid and assistance, then after seeing no one, she took off running. I wanted to die. For a piece of pussy, the young homies put a girl into our mix who was never a full breed, with no consideration of future detriment. It was one hell of a lesson learned.

Whenever homies decided to put on a female she had to know and understand struggle. Not because struggle made them vulnerable, but because it meant they identified. They walked the same school hallways, were rejected by the same teachers, and wanted a way out of the same 'hood just as bad. The homegirls rolled with the punches and did what they had to do to eat. Maybe the Bloodettes felt they had something to prove, but they were down for whatever. The city held some venomous homegirls who kept a steady GemStar Razor and swung loose from the hip. A pretty face didn't mean they weren't poison. Bloodettes were flat out cold-blooded. They didn't want to be seen as weaker or less than one of the homies in any light. In some cases the roles were reversed. Some went even harder than some of the homeboys. Homegirls would call out homies for a fade on the regular.

Bloodettes took what they wanted and needed. Their wants and needs ranged from dollars to dick. Some hustled, others robbed and boosted, and some stripped. Their flaws went unjudged. Instead, I loved their intentions. I loved them all. I will die knowing they loved me back. The list of reputable Bloodettes ran for days. A few I am certain are cemented: Bak, KiiKii, Lee Lee, Qua, Big Hak, Twiin, Nellii, Riika, Miika, Assatta, NaNa, Mrs. and Lady Lay, Mrs. and Lady Killa, Fee, China, Tah, Jada, Princess ii, and Monroe. In one way or another, they are all equally significant as any Blood. Salutations to the sisters far and wide—keep it thorough.

Male or female, Blood on your hands and actual proof you yourself had put work in was the only way to be recognized for work put in. Whether it was whispered or spoken aloud everyone was in search of recognition and status within the gang. Status meant superiority and the right to reign supreme in your life under Blood. Power was illustrated by going from nada to that deal. How did one accomplish this goal? Either you were supplying suppliers or outlining bodies in chalk. These rites of passage sent hordes of gang-bangers into the streets stacked in tagged, rented, and stolen vehicles with music blaring through the speakers—basically, anything that brought a man's mind closer to murder. There were no remorseful souls. It was Murder One—all in the name of Blood.

National Geographic couldn't portray more suspenseful episodes of a predator angling down on its prey. Everything would be blank, then all of a sudden gunshots, screams, return fire, the sounds of glass breaking, cars and homes being hit, tires screeching, sirens, and Su Whooping. Adrenaline rushing, the high boosted—not from the seriousness of the moment just passed but in anticipation of what the morning paper would read.

With both red and blue prowling the streets blinded by colors the murder rate was increasing.

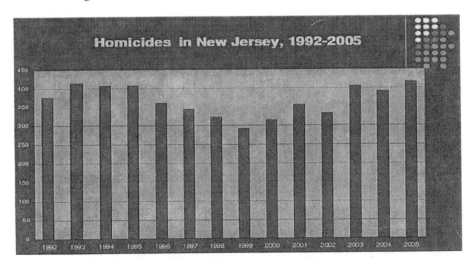

Source: NJ Department of Health and Senior Services

It was 2000 and I had not been home from my Caldwell bid for a year, and events were unfolding horribly. In the midst of the nonstop gang-banging, the word was out about the Feds' secret indictment. Nobody in the streets wanted to hear such an ugly monster was lurking. Homies were constantly getting arrested and frustrations flared and concerns arose. With the extra eyes around, the teenage socializing became less frequent. 'Hood love remained unconditional, yet with prison being the last place one wanted to spend their best years, it seemed in the best interest of whomever to lean a little toward the background. This meant the days of Troub and I joined at the hip had to stop. There was no question, the law, and everyone else for that matter, had us connected to and held us responsible for tormenting the city's streets.

I didn't mind playing the background. However, to fall back meant to do away with the responsibility that came along with being considered one of the big homies—something I could not do. The entire 'hood shared importance. The title meant nothing, if one did not contribute. It was never a one- or two-man show. Still, it was seemingly the two —Troub and Mass. For the most part we were inseparable, but as we grew older we gained responsibilities and even different outlooks on certain things, and with the law out to seal our fate, the streets would perceive we grew apart. The apparent distance between us caused some to whisper we were beefing, or separating, or both. We paid no mind to any of it and kept on doing what we believed to be right by the 'hood.

Since I could remember, Troub and I always had a plan, even when we played Pop Warner football for the Rams. These days were no different. We wanted to strike gold and make a grand escape. Aside from hustling and go-getting, we loved, admired, and cherished the "B" and those who rode the "B" alongside us. I have no doubt the love was mutual, and this made it all the more respectable when the turf named Troub the Five-Star General of the set. As Five-Star General Troub was equally as important and influential as 101 or Superior of the set. The only "real" difference is the title. Who we were was already solidified, minus the status, but for the sake of understanding let's just say it was a great accomplishment. Moving up in the gang the way we did was like becoming CEO from the mailroom. The good times and the hard times taught us invaluable lessons and delivered great responsibility. In the end, the 'hood wanted us there.

While we tried to keep a low profile, bandanna-covered faces clutched an array of automatic weapons locked behind limo tints until their mark was spotted. The outcome, bodies lined in chalk, "In Memory of . . ." pasted on the front of what were once plain white T's. So for us to lay low didn't mean danger didn't exist.

It was summertime sticky, broad daylight, the noise of the neighborhood kids who were out of school was loud and clear. Sounds of hustlers making pitches echoed in the background. Two individuals sat in front of Lamont's driveway. Lamont was the 'hood question mark. When he wasn't high you couldn't tell if he was straight or gay. One of the individuals sat casually on a young homie's dirt bike and talked to the other who was perched on the trunk of his vehicle. Both had come a long way, from nothing to something, and sat discussing the next chapter of their lives. I heard when the time was right both had big plans to get as far away from the madness as possible. But, as the streets would have it, they would have to make it through the next twenty-four hours. Danger seemed distant. Nobody paid attention to anything other than the conversation, when mid-sentence the eyes of the guy on the trunk of the car grew big and a calm "Oh shit" escaped his mouth. His body language told the story. Something wasn't right. The other person turned to see what stole his homie's attention and was met spot on by an automatic rifle staring out the backseat of a candy-colored sports car. A blue rag dangled from its nozzle and blue rags covered the faces of three men inside. The two were caught off guard with no time to react. A sudden move was sure to send the AR roaring.

Crips had ventured into the 'hood on a hunt for a victim and stumbled upon the two. Immediately, it was Slob (a term of disrespect toward Bloods) this and Slob that, yet the AR stayed quiet. The two whose lives could have ended that instant never said a word. Any gang-banger who truly loved what he stood for could attest to the fact that chills run through their bodies when another throws disrespect their direction, let alone on their own turf. It must have been painful to get banged on in your own 'hood. The two exchanged looks and knew this pretty summer day was about to get ugly.

The Crips never fired a shot. Instead, they continued to taunt the two individuals, not aware the two they disrespected were not going to let it pass. As soon as they bent the corner, the two individuals ran to a parked vehicle and took their respective seats—one in the driver and one in the passenger. No music, just heavy breathing, the car took off in search of the opposition. Gang-banging wasn't a 42 and 0 sport. Wins and losses went hand in hand. Whose gun went off first often provided the upper hand. The two individuals rode around and did not spot their target. Both were extremely upset the candy-colored sports car got away. They could have hit a Crip 'hood in retaliation, but since gang-banging wasn't atop their list of priorities as it once was, they decided against it. It was the blatant disrespect that sent them into the streets with loaded weapons in the first place. Maybe for them it was a good thing they didn't spot their target.

The moment began to settle, and the two headed back to the 'hood. Then, just when they thought it was safe, from the opposite direction, they spotted the candy-colored sports car. "There they go," one shouted to the other. They made a flash U-turn as if they didn't care who saw them. It was about to go down. No talking, no stare downs, straight action. There was just about a ruler's length between the cars at a red light. And BOOM!

Both sides were tapping triggers, ducking, still firing, wishing, hoping, and determined to hit the other. Car windows were shattering, slugs penetrating the steel of the adjacent G-ride, sounding off with heavy bass. All this happened within seconds. The driver of the two yelled, "I'm hit!" The passenger took one last look at the now Swiss-cheesed gunpowder gray sports car right before they pulled off, burning rubber down the city streets. Nobody knew whatever happened to the participants on either side. Still, the reality in the streets was that gang banging was at an all-time high in the East.

Every gang was dealing death and dismissing the repercussions. Each day it was a different block with colored rags left in the streets as a sign of "who done it." Local newspapers ran the headlines. Families dreaded their losses. Mothers cringed at the sound of gunshots outside their windows and panicked when the phone rang, worried it would be the morgue calling her to identify the body of her fallen seed.

Sad to say but funeral parlors were left to reap the benefits, and prisons became even more packed. Let my mother tell it: The streets were so deadly parents whose kids were banging began to be more at ease with their young in prison instead of in the streets. It was real life, real guns, real death, real pain, and real suffering.

Death nearly found its way to my door. I'm still amazed the heavens didn't answer. It was just after 10 PM. The corner store on 15th Street was closed, and the strip was pitch black. Me and a few homeboys were out to make ourselves available to those who needed what we provided. We passed cigarettes dipped in PCP back and forth and fell even deeper into an irreversible trance. Even from a distance, the 9mm handgun on my waist was unmistakable. I cared none. But as the high began to set in, so did paranoia, and one or two homeboys suggested I stash the gun in case the Gang Unit ran down, which was more than likely. I went against my better judgment as it related to the code of the streets, and I slid across the street and tucked my burner underneath the porch of an abandoned house. I was high out of my mind and dismissed what I shouldn't have.

Back at it, smoking and joking, I stepped off from the homies for a brief second to put a bug (talk) in my young homegirl Mudda's ear about my developing feelings for her sister Neisha. While we walked and talked I happened to notice a car bend the corner in slow motion. I watched the car thoroughly. After bending the corner, the car came to an abrupt stop. Mudda and I were spot-on targets. The backseat passenger jumped out of the car, shotgun raised, and from where I stood I could hear the "Clack Clack" as he slammed a slug into its mouth and released a monstrous roar.

My first instinct was to push my homegirl down behind a parked car. All the while I could hear the impact of the shotgun slugs ripping into the house behind me. I imagined what the slugs would have done if they had hit me. I ducked down and took off in a slow jog behind the cars toward the abandoned house where I had stashed my gun. Now, with my high dumbed down, I realized how I shouldn't have put my hammer away in the first place. There I was, unable to defend myself or the 'hood—never again!

By the time I made it to my stash, the roaring stopped. In total there were seventeen shots. Luckily, nobody was hit. Those who took up arms in the 'hood weren't exactly always marksmen, especially when gone from drugs and alcohol. But the fact was they brought disrespect to the doorstep of the Double ii Bloods. We didn't have any specifics on who was in the car. Truthfully, it didn't matter, for the enemy had no face. I rocked red, so if you banged blue, it was reason enough. I knew I wouldn't sleep until my gun went off.

I stood in the center of the intersection of 15th and William Streets with blood in my eyes, praying whoever was in that car had the heart to double back. I began to walk in the middle of the street, gun in hand and to question homies why I didn't hear any return fire.

During this episode, a few GKB (Gangster Killa Bloods) homeboys from nearby The Bity who heard the shots pushed through to provide some aid and assistance. They rolled down their tinted windows and asked, "What's poppin?"

"Another day in the neighborhood," I replied sarcastically.

They revealed a car full of hammers that said all that was needed.

"Let's go!"

Just before I could get in the G-ride, an E.O.P.D. squad car pulled up sounding its sirens. The homies pulled off, not wanting to take any chances, and I walked away. It was clear the police were responding to shots fired. I hoped they didn't jump out in search of a victim, firing shots of their own. The police rolled away, and it wasn't minutes before I heard another horn. I turned around and spotted another GKB homie from The Bity rolling with one of the young homies from my 'hood. I hopped in the backseat and told them to drop me off in the Bity so I could meet up with the other GKB homies.

Once inside the car, I noticed we didn't move. I looked up and from the rearview mirror I caught the homie's eyes, frozen like a deer in the headlights. I turned my head to see what had him on froze, and I was greeted by Newark's Gang Unit boxing us in from all angles. There was no escape. My luck with the law had once again run out (8/21/00 Age: 20 Possession of a weapon for unlawful purposes, 9mm handgun, NJ Superior Court, Essex County Accusation No. 00-10-1062A)—my third adult case.

Days later, while sitting in the County Jail, I was given a bail but was held on a detainer for a violation of probation. Within a week I was back in Caldwell's Jail Annex Satellite 2 working out, playing Spades, and eating hookups, culinary arts prison style: ramen noodles, mayonnaise, mustard, chicken or fish, salt, pepper, and sliced bread.

I was already in contact with my lawyer, Paul Bergin, to clear the violation of probation, and I didn't plan on being in jail for long. I knew once my lawyer got a handle on things the gun charge would be nothing to worry about. Pistol cases flooded court dockets in Essex County. Anywhere else a gun charge would have been headlines but in Essex County it was barely a blip on the radar. I waited for the process to work itself out and took advantage of the opportunity to rough it out with homies from the set, Luck Looch and Na Black (RIP), who were both finishing up violations also.

During this Caldwell bid, I met Brick City Brim's big boy Killa Reek for the first time. The atmosphere was crazy. Nobody wanted to be in jail but with the way the police were slapping silver bracelets on just about everyone, once inside it was just like what Pac and Snoop described in the song "Two of America's Most Wanted": "nothing but a gangster party."

In jail, a place where I couldn't see any upside, homeboys shot the breeze, cracked smiles, and once in a while made jokes. The free world had become so treacherous, smiles among homies were rare. Who had time to clown? But maybe that's what jail had become for some, a joke. So for some, a Caldwell bid was time to relax without having to worry about the gunfire. In jail, though surrounded by different styles of criminal, one thing always in play was respect. Men respect men and if you carried it as such, your bid ran smooth.

Caldwell didn't cuff serious offenders, so most inmates had short time. I learned very few of the inmates had gotten their hands on that new weed flooding the streets—that 189 or that sticky green named after a street in the Washington Heights section of New York City. I did not intend to flood the prison with weed, but I knew the homies Na Black and Luck Looch wouldn't mind a taste. After a few phone calls, things were set. We arranged for a 'hood-hopper to pay a visit to another inmate who didn't mind getting his hands dirty. Plans were in place for the upcoming weekend visits and that lifted everyone's spirit. On the streets people got high to escape reality. Imagine what it would be like to get high behind the wall—tolerance down and all.

The Friday before the visit I had a long line of friends who could not be avoided. It was no secret. The word spread. You'd be surprised at the gossip that takes place among men. Those in jail know what's happening in the world before those in the streets. With all things considered, I kept a straight face and refused to let on if I was behind the move or not. The last thing I needed was for an envious or spiteful inmate to drop a note (inform police) and ruin everything. But to everybody's delight, the plans went off uninterrupted.

Saturday rolled around and prisoners were up bright and early ironing their pumpkin-orange jumpsuits, paying a visit to the unit barber for a quick edge up, and burning up the telephone lines with hopes their shorty wasn't out clubbing the night before and bumped into a Jody (Jody is an anonymous name inmates attach to the man their "girl" creeps with while they're in prison).

"Butler, visit!" the CO shouted through the iron grill that secured the unit.

Five to ten minutes earlier my man who was going to catch the drop was called down. All eyes were on me. Smiles were plastered on the faces of other inmates who were in the know and anticipated my return. I smiled back. It was better that the attention was on me anyway while down in the visit hall. I took my seat in the visit hall and kicked it. The entire time I kept a clear visual and paid close attention to monitor the transaction. When the move went down my man shot me a quick wink, got up, and hugged the 'hood-hopper and ended his visit.

Hopefully, he wouldn't be busted during the strip out process. Bringing drugs into the jail could lead to criminal charges. And nobody needed a case on top of a case. Meanwhile, I enjoyed the remainder of my visit. When the visiting hours were complete I couldn't wait to get back upstairs and blow the house down. If Paul Bergin couldn't work his magic by the next week and I was to find myself still stuck in the Well (Caldwell), I let my shorty know to come back. She whispered, "I got you baby."

Ain't nothing like a down-ass chick.

Any joyous emotions a man could experience on visit were destroyed once your visitor left when, before returning to your unit, the CO ordered you to strip in front of all present and called out, "Lift, turn around, squat, cough—now get dressed!" It was a humiliating process that had to be done week in and week out. I buttoned my jumpsuit in a hurry, having satisfied the CO's needs and took every other step up to the top. "Butler, back from visit, let me in!" The CO opened the unit gate and my "main man" approached. Playing the game, he spoke, "I seen you and your shorty down there. How was your visit?"

"Everything is everything. And you?" I replied. "I saw you cut it a little short."

"It's all good," he replied. "Wifey had to get back, her Moms was tripping about babysitting; but dig, let me holler at you for a minute."

I told him I'd meet him in his cell in a few and brought our brief discussion to a close. I went and changed out of my jumper into some more comfortable attire (sneakers, sweats, and tank-top) and headed to his room. When I entered the cell he was seated smoking a Black & Mild cigar. He was just as eager as I was. I stared at the weed spread across his bed like it was gold. In fact it was. Be it weed, coke, dope, PCP, or pills, the value of drugs multiplied behind the wall. Take a nickel bag from the world and you could move it on the inside for fifty, regardless if it was top-grade or backyard boogie. We caught a contact high from breaking down the weed alone. We stashed a good portion and headed to the showers to put the rest in the air.

The showers located at the back of the unit provided enough room for a group of us to roll up and chief like Indians in a sweat lodge. The steam from the showers helped keep down the smell. There were a few fistfights to get back to the showers to blow rings and things. When the spliff was finished, we were all high like eagles with chinky eyes, the giggles, and the munchies. One by one, we stumbled out of the shower area and rode the high out for the remainder of the day. We played Spades, ate hookups, shot dice, watched videos, and chain-smoked Buglers and Black & Milds to try to maintain the high.

During these few weeks in Caldwell I established an everlasting relationship with the woman who would later birth my son, Alneisha Hall. Since the very first day I stepped foot Down the Hill, my heart raced whenever I saw her. I would lay back and listen to just about every homeboy from the 'hood talk about claiming her as his own. She was reserved and quiet; you know the good girl who just so happened to grow up in a bad environment. Raised in a house full of women, she carried herself with class. My appreciation goes out to her family—Grandma Hall, Mama Hall, Faye from around the way, and Tawanna.

Saleema and I had been on a downslope and our relationship was just about over. A few weeks before my arrest I finally worked up the nerve to ask Neisha out, something I didn't do too often. Neisha, with the encouragement of my big homegirl Toya, who was the mother of my homeboy Beemo's kids, finally accepted my advances. Neisha was still somewhat in a relationship of her own, and our friendship was slow to take off. It didn't help I was sitting in jail. I convinced Neisha to come and visit, and I expressed to her my desire to be with her and only her when I was released. With no definite answer, I was left to linger in limbo in Caldwell's jail until my bid was over.

This Caldwell bid was a piece of cake. These short stints on the inside—or skid bids—became so common many got the impression jail was prison or the penitentiary and only consisted of quick ins and outs with familiar faces. The end of the road never truly registered. Lightweight bids and slaps on the wrists by the courts did little to deter. Still, I couldn't wait to get home. And on September 14, 2000, I was free to go.

Now that I was home, I was determined to see if what I was feeling for Neisha was real. I didn't expect much and played it cool. I never shared when I was getting released. So I hit the corner of 15th and William and she had no clue I was out. Mama Hall spotted me on her way home and questioned if Neisha knew I was home. I replied "No" and doubted it was a big deal.

Minutes later, I stood at the phone booth on the corner of 15th and William Streets and glanced up at her bedroom window. I saw her head pop out and she yelled, "Come here!" I approached without delay and she came running out the house still in her nightgown and jumped straight into my arms. It was Romeo and Juliet 'hood style. I felt like the luckiest man alive. It was no longer a question and no longer a secret. The 'hood stood in amazement.

There it was for all to see, I was hers and she was mine. This thing called love was not familiar territory. I chanced it, though I was not ready. At this stage of my life she could only have a portion of me, as my love for the streets, gang-banging, and all that came with it were still heavily entwined. Still, I felt like I conquered certain emotions and filled a void. Nevertheless, I went right back to the jungle to tame its beasts. The fruits of my labor were paying off. It appeared I was closing in on my dream to make it out of the ghetto or at least remove my mother from its grasp.

I was naïve to the workings of the Feds. I honestly believed there was no way they would be targeting me. The telltale signs were recognizable but since their truths weren't beneficial to my movement I swept them under the rug. I failed to value what we as Americans often take for granted, freedom! As it is declared, we have a right to be free; however, as showed by history and articulated in the 13th Amendment, such rights can be snatched away in an instant. Years later I would learn that many men before me, as there will be many men after me, failed to cherish their freedom until it was lost.

The Feds were chasing for months trying to get their hands on the man or men behind Cash Money, which had become a brand name in the 'hood, one of infamy. Cash Money was a business in itself, and it literally sold itself. This brand of heroin equaled sure success in the streets. We had the patent on a product accessible only to elite heroin pushers.

The Feds' investigation was encouraged by their newly attained knowledge that a young kid around the age of twenty, 145 pounds, with short dreads and tattooed tear drops by the name of Massacre assumed leadership of the Double ii Bloods.

Little did I know someone from the set had already been picked up and charged Federally under this "secret indictment." With one of two options, this person chose the lesser. And out of the precinct walked a Federal informant. One of our very own began providing the Feds information dating as far back as 1993.

I would have never guessed this informant to be one who I basically took in and gave money to feed his family and leverage when he claimed that his world was off balance. I pretty much looked at the dude as a brother.

This informant handed over information on the birth of the Double ii Bloods, its structure and beliefs, down to who called shots and who put in work. There was no way the Feds could not pursue the information. It wasn't "simply" a gang issue. They were served proof on a platter by an inside man that the Double ii Bloods were running a lucrative heroin business that, by their estimates, grossed upwards of $30,000 a day and controlled the drug trade of East Orange and surrounding areas.

I carried on, eyes wide shut to everything except red and green. The struggle continued and whatever one felt was needed to overcome the struggle stayed in motion. Indifferent to a judge, jury, prosecutors, and jail and activity resumed. Until…

{Federal Documentation Ref: October 19, 2000 murder of _____ by Tewhan Butler. Several months later after _____ (___) was killed, Tewhan Butler had an altercation with a local man named _____. _____, known in East Orange as "___" was a long time resident of East Orange and had a tough reputation of being able to hold his own when necessary. Additionally, _____ had his own ties to the rap group ____. He was a spokesperson or promoter for the group. _____ had grown up with the guys from _____. He remained friends with them. In October 2000, ____ had just returned from being on tour with the group…when ____ returned from the tour, he and defendant Tewhan Butler had an argument concerning drug dealing in Double II territory. Tewhan Butler and homicide victim _____ had a heated argument just a day or two before _____ was shot twice in the back of the head…in the early morning hours of October 19, 2000 (around 4 A.M.), ____ had walked over to the Pit Stop Gas Station, at 47 Park Avenue. As ____ sat there on the crate unaware, Tewhan Butler circled the block in a car. Because he knew _____ and they had just argued, Butler would have to come up on _____ from behind. When the time was right, Butler got out of the car. He placed a covering over his head and face and pulled a gun from his waistband…then, gun drawn, defendant Tewhan Butler walked up behind ____. From only feet away, Tewhan Butler fired two shots directly into the back of ____ head, killing him. When police found him at Pit Stop Gas Station, _____ was slumped over the island at the end of the gas pumps. The crate he had been sitting on was knocked over on its side. ____ died at the scene. Medical examiners determined the cause of death was gunshot wounds to the back of the head.}

On October 20, not even twenty-four hours later, I stood in the driveway of Neisha's family house with one of my homeboys, Chavell.

Chavell was a 'hood pretty boy and ex-star athlete who threw in the towel for the streets. We were working the early morning rush when all of a sudden we noticed an E.O.P.D. squad car patrolling more frequently than usual. We figured something was up and cleared the line of customers from the driveway. We were on a slow creep to the front to see which direction the police went when we were met by a pack of uniformed officers charging toward us. We turned around in a hurry and prepared to make a run for it to no avail. Another load of police swarmed from the back. With nowhere to go we raised our hands in unison as they approached with guns out and extra caution. Superior officers back at the station must have warned that I might be in possession of a weapon and uncertainty lingered. Although they had the upper hand, I could see the fear in their eyes turn to looks of relief when they finally placed the cuffs on my homie and me.

Once in the backseat of the squad car I noticed a group of officers huddle up and look at a photo and back at me. I was able to read one of the officer's lips and made out what he said: "We got our man."

When we arrived at E.O.P.D. for the umpteenth time a duty officer stepped to the bullpen and stated if we cleared the record check we would be released.

I was positive I had no warrants. After twenty minutes or so the duty officer returned fumbling with his keys. He opened the gate, and we both got up to leave. "Not you Butler, only your friend here is leaving."

I was crushed and in the back of my mind I knew exactly what they had in store for me. Emotionally drained, but too strong to let them defeat me, I held my head high as I sat caged by myself for hours and hours on nothing more than a complaint. "Our" men in black and white who are to protect and serve walked in one after another, passing judgment and labeling me guilty. It suited their preconceived notions of the man I was.

I had just turned twenty-one years old and was still basically a baby. Yet I had become a threat, though I would not realize it until years later. I wasn't overly aggressive, extremely violent, politicized, or enlightened at this point. I was a threat because I didn't promote passiveness. I understood right from wrong as it applied to our way of life, and I encouraged my homeboys to go and get no matter the means. Moreover, I was a threat because gangs were spreading and gaining control of neighborhoods along the East Coast. Politically speaking the world hadn't seen a movement of this magnitude by black youth within urban America since the BPP (Black Panther Party) and the BLA (Black Liberation Army) in its power and ability to mobilize and influence community. It just so happened, from one generation to the next, the cause(s) digressed from politics and civil rights to strictly about money. "By any means" necessary still resonated. However, history's lessons taught our government that the new era of young black militants (Bloods and Crips) had to be stopped before they smartened up, stopped going at it with one another and began to attack the injustices that crippled our kind.

To say the least, the law was gunning for me. They needed their poster boy. As delivered in doctrines as far back as Hannibal's reign—you kill the head, the body will crumble. I was everything but spit on, then processed and booked on charges of first-degree murder, third-degree unlawful possession of a weapon, and second-degree possession of a weapon with unlawful purpose.—my fourth adult case.

That night it was impossible to sleep in the basement of the filthy East Orange precinct. Somewhere between dusk and dawn, I was told to cuff up and led to another part of the precinct I had never before seen. I found the surroundings humorous. It was obvious someone watched far too many episodes of *Law & Order*. The room was freezing cold. The lights were dim. Inside sat what I figured to be their top detective. I stared straight into his eyes. I was all ears and desperate to hear what they claimed to have on me. Detective whatever-his-name went into his charade.

"We got you! Confess! The mask didn't work. We have witnesses. Confess, confess, confess." With nothing to confess, I sat in silence until he grew frustrated and ordered I be taken back to what they considered to be a cell.

Interrogations were more like accusations. It's you, the accused, and the law, the accuser. What? When? Where? And Why? Rang more like you did it, you did it, you did it, and now you're going down. Alibis only got twisted and fashioned into admissions of guilt. Then a jury of twelve is left to believe either you the "defendant," who was defamed by prosecutors in opening arguments, or the law and all its "righteous officers." Just look at the number of cases overturned for prosecutorial misconduct and deception. Now imagine the full scope of what hasn't been uncovered.

The morning after the interrogation, I was picked up at the East Orange precinct by Newark's Robbery/Homicide Squad and taken to Essex County Jail. This was after I was asked for my alibi, then denied the opportunity to present one.

In Receiving & Discharge of Essex County Jail I learned my bail had been set at half a million dollars, $500,000 cash or bond. I wasn't worried about posting bail. The money was there. The thing was, similar to my last situation, I already copped out to a 364-day custodial term and was to be sentenced in a matter of days on my third adult case, possession of a firearm.

Essex County was famous for piling cases on top of cases without question to how one was able to cycle through the system so frequently. In any other county, I probably wouldn't have made it home from my initial gun charges or never had been charged in the murder. Whether it was legal strategy from the prosecutor's office, a catch-and-release policy due to the courts' overwhelming caseload and constant overcrowding at the Essex County Jail, or simply the consequences of poor police work, one thing was clear: You were sure to get a bail in Essex County.

Now, I could post bail and take off running, or I could sit tight, wrap up the 364 and hopefully have an attorney clear for a bail reduction in the process and give the heat the law was laying on some time to die down. I chose the latter.

There I was in the wild ass Essex County Jail again. On this trip in the County the thin line between consciousness and a corrupt mentality grew even thinner. Feeling the County blues dressed in my County greens, I exited the elevator on floors eight and nine with bed roll in hand. I headed to the officers' booth and showed my red ID band. I was assigned a cell.

The cells were six by eight and the color of piss. A steel bed occupied more than half of the cell. In the other half was a raised flat shelf and a connected seat and toilet. Iron bars separated COs and prisoners. The section where COs patrolled was called the catwalk. The dugouts and sally ports were death traps, and the entire tier was a blind spot. The most comforting part of the County was at night when the cell gates were locked. Then again, fear could keep one awake as the gaps between the cell bars were so spaced that it was nothing for an unfeeling convict to reach in and douse a cell with a prison-made concoction, sending inmate and room to the high heavens. Many nights I remember the deafening screams of inmates being awakened in the wee hours of the morning by raging flames after their cells were set ablaze.

In jail, true colors get shown. You either man up or fold. You could literally find yourself hand-washing dirty drawers, getting punked for commissary, or worst-case scenario, out in pink panties (treated like a female). You could see firsthand the men who were stand-up and those who lived like cowards. You discovered a soldier's true worth when placed in the line of fire, and the County was an all-day war zone.

In an attempt to keep the violence down, the administration housed the majority of Bloods on floors eight and nine and the Crips on floors four and five. Bloods from all over the city were on floors eight and nine. Most I didn't know personally; only one was actually from my neighborhood. For me that was more than enough.

There would be fights over the TV. Crips would get caught slipping on Blood floors, which was practically the entire jail except four and five, and be beaten to near death. Unclassified Bloods would be sent to the lone Crip floors and be knocked unconscious by socks filled with bars of soap and branded, literally burned, stabbed with homemade shanks, bones broken, and in some cases even killed. It was a deadly contest with both sides out to make statements with their brutality. At night, word would pass through the windows, "Yea we just caught your crab ass homeboy." Or "That's right; we just served your slob ass homie." The disrespect only made it worse on the next to get caught slipping.

The only homies from the set in the County at the time were myself, B-Blood, Lil Reef, and Too Gee (Omar Broadway), who was stuck in the hole on the twelfth floor for throwing baby oil, Magic Shave, and boiling water on another inmate who bragged about shooting a homie from the set without any knowledge of who he was around. Too Gee made him pay the price.

Inside the County Jail in late 2000 the Bloods were disorganized. Many East Coast sets were still finding out about each other and had yet to establish formal ties. While set tripping was deemed a violation, its occurrence was taking place more frequently. Dozens of Bloods cooped up and turned out on drugs and drama. With no enemies around and stress weighing, the small things easily became major. Sets got thick and homies started banging on each other.

There were a few among the population who were in position to establish some sort of order. I realized this was my temporary place of residence, and I called a meeting in the middle of the dayroom and explained while it was OBCC (Only Bloods Can Control), disorder disrupts and causes even the strongest empires to become weak.

Blood was feared throughout the jail, but the thinking man knew it was much more valuable to be respected. We needed to move differently to gain respect.

With a now-more-than-ever attitude, I set caution to the wind and added another chapter to the history of the Double ii Bloods, which by then had been seven years strong on the East Coast. Add in the time we had risen from our roots in Inglewood, California, and the family had fifteen years under its belt. Eight years from inception in 1985 until it reached us in Illtown, New Jersey, in 1993. Now, seven years later, in 2000, I felt the need to spread our wings again.

Up until then, anyone who wasn't basically bred Down the Hill had no chance of throwing up the D two ii's and the B. We weren't in competition, so numbers meant nothing. It just so happened we were the only set stationed in our neighborhood. The decision to branch out and expand beyond Down the Hill had its pros and cons. It meant more opportunity, and it also meant more risk. The rewards seemed to outweigh the risks, and I chose to seize the moment. I knew many would disagree. Personally, I wasn't on a hunt for crooks as much as I was for solids.

The County Jail served as a perfect place to recruit and expand. Like clockwork, I sat back on floors eight and nine and paid close attention to the men around me in search of those who had not only muscle but also a mind.

One day, I was sought out by Brick City Brims' Quick Brim with regard to two individuals downstairs on floors six and seven who were representing the set (ii) under false pretense. I had no idea who the two were, but I was positive I would find out sooner than later. Everybody knew false claiming was a sure way to get served. I thought whoever these two were, they either had a lot of heart or were flat-out stupid.

I wanted to get my shot at these two and see what they were about. When I saw CO XXXXX (name intentionally omitted) on my way to rec, I jumped at the opportunity to get them moved.

"Ay, I need you," I got at the CO—one of those slick-talking COs who thought he was the coolest thing moving.

"Butler, you always need something. I ain't got a damn thing for you," he shot back.

"Yeah aight. Tell it to one of these niggas that don't know better. But look, this ain't nothing major. I got two homies downstairs I need to get moved up here. I already got cells for them and everything."

He eyed me with suspicion. He knew most times we made moves to get dudes delivered it was for physical retribution.

"Nah, it ain't like that. That's my word."

"Nigga fuck that. I been around y'all enough to know what's up. Put it on Blood," the CO replied.

It was crazy how the police observed us and knew so much. Even when we thought we were being slick, there were those who paid attention to our every move and let nothing get by. Good thing, in this case, the unnamed CO wasn't tripping. Nevertheless, he was still the law.

"Man, you bugging. I ain't putting shit on Blood. Get yo ass outta here wit dat shit. Real talk though; I got a couple packs of Newports for the move. What's popping?"

"Now ya talking. In a couple of days or so I'll have 'em up here. I can't do it today cause the lieutenant and them been on my back lately. But I got you. Just have what's mine when they get here."

"Yeah aight. You keep talking shit you might not get nothing."

"Alright Butler. Stay out of trouble up here. I hear they talking about making some sort of gang unit. It's too many of you goddamn Bloods and, if you ask me, all y'all locked the hell up in this one little ass County Jail."

When the CO walked away he threw up a hand sign that resembled a "B" and started laughing. Maybe in another lifetime he was Damu. Who knows?

"Keep bullshitting. One thing for sure, they got room for your ass too," I yelled.

Days later and in exchange for a few packs of cigarettes, the two were moved up to floors eight and nine.

When the two arrived, to my surprise, one was a childhood associate from my days back at East Orange High. He went by the name of Boxing Rock. He was an avid boxer with quick hands and a sharp tongue. He was a Muhammad Ali--type trash talker. I wasn't familiar with his counterpart Baliown but he grew on me. He was a big young boy who stood six feet something, 200 pounds and some jingles. I learned they had been stuck in the County Jail quite some time awaiting trial on robbery and assault. A charge that years later, minus the fact I had no clue as to who they were or where they were at the time, I would be accused of ordering as work put in to join the set.

I expressed the seriousness of false claiming. They proceeded to tell me they weren't false claiming. While downstairs, Damus took note of their fearlessness and began to press them with offers to join their gang. Of course, after they were either jumped in or put in work. The two respectfully declined by stating, "When I come home it will be under no other set but Double ii." Both were originally from Illtown and felt it only right to represent a gang that banged from Inglewood to none other than their hometown of Illtown. Most sets took their refusal as a sign of disrespect. Turning down Blood was just something you didn't do. Each set believed their 'hood was the hardest, toughest, most dangerous, and put the most work in. And in these times each set had crowds of prospects waiting in the wings to join, but these two were different. They swam upstream as opposed to simply rolling with the tide—exactly the way we did things from Inglewood to Illtown. I liked them already.

These two became the first homies adopted into Double ii who weren't direct descendants of the turf. Together, in the County, we became a force to be reckoned with. We were small in numbers but big in heart. Everything we did was as a unit. We came up with a new way to throw up the set to differentiate between those of us who were actually gang-banging and those who simply represented. They were right there beside me when the County decided to turn floors eight and nine into a gang pod.

Essex County entered an agreement with the state's Department of Corrections to imitate Northern State Prison's Gang Unit at the County Jail, and we were its first occupants. Among the list were homeboys like Boxing Rock, Baliown, B-Blood, Laydown, Reef, K.O., Life, and a gang of others. The unit was "23 and 1" lockdown (twenty-three hours or more in your cell a day). Their justification was to label the Bloods as a *security threat group*. Once validated you were categorized as a threat to the general population. The label stuck for a lifetime. These classifications were life-altering, similar to the way kids were classified in school. In prison these classifications subjected us to wicked torture created and reserved especially for gang-bangers and other "threats." Our overall attitude changed. We became more militant.

On this same bid, the County Jail administration thrust a so-called position of power upon me. Given my desire to stand on principle and what I believed to be right, along with my voice of reason, when incidents occurred, I was the first person the administration ran to.

"Mr. Butler your homie, inmate such and such is upstairs, downstairs, or in the hole acting out and claims he will not quit until he speaks to you. Can you calm him down?"

I was nobody special. I was no more important than the next Blood serving time. But because I never wanted to see my people destroyed (physically beaten, psychologically played on, or worse) I would run. I felt it was my duty as a Blood to keep my people afloat. That was until, no matter how critical the situation, I decided to let things be and play themselves out the way they would. It wasn't that I didn't care. It was because I started to see the way the law used me and saw me as nothing more than a tool. They didn't care about me. All they cared about was the orderly running of their institution. When I stopped it became, "Mr. Butler you are perpetuating this violence, extortion, and robbing in our jail. You are responsible for this unwanted behavior."

Part of the stigma attached to my name originated in the County. This was how I became the man allegedly responsible for much of the madness that would follow. What was kept from the people were the many times I put my head on a platter in attempt to resolve issues and bring about a peaceful situation for everyone.

Me and Hakavelli, Threat Ru, Quick Brim, and others put egos to the side and started to form as one. We studied together, educating ourselves on history that was not offered in our school system. We worked out together. We broke bread together. And at night, we roll-called together. Though we did it for ourselves and for our cause, you would have thought the jail staff would have welcomed such change, because violence in the jail declined. But to no surprise it worried the administration. They began to ask questions like "Why are the Bloods so quiet? What are they up to? Who is behind this? And who is running that?" The situation was like something ripped straight from the pages of books that lined my cell: Elaine Brown's *A Taste of Power*, Eldridge Cleaver's *Soul on Ice*, George Jackson's *Blood in My Eye*, and the list went on.

As Thomas Jefferson once stated, "Dissension is the greatest form of patriotism," and I took to the struggles those before me endured in their attempt to rid the nation of its oppressors. With each page I read, I noticed the similarities between what they went through and what we were going through. I saw the similarities of how war was waged—the police intimidation, the arrests in abundance, falsified documents to divide the people, outrageous bails, isolation, and brutality.

The system preferred we remain unorganized, uneducated, and sparked with savagery. They feared unity and cooperation among our kind. It was easier to control, abuse, and conquer the ignorant, undisciplined, and divided. With no incidents taking place, there wasn't much they could do. But if they wanted you bad enough you could trust they would find a way.

Homies like Boupdaville, Tec Tutt, Monster Ru, and others were already trapped off, and my turn arrived as I enjoyed a visit with loved ones. I knew something was up when my visit was cut short. I didn't give it too much thought. It was clear I had been sitting directly in front of the officers for the last forty-five minutes and had no direct involvement in whatever took place. None of that mattered. When I exited the visit booth, I was greeted by a female sergeant and the Goon Squad (response team).

"Butler, place your hands behind your back."

"For what?" I questioned, knowing I had done nothing wrong.

"Just do as I say and we won't have to use force."

Here they were, looking for any sign of resistance and a reason to get aggressive, power-tripping as usual. I understood there was no need to engage in a physical confrontation I knew I couldn't win, and I turned around to cuff up. I noticed an inmate standing in the Southside's sally port who attempted to hide his face. Too late, I knew exactly who it was. It was a kid I went to school with who had come in a few nights prior. Though not a Crip, he was guilty by association, so first sign of me not being around, the homies roughed him for his brand new Air Jordans. Scared to death, he hit the gate and gave up the only name he knew, Mass. It didn't matter I was nowhere around and already had more shoes in my cell than Sneaker World. I had mesh bags full of food from commissary, cartons of cigarettes, shoe sizes 8 ½, Air Max, Air Jordans, Bo Jacksons, Penny Hardaways, and all the throwbacks, New Balance 992s. You name it, I had them.

Since I was in the County I had yet to receive a write-up, but for reasons unknown at the time, staff and COs alike were instructed to keep a log of my daily activities. Now based solely on another inmate's mention of my name, and I was off to the hole—the twelfth floor of the County.

The twelfth floor held nine dungeon-like cells. Any and all disciplinary infractions led you there. Property or cosmetics were prohibited. In the hole, it was just you and your thoughts. And for the next thirty days this was where I was held on write-ups from possessing gang paraphernalia to extortion. I also found out I was indicted for my fourth adult case, first degree murder.

I was smothered in the filth of the hole when my unmovable iron door began to shake.

"Ay B, I got to holler at you," voiced the hole officer who opened and left my cell door wide open. I wasn't sure what he wanted but it could've easily been a set up to lock me out of my cell for a shakedown. I was hesitant to exit. I used a plastic mirror I had stashed to peer out on the tier.

"Ay B, let me holler at you," the CO said again. Finally, I stepped out. My eyes adjusted to the light, and I yelled, "What?"

"I have some serious news concerning your father," he replied.

We were on opposite sides of the spectrum and had nothing in common. Therefore, any remark about family was a personal matter and completely out of line on his part. I knew it was the Chaplain's job, not the CO's, to report family emergencies.

"Ay B, if you don't want to talk, you don't have to. But I've been given instructions to let you out to use the phone. I've been told your family will be awaiting your call."

"Whatever," I responded.

I wasn't in the mood to hear anything else he had to say. But I thought maybe my father was back in the hospital. My father was diabetic, and I was used to him in and out of the hospital. Occasionally, he even went into diabetic comas. But damn, call home. Was something not right? Butterflies floated in the pit of my stomach.

A month or so prior my father just visited me alone. I felt it was the first time we really kicked it. Now out of nowhere my door was busted open for a "special call." I tried my best to stay focused, yet I feared what awaited me. I hesitantly exited the tier and walked towards the phone. I stood in front of the phone and dreaded the unthinkable.

Finally, I dialed home. Three rings and I heard a female's voice answer as the operator chimed in. I heard whispering in the background. Then, in a voice of fear and sorrow, "It's Tewhan, oh my God, oh my God, should I tell him?"

The voice on the other end didn't realize she already accepted the call. I was tired of the charades and lit up, "Tell me what!"

"It's your father, Tewhan. He's gone."

"Gone?" I managed to reply. Impossible. In my eyes my father was made immortal, an original gangster, unfadable. I couldn't believe it. Along the way, we bumped heads and that prevented us from doing and becoming so much. Now, it was clear, we never would. Since I could remember, I secretly wanted to be just like my dad. I never had the heart to tell him. I felt regret. I was crushed. At the age of forty-one my father was dead from complications related to diabetes.

I knew my moment of mourning would have to be put on hold.

"Where's my mother?" I questioned

"Tewhan, as soon as she gets back from the funeral home we will be down to see you. Are you OK?"

"Yeah, I'm good. See you when you get here."

It wasn't until I disconnected I realized it was my godmother Candace I had been talking to.

An hour or so later I was shackled and led to a visitation booth where my mother and godmother sat waiting. As soon as I entered and saw the look in my mother's eyes, it took everything I had to not break down. My parents were separated since my Caldwell bid in '99. Despite being physically apart, the love they possessed for one another was always apparent. But now the man my mother spent the past twenty some odd years with had moved on. She was emotionally scarred and needed to be consoled. The visitation booth's Plexiglas window only deepened the wounds. Opposed to words, we spoke with our eyes and promised to remain strong. It wasn't long before COs interrupted our visit to return me back to hell on earth, the hole. When I was shackled and dragged away, it was like removing a newborn from its mother. I was locked up. My father had just passed. There was no telling how my brother was coping. I had to get out the hole and out of jail.

I went through a few days of psychological evaluations and other assessments, and I found out I would be going back downstairs to floors eight and nine, the Gang Unit, cell 826. I was more than pleased to know I would be back where I was housed before I went to the hole. I hurried on to the elevator and shot the breeze with CO Kojack and told him, "Take me home."

"Things done changed on eight and nine, young blood," Kojack said as I was getting off the elevator.

I didn't know what he was talking about. I reached the officer's booth, my band was checked, and I strolled in with property in hand. When I arrived at West End's back gate, it looked like a hurricane had swept through. There were spilled dinner trays, splattered milk cartons, cigarette butts, and floodwaters everywhere. All was a result of inmates bucking for being locked down in their cells for absolutely no reason at all.

I was told if I kept cool I would be allowed the opportunity to attend my father's funeral. I have no idea why I fell for the nonsense and got my hopes up. On the day my father was buried, the prosecutors told me my charges were too severe and therefore they could not grant me the privilege to say good-bye. Again, I felt manipulated. I wanted to explode, but I would have made the rest of my stay a nightmare if I did. It was the brotherly love granted by each and every Damu in the Gang Unit that made it possible for me to get through emotionally and mentally. Still, I couldn't wait to be set free.

After months of sitting in the hole and the Gang Unit on nothing but an arrest sheet regarding my recent offense, and stressed out over my father's recent death, I was presented with legal documentation that revealed the names and statements of those who were assisting the law.

That same day, on my one hour out to shower, use the phone, and stretch my legs, with no clue the phones were tapped as part of an investigation into another Damu who was housed in the Gang Unit, I called home to speak with my younger brother.

Had we known the phones were tapped, much of the conversation would have never taken place. We should have known better. Regardless, this conversation and the law's interpretation was a sure shot to prison.

PLANT #2 (973) 596-2484   DATE: 3/27/01

TAPE #120   TIME START: 13:22 HRS.

INTERCEPTION #1492   TELEPHONE # (973) 673-XXXX

CASE # SI 04-01   TRANSCRIBED BY: INV. TREVOR LAVINE #206

                              ESSEX COUNTY PROSECUTOR'S OFFICE

                              MONITOR: S/I CHRIS FERNICOLA

                              DIVISION OF CRIMINAL JUSTICE

SUBSCRIBER: R D SMITH

                               84 ARSDALE TERRACE, FL. 3

                               EAST ORANGE, N.J.

M: Tewhan Butler, aka Mass

S: Steven Butler

OPER: Operator

Oper: Bell Atlantic has a collect call from inmate Mass at the Essex County Jail. To refuse this call, hang up; if you accept this call, do not use three-way or call waiting features or you will be disconnected. To accept this call dial "1" now. [Prompt given.] Thank you.

Counter at 002 to 012

M: Yo.

S: Yo.

M: What's poppin'?

S: You go to court Wednesday, right?

M: Tomorrow, yeah.

• Conversation about how much money unidentified male will give mom.

Pertinent counter at 026

M: When the last time you talk to for real.

S: Last night. Yesterday.

M: Yesterday?

S: Yeah.

M: What he talking about?

S: B-O-N [Bureau of Narcotics] motherfucking beasting out that motherfucker.

M: Yeah. That's why, that's why, that's I've been trying, trying to catch you man. Don't be, don't be slippin' cause you got the motherfucking G-ride going out all in the early daytime yo.

S: Yeah.

M: If I be, be trying to call sometimes you don't be answering the phone mommy be like you be coming like five bouncing right back out and shit, don't be, know what happened the last time.

S: Hell yeah.

M: Shit, we both would have been gone, nah mean, fuck that daytime shit.

S: Hell yeah.

M: Just stay to your regular shift know mean.

S: Yeah.

M: Just G-mack you and the homies stay in the G-ride or whatever, ride around or whatever, nah mean. Do y'all thing till late night, then come back out, come out on your regular shift know mean.

S: Yeah.

Non pertinent counter at 039

Conversation about M's bail being paid

M: Y'all bout to pay my bail tomorrow so then I know [inaudible] now my bail gonna be paid so then I only got three months left and you go out there on some early day shift and get bumped.

S: You know mother fuckin [S/L] Slash had got bagged and shit right.

M: Yeah, for beatin up Lamont?

S: Yeah.

M: Ah that nigga crazy man. Y'all niggas crazy. Word up. Somebody dropped the charges though?

S: Yeah.

Pertinent counter at 071

M: Mommy told you the name of the broad that had got the statement against me right.

S: I heard _____.

M: Yeah, _____.

S: Yeah.

M: Um, Chavell know her.

S: Chavell know.

M: Yeah. Chavell had came down here to see me and shit.

S: Yeah, it was, it was a [inaudible].

M: Yeah.

S: Chavell said he know her.

M: Yeah. He said it some ol fiend burned-out broad, nah mean.

S: Where she live at?

M: He ain't, he said he, he said she stay with some fiend nigga nah mean, but he know, he know everything, nah mean.

S: Yeah.

M: He know everything and you know Fiend Dot.

S: Who?

M: Fiend Dot.

S: Yeah, yeah.

M: From Roseville that look like, that look like she got that shit.

S: She know her?

M: Yeah. She know her too. She the one that pointed her out to Chavell.

S: Oh.

M: She know her too, nah I'm saying, word up. I ain't gonna, nah I'm saying, tell you what to do over the phone, nah I'm saying. I just probably, I'ma just tell

Neisha, um, she just left today but I'ma tell her Thursday nah I'm saying. Y'all could hook up with Dot, make something happen, but either way she, she ain't holding no weight, nah mean in trial anyway, nah I'm saying, he said Chavell said he know the broad, she burnt out nah I'm saying?

S: Yeah.

M: So that's something light. I'ma get my paperwork and shit tomorrow when I go to court.

S: Yeah.

M: Nah mean, hopefully they drop the shit down some [inaudible] nah mean?

S: Yeah.

Non pertinent counter at 088

Weeks after that conversation, the court ordered the County's Gang Unit emptied as a result of unconstitutional findings. But in reality they just changed the name. For the moment, we were all returned to general population. I was on the mainline (general population) for less than a month when I received an unexpected visit from my mother.

As soon as she walked in, I noticed an unsettled look on her face. I sat down and picked up the receiver. She began telling me how helicopters had hovered above her house and dozens of police kicked her door in looking to arrest my younger brother. Honestly, I knew there was no telling the things he could have done, but what I couldn't figure out was how they didn't know he was already in the Youth House. Shortly after our phone call he went against my advice in the phone call and hit the strip in the daytime. He got caught slipping again and charged with possession with the intent to distribute.

I did my best to calm my mom's nerves. We exchanged words of faith and fortitude for the remainder of the visit. I returned to my cell right on time for 3:30 freeze count—a regular lockdown for a head count to be certain no one has been harmed or escaped. Every man is to be accounted for.

After count settled, all I could do was hope my brother hadn't dug a hole he couldn't get out of. I thought of what could have led the law to raid my mother's home. While deep in thought, the Goon Squad came to my cell door and demanded I lie down on the ground, face toward the toilet, palms up, and no movement. I didn't know what all this was about. But I did realize being a self-admitted Blood was enough. I went through the motions and was led back to administrative segregation on floors eight and nine, the former Gang Unit.

As I was hurried down the tier I noticed a different Blood homie in each cell I passed. Some were previous occupants and others weren't. For the next few hours I just sat at my cell gate and hollered back and forth with the homies as we tried to decipher what was going on. My mind was racing a million miles a minute.

Around eleven o'clock that night, things started to make sense. Some who were arrested earlier that day and just came in shared stories exactly the same as my mother's. There was an obvious connection. Outside of us all being Bloods, neither I nor my brother had ties with some of these men. I refused to let it drive me crazy and stopped trying to figure it out. Why worry over that which you have no control? When misfortune comes one must remain with head up, chest out, and all ten toes firmly planted. I did not accept my situation, but I understood how to deal with it. I went to sleep and hoped for the best while expecting the worst.

The next morning I was greeted by the worst. I awoke to the tier officer banging on the cell bars yelling, "Everyone get ready for court. Everyone!"

It was no coincidence we all were scheduled for a court appearance the same day. When we arrived at the court building there was a line of pool attorneys and public defenders, all of whom suggested we waive our appearance due to the heavy media presence in the courtroom. After we all agreed, we received our arrest sheets and were sent back to the jail. There were forty-four co-defendants. I didn't know over seventy-five percent of them. Plus, for me, there was an additional $250,000 bail, additional state charges from conspiracy to commit murder, racketeering, and possession with intent to distribute—all a result of the earlier phone conversation with my brother.

Seven months in on my 364, a little over a month left before my time was complete, and the state came with a racketeering charge (RICO—Racketeer Influenced and Corrupt Organizations Act)—my fifth adult case. The racketeering statute had been used to attack organized crime and dismantle the Italian Mafia—the guys we used to imitate around the Laundromat table as kids. Now, the State of New Jersey and its war on gangs, for the first time in its legal history, was out to set precedent and charge, indict, and convict numerous members and associates of a street gang on racketeering charges.

Later that night, in the isolation of the County's Gang Unit, we heard uproar from the general population's dayroom area. The screams were loud. We could hear in the distance, "Oh shit, that's the homies" and after population returned from the dayroom other inmates hollered downstairs to enlighten us.

Come to find out, the homie Duke Dave went against the consensus and decided to attend the arraignment. As a result, he was cast on the five o'clock news and labeled as New Jersey's original gangster. His decision rubbed some the wrong way, but didn't bother others. Along with the titles placed upon his name by the media, they also spoke loud and clear on the match that sparked the fire. After Duke was sentenced for an unrelated offense, prosecutors accused him of mumbling threats to the prosecution and the judge. Ironically, no one heard these alleged threats except the prosecution. Still, they used it to launch a targeted investigation into the entire (gang) population on floors eight and nine. Keep in mind the Gang Unit had been ruled unconstitutional and ordered emptied, but it had simply been relabeled Administrative Segregation and still held nearly all, if not all, gang members. I didn't let it get me down. Instead, I thrust myself deeper into liberating literature and history, reaping its benefits and loving its lessons.

Before I knew it my max was up, and I G-strolled out of the County Jail. Those eight months seemed like forever. I knew a lot changed while I was gone, but I couldn't wait to pick up where I left off. My drive to get rich was the one thing that remained unaltered. I stood still for a minute and closed my eyes. Before I could think, I was snapped out of my daydream by the sound of my name and the honks of a car horn. I looked around and noticed an all-white Cadillac. I knew exactly who it was. It was apparent the love of my road dawg didn't change either. Just as last time, I was welcomed home by none other than the homie Troub. I hopped in, and he drove around and brought me up to speed on the town's latest occurrences.

Troub told me that since the publicity stemming from violent turf wars and the state's recent RICO sweep, Essex County formulated a bunch of different task forces aimed directly at curbing any and all gang activity. I heard this and knew I had to step out with a totally different approach. But all that would have to be figured out later. I was heading home to my first lady and second in charge—Momma Dearest and Alneisha Hall.

8

Only God Can Judge Me

MID-JULY 2001, THE morning after my release from the County, I woke up at my mother's house on Arsdale Terrace with money on my mind. It was back to the basics! When I hit the streets, most people couldn't believe their eyes. It was like they saw a ghost. I was home! There were so many stories surrounding my arrest nobody believed I would see daylight again. And there I stood, back where I rightfully belonged, the trenches of Down the Hill.

While in the County I evaluated and re-evaluated much about my past, present, and future. Now, I was out and after a few conversations, I knew the findings of my evaluations were correct. With pending charges of first degree murder and the State's racketeering case and the law lingering, I would have to keep a low profile and lighten up on the gang-banging to get money. It sounded easy, but it seemed impossible to turn it off like a light switch. And even if I could, it wouldn't stop the enemy from coming for my head or riding on the set.

The night was hot and humid. The Blood Country just dipped off and left me and the Blood Trigga Slash in front of 6th Avenue's Middle Bar passing back and forth a blunt and Trigga Slash's newfound favorite Remy Martin V.S.O.P Cognac.

Trigga Slash was a 'hood reputable. He was also a rapper. You could hear his lyrics on early Naughty by Nature albums. He was a 'hood entrepreneur and took no shorts. Trigga Slash was kind-hearted but a ticking time bomb. You best not rub him the wrong way.

Moochie and Archie, two GKB homies from The Bity, pulled up. We kicked it for a few, then they suggested we play it safe and hit the Patio for a few drinks and games of pool. I wasn't doing much and was cool with it. Trigga Slash opted to kick back and play the turf. I jumped in the backseat and called back to Slash, "You good, Blood?"

"Yeah, I'm straight", he replied.

This was the 'hood, why wouldn't he be? But that would be the last time I heard Slash's voice. Moments after I departed and sat in the Patio, Slash was shot multiple times and killed in a drive-by shooting at a phone booth on 6th Avenue in the heart of the 'hood. This situation left me crushed. However, as time went on, what left me even more scarred was when perception and reality began to walk hand in hand.

At this time, my name was in circulation for more than just being a hustler. I was already tied into a murder case. Violent behavior had grown on me and this was no secret. Yet, the image of who I was, or believed to be, was a consequence of imaginations gone wild and shameless, sensational and suggestive storytelling. The creative inventiveness of idle minds in the 'hood made this next bit of news near believable. It just about set the streets of Down the Hill ablaze. Immediately after Trigga Slash's murder my name was linked. There were rumors the killing was a product of debt. Ironically, nobody knew if I supposedly owed him or he supposedly owed me. There was no truth in either scenario.

I got a phone call from a person who I idolized growing up and was told to meet him at the Patio. I was unsure of the reason for the meeting but showed up all ears to hear what could only be serious business. The news he delivered all but broke my heart.

"You know word in the streets is you hit Slash."

Instantly, I felt disrespected. I appreciated him making me aware. To walk around with a bullet with your name written on it while you alone had no clue was an accident waiting to happen. If I knew nothing else, I knew the potential of getting caught slipping. But damn, here I was mourning and trying to unearth ways to avenge the homie's death and the look in this dude's eyes spoke of the uncertainty he held in my world.

At this point in my life, and all I had been through, nothing was unbelievable. But could my own neighborhood actually be under the impression I had become so venomous I recognized no one as more important than a dollar?

My hurt quickly turned to anger. I thought to myself, do I try to make sense of it all by explaining what I didn't know? Did I hide out? What was I to do?

Fuck it! Gun on waist, I guzzled down shot after shot of Hennessy with no chaser and went to my car parked out front and snatched up my bulletproof vest. I put it on under my clothing. I exited my vehicle and took to the street's yellow lines. Up 6th Avenue I went; 10th Street, 11th Street, across the tracks; 12th Street, the sight and sounds of the normal crowd of people who flooded the 'hood grew louder as I got closer; 13th Street, at any time one of my own tucked away in a cut could have easily taken aim and sent me to the place of no return; 14th Street, there was no turning back. I was met in the intersection of 14th Street by the Blood Country who was the one person besides Troub I knew I could depend on. We walked to 15th and William Streets to Sabora's hut.

Sabora was another of the Triplets and an auntie to the 'hood. She was related to my old girl Saleema and the mother of my two homegirls Dirah and Bree. In the game, there's nothing like family. When situations got ugly, or police ran down, their apartments were all access.

Me and the Blood Country hit the front of Sabora's and there sat Flocko—all 200 plus pounds of jailhouse weight. He just came home from a stretch out in Delaware. Flocko was a Spanish-looking cat from the Steel Click section of the 'hood with long hair and a fuck-the-world attitude like us all. Uncle Rat was also on the porch—the same Uncle Rat who set it off at the Ja Rule concert. Two words to describe Uncle Rat—no nonsense.

An argument ensued regarding the loss of Trigga Slash. Without the love Flocko and I have for one another, if the pain of that moment was tapped, somebody would have died that night. Uncle Rat, who was no stranger to such controversies and not blind to what was actually going on, intervened and stated he didn't believe to any degree that I had done such an ugly deed toward one of our own. With God's will, guns remained tucked, and though Flock and I nearly came to blows nothing jumped off. However, all did not feel the understanding we built.

In passing days, I was approached by quite a few, yet my latest visit came as the biggest shocker. Bad Newz and I stood on the corner of 15th and William Streets with our feet glued to the blood-stained sidewalk overseeing the steady flow of drug money. By then, hustling shifts were implemented to limit crowds and commotion on the corners to lessen the police presence and keep homies out of harm's way. Our corners weren't hangouts; they were places of business. We stood alone as a result.

I stood on the corner and flirted with Neisha from a distance as she sat in the window of her grandmother's three-family home when Treach from Naughty by Nature pulled up in his Lexus truck with a look to kill on his face. He aggressively called Bad Newz to his driver side window, and they talked for a minute or two.

I had an open mind but knew the rumor mill wasn't silenced. I paid close attention when Bad Newz finished their conversation and walked back toward the curb, avoiding eye contact with me at all costs. Treach jumped out his wildly parked truck and approached after Bad Newz. Body language could either work for you or against you. If I hadn't had a tremendous amount of respect for Treach, this day it most definitely would've worked against him. The heat on my waist was still warm from the night before.

Immediately, Treach went off: "F" this, "F" that, what the "F" happened to his homeboy; talking about how he ran this, and somebody better have answers. Of course, I was who he referred to.

I swear I understood what he was going through. The good ones always seem to die young. Yet, his approach was all wrong. We weren't the same kids who were sent on trips to the store and chased around the 'hood. I thought this was clearly understood when a few years earlier we as GRatz said fuck it and mobbed to 18th Street with the sole purpose to exchange fair ones with the older homeboys. And if my memory serves me correctly, fifteen-, sixteen-, and seventeen-year-olds lined up no longer afraid to lose and challenged the authority of our predecessors. We were now grown men in the 'hood, making our own way and giving the turf a name where it counted the most, in the streets!

With all due respect, while Treach was out doing concerts, shooting videos, and making movies, we as Bloods, gang-bangers for real, were out and about with our lives literally on the front line. I felt he needed to know this. I could bite my tongue no longer. Not today. So, I told him to his face what most in the 'hood whispered behind his back.

First, I let it be known he didn't run anything in respect to the "B." I then expressed how most of us felt let down and that he had picks when it came to reaching back. Please understand he did do a lot but what I knew that day was surrounding circumstances were a million times more egregious, so whether I was right or wrong, I felt enough was never enough. Enough would only be enough when one man, alone, could no longer separate or determine what we created.

I thought about the hardships one would experience on the wake-up, breath stinking, to put on the same clothes worn for the past week and lace up their Timberland boots to J-Cole and "face a cold world, no blanket." The thoughts of those who lived the life, while we looked for life, and lost it in the process, had me feeling some type of way. Treach stood somewhat amazed at how I laid it all out. There was no movement. Not a word between us for what seemed like hours. He turned and left, stating, "I'll be back."

This shit was crazy. In the 'hood, "I'll be back" was a threat. Threats meant murder. I didn't mind going to war with the world, but I dreaded the thought of going shot for shot with a homeboy. If death was what awaited me, I was willing to accept it in hopes my ashes were smoked and the truth of my undying love for the set would be revealed. Though Treach never returned, tension was brewing.

Days later I pulled up in Troub's BMW 325 in front of Cotton's Funeral Home on Main Street in Orange to pay my respects to Trigga Slash. I stepped out in a brown Dickies suit to honor the fallen, red Chuck Taylors, and a red bandanna to hold high the "B." Dozens of Bloods from Piru, GKB, Sex Money Murder, and Nine Trey were already there and anticipated my arrival. My heart was warmed by the sight of everyone who came out to send the homie Trigga Slash off.

The streets were still abuzz with different scenarios as to what happened to the Blood. Word also spread about the internal drama between me and Treach. After paying their respect to the homie Trigga Slash, Damus in attendance who were forever loyal to the "B" made it clear they were on deck and ready for whatever. I didn't come for any problems so I made my way toward the homie Slash's coffin and stood there for the entire service. I deliberately ignored any questions related to the unfortunate dilemma with Treach. It was a sad day. Revenge was a must. And after my own investigation I knew exactly what direction I was headed at the conclusion of that service.

After, I heard the whispers and saw the finger pointing. I did my best to overlook it all. I knew those who truly knew me, knew better. I stayed around to kick it and thank those I could for showing up. It was in these moments what can be construed as a light standoff occurred. I don't believe everyone fully understood what was going on. It wasn't a big spectacle with loud talking, but the eye contact between Treach and I said more than words could ever say.

I knew in my heart what could have easily transpired. So, I peaced the homies and told a few where to meet me later on and rolled out. The entire ride home I banged my head against the steering wheel lost in a mix of unpleasant speculation. I rolled behind tinted windows, filled with uneasy emotions, and ready to die. I never felt more alone in my life. Stressed beyond belief, I lit a blunt of that '89, pressed play on the CD player, and blasted 2-Pac's "How Long Will They Mourn Me." A lone tear fell from my eye.

The love I had for my gang was overrun by the fear that my gang no longer loved me. To love with the uncertainty of knowing if I was loved back left me raw. The 'hood was all I cared about. It was my flesh and blood and though things hadn't fully escalated, I felt betrayed. Full tilt, the pain I felt had to be unleashed. If I was to sit on this hurt any longer I might've imploded. That night word was Newark and Irvington went up in smoke.

Things were eventually cleared up with respect to my name being linked to the homie's murder. No one wanted to look at what could've been, and we kept quiet and left well enough alone. Trigga Slash's death is one of many that remain unsolved.

I still believed it all to be worth it, and I continued to roll with the punches. After a couple of months of lying low and letting the game come to me I began to encounter a dilemma. Since I came home I found myself echoing the earlier phone conversation from jail with my brother and repeatedly telling the younger homeboys from my neighborhood to stay off the corners and off the strip. The death of the homie Trigga Slash should have been reason enough. Still, I noticed more and more of them trying to pick up and take on the drug trade.

At just the right time, I pulled up on a group of young gangsters from the 'hood and hopped out demanding they all stay put. I knew they expected some style of physical discipline, but this time I tried a different approach. I asked, "Why y'all still out here like this after time and time again we told y'all not to?"

In my head I was tripping at the fact I sounded like somebody's father, yet with all sincerity I wanted to know why they wanted the life of another. The young homie Lil Leem aka Hip Hop, Saleema's little brother who was like a little brother to me—the same young homie I practically raised as a child, the same little homie who years back was so intimidated by the law's screams during my '98 raid case he tucked our dog inside the apartment's bathroom—was now fearless and stepped up to make it clear he wanted his piece of the pie. I was amazed at how so much changed, but, then again, that's what the streets do.

Young Hip took to the forefront and presented me with questions and the views of his generation:

"It's hunting season out here, big bro, and you know that. Ain't nothing you or us ever seen accumulating capital like this corner. Why should we have to walk around hungry, wearing hand me downs, looking like nothing while everybody else gettin' it [money]? If not like this [hustling], Big Bro, then how? They tell us we gonna die young. If that's the case, grant it; but I'll be damned if we got to accept dying young, broke, and repping anything other than the Double ii Bloods."

"I feel you," I said. "I know shit ain't easy out here, but who would I be if I didn't at least try to show y'all something other than the life?"

Listening to myself talk, it reminded me of the older homies who tried to talk sense into me back in the day. At that point, I was beginning to understand. In the 'hood we had a unique way of displaying our love, and sometimes we did it through aggression.

"But bro, if you was feeling us you wouldn't be trippin' off us being out here trying to get this money. You know I been around you for years. What I'm doing ain't nothing different than what you, my brother, and all the other homies around here been doing."

With a smirk I replied, "You right, but who we are and what we did don't mean ya'll got to be the same and do the same shit. Now, it's different. Repping don't mean gang-banging. Hustling ain't the only way to get rich. I love ya'll lil niggas. I know ya'll love me. Am I asking too much for ya'll to fall back off these corners?"

"Big bro, I love dat nigga back, but out of respect for you, I aint gonna tell you that this is the last time you'll see us out here."

Wow, the truth wasn't always soothing. Lil Leem's response left me crushed, but every part of me understood what he said. I still tried to talk to them on other ideas. I stressed the importance of school, life, and more. I could see it was all going in one ear and out of the other. They wanted to know the quickest way to get behind the wheel of the Cadillacs and the BMWs that lined our streets. They wanted to know how to come up on the reputations of homies like Auto and Dream, Soup and Rat, Buckshot and Trigga Slash, MD and Lil Steve, and Troub and Mass.

How could we deny the young homies the opportunity to bang as Bloods when they were born and raised in the 'hood? They expressed the feeling of rejection for not being accepted by those they looked up to. Did I understand? Yes! I understood, but I wanted more for them. I too grew up wanting the finer things in life. I too wanted to be recognized by my bigger homeboys, and I too believed moving that work increased my chances of making it out of the 'hood.

Poverty and lack of identity are a man's worst enemy, so as each of them took me through what they felt, I wondered what would be if they were left to find their way in the streets on their own. I could let them go, or I could try my damnedest to help them make the best out of a bad situation. With my twisted way of thinking at the time, together we took off hustling and gang-banging.

With the emergence of the 'hood's next generation, there was no way I could lay low. Their perception of the game and of Blood was totally misconstrued. They were red ragging as if it was a fad and not a way of life. They hustled for sneaker money and hotel costs. If some form of discipline wasn't instilled, their recklessness was sure to be their downfall. And their demise meant the death of the gang. The love I held for my turf wouldn't allow me to see such a thing.

Right around this same time, I was blessed with the news that Neisha was expecting. If you asked me, I thought I couldn't have children, so I was shocked when Neisha began having morning sickness and mood swings. Almost in the same breath, a girl I met at my homegirl Sha's house, Princess, offered me the same story—PREGNANT!

I know you are probably wondering "what the hell?" After Princess and I "hooked up" we basically went back to our daily lives without one another. We were none other than two adults who did what grown folks do, and that was that. So when I was informed Princess was pregnant a few red flags went up immediately. No, I am not suggesting Princess is anything other than a woman. It's just our "situation" called for skepticism on my part. During this time in my life many women were appearing and most were under the impression that there was something to gain. Princess and I went back and forth with her trying to reassure me the baby in her stomach was mine. This conflict went on all the way up to my daughter's birth and even after.

The drama was overwhelming. I had just started to feel ready to become a one-woman man, and the consequences of not protecting myself caught up with me.

Princess wasn't a bad girl, but emotionally we never connected. Sex to me did not mean love, and I feel it takes love for two to create a child. I expressed my feelings to Princess, maybe not in the best of ways, and so Princess reacted hastily with basically a fuck me and what I had going on attitude. Rightfully so, all she cared about was her and the unborn child. I couldn't blame her.

I didn't know how I could break the news to Neish. So, I ducked it for as long as I could. That was until the streets began talking and Neish approached me with tears in her eyes and anger in her heart. I don't believe she was a woman scorned, but after all we had been through, she was absolutely disappointed. Neish was soon to be my fiancé and one day my wife but now she was having second thoughts. We were all in the same town, only blocks away, and I had two women pregnant at the same damn time. Imagine life's difficulty at the time from just this situation—let alone what was going on in the streets and with the law. Talk about drama.

I never saw myself becoming a father, let alone in this fashion, but the idea of having a little me running around was a beautiful thing. At the same time, fear crept through me every time I thought about the chills and shivers of a cold world my kids would be forced to endure. What would it mean for my children to be born to a parent who is a gang-banger? Would their lives be their own or would they be doomed by the choices I made?

When I first entered the game, none of those thoughts crossed my mind. I lived for my gang and me. I was a few months away from bringing life into existence. My life was no longer mine; it now belonged to the little ones growing inside the wombs of their mothers. How could I or would I clean up my act while my hands were dirty and my feet were muddy? They say "It is in your moment of decision that your destiny is shaped." My choices would either heal me or kill me. My attitude was for my seeds to want for nothing and have the very best of everything without having to endure a lifestyle similar to mine. And with this mentality, I lunged deeper into the land of crack sales and dope deals.

I hit the strip for a list of other reasons. Selfish: I thought of quick money. Fearful: of life without my homeboys. Since our youth we were inseparable and validated each other's existence. Blind: My one-track mind wouldn't let me see any other way to provide.

Through it all, I tried to prepare myself for the arrival of my baby boy and my baby girl. I wanted to be around when they both arrived, and I couldn't wait to remove the legal issues hanging over my head. The worries of leaving my children behind were stressful. I began stressing my lawyer concerning my day in court for the October 19, 2000, murder charge.

I was already assigned two different trial dates only to show up and have them postponed. They wouldn't dare share, but it was evident the State's murder case was extremely weak with no physical evidence, and revolving around hearsay from two supposed eyewitnesses, both of whom offered up contradictory statements. At first, neither saw anything. However, after they were picked up again on outstanding warrants, they gave up my name and were released. At the precinct, when the two supposed eyewitnesses were asked why they did not provide this information during the first interrogation, they said, "Because he [Mass] is the leader of the Bloods and I knew he could have something done to me." One even went so far as to say, "I once asked him [Mass] what his teardrops [my tattoo] meant and he told me each represented a person he killed." I knew the truth and to me their case was a joke. But picking twelve was a crap shoot. The state feared their case wouldn't stick, and the Feds were in the background equally unconvinced, so they sent their informant.

On a normal day in the 'hood, I posted up with a gang of the homies. Someone asked how things looked with my case. Confident in my surroundings, I spoke freely and shared, though I hadn't received an offer. "If they threw me ten years or less I would take it simply to put it all behind me," I told them. From a legal perspective, a man only does time for a crime he committed. On a street level, not always, but a lot of times, men and women alike admit guilt to get out of the way before the gavel came crashing down and risked forever behind bars. With their informant in the midst, this became my confession #1.

I wish I would have known that one who I considered a brother saw me as an enemy and was working to set me up! I loved. He hated—not only me, but also himself. Then I didn't know, but today I wonder what our friendship meant to him, if ever anything.

Whether I stayed active or got low, the script was already written by another cowardly and treasonous homeboy turned informant who chose the game but didn't know its rules. He got caught up and dismissed our vow to "let no man separate what we create."

Little did I know, penitentiary chances had become a sure shot.

9

LOYALTY

I was no longer as active in the street as I once was. But my involvement could not be disguised. Even if I allowed my gun to go warm I still felt the need to be an integrating force within my neighborhood. I never wanted my gang to be overcome by dissension. If it meant I had to pass up the opportunity to ride off into the sunset and remain confined to Illtown, Down the Hill, then that's what it was.

A fool suffers more than necessary. So while I was true to what I stood for, I was a fool in my display. But still I could not come to terms with leaving behind those I considered to be my brothers. The door was open, and the road was clear. I should have been experiencing the fruits of the road less traveled, leaving footprints behind for the many who searched for an out to follow, but I lacked direction. I was so close to the problem, yet even closer to the solution. Thing was I didn't know it. I was actually feeding and preserving the treachery I rebelled against. How could I want to better our current conditions, but refuse to better myself?

A homeboy of mine once told me, "Before placing the world on your shoulders *you* must first build a strong foundation on which you and others can stand." He put emphasis on "YOU." All the answers would never be found within. My principles and ambitions would have to become my foundation.

I couldn't fight it any longer; these thoughts had been on my mind for quite some time. Since I first felt truly compelled to let go, I realized the forces of negativity never let up. You just have to find a way to remove yourself. An older homeboy, who already left the streets alone to pursue more positive and productive outlets, suggested to me it was time to settle down. I finally decided to do just that. My actions were spontaneous. When I awoke that morning, the first thing that came to mind was marriage.

I had never missed one of the 'hood's Sunday meetings since they had begun. I never even entertained the thought. But on that Sunday, I would have to. It was the beginning of a new life for the man known as Massacre.

I called my homeboy So Fat to pick me up. He answered his phone,

"What's poppin', big homie?"

"That Wood Gang!" I replied.

"All the time," he shot back.

"Come pick me up, I'm over here on Arsdale Terrace. I'm trying to go see a few things."

"Trillz, say no more. I'll be there in a minute. Listen out for the horn."

"Aight, I'm waiting on you," I replied.

When the brief conversation ended, I hit the shower and freshened up. I stepped out feeling like new money and lit up the rest of the spliff I had from the night before. As I sat and inhaled that Little Bricks' sticky, I secretly watched Neisha. When she got out of bed wearing that pregnant glow and baby belly, I knew then and there exactly what I had to do. The vibration from my phone and the sound of a horn outside broke my train of thought. I answered the phone, "I'm on my way down."

I exited the house, throwing up big B's with one hand and the set with the other. I saluted the homie and jumped into the passenger seat of his kitted out Supra. Our first stop was cross-town to John's Place for their famous ox tails and rice. After we were seated, I broke the news.

"Today, it's me and you. I'm trying to go hit the Jewelry Exchange and do a little ring shopping."

"Ring shopping? First off, we got a 2:35 meeting in about an hour. Second, I ain't never seen you with no jewelry on besides a watch and the O.D. piece you had made for your birthday back in 1999. Besides, whatever happened to that chain?"

As a tribute to the death of my beloved brother Marcus "O.D." Allen, I purchased a white gold and 14k gold chain with a medallion fixed with invisible set diamonds that read "O.D."

My road dawg Country felt he was not being rewarded enough in business and had recently dipped with my chain and about $10,000 dollars in cash. He opted to end a friendship instead of talking things out and working through whatever was on his mind. Country never returned to the 'hood and in 2011, during my current incarceration, I found out he was killed.

"I ain't really trying to go into all that. That shit makes my blood boil every time I get to thinking about it. But, trillz, I never been big on jewelry. This trip ain't about me though. I'm trying to snatch something up for ol' girl back at the pad."

"Ol' girl back at the pad?" So Fat responded, laughing me off in between sips of his Uptown (iced tea and lemonade mix). "What kind of ring? I know you not talking about the lovey-dovey marry me be my wife type ring."

"Why not? A nigga can't decide to lay it down? You know she pregnant and all. I can't continue weaving in and out of traffic navigating my way around enemy 'hoods and ducking the law for the rest of my life, homie. I'm still young, but I been around the block and back."

"I guess you right, but this the life we chose," replied So Fat.

"Yeah, homie, you right, it's the life *we chose.* But what about the young homeboys who out here trying to emulate the lives we live? I done put hundreds on to the 'hood and whether they thought it was the right thing to say or truly meant it, ninety to ninety-five percent of them jumped in that circle and when asked why they wanted to become Blood, their answer was to override the oppression and uplift our kind. Listen Blood, contrary to what you may believe, since we picked up our rags, most of what we done been more oppressive than not."

So Fat: "I can't deny that, but as products of our environment, how can't they respect us getting it how we live?"

"This ain't about them, it's about us and ours. Think for a second on how we living and how we want to be living. It's two different realities. Nothing we got gonna amount to shit if we still around when them boys come knocking. And trust when they come, the last thing on they mind gonna be respect. But listen Blood, I'm still me, just with a more advanced mind-frame. Before we G-stroll hold this: You ever heard the quote: 'a person's thoughts are made in the fashion of dry land'? The mind is capable of growing as it is properly nourished. Circumstance is utterly important to the mind's development. Circumstance feeds us the life lessons that bring us closer to a promising stage of existence. One struggle will inevitably give way to another, yet our goal must be to evolve and never become stagnant."

"Enough of the philosophical shit Blood, let's hurry up and get to the Jewelry Exchange so I can see if you really serious," So Fat replied.

"Fasho wit it!"

On the way to Jewelry Exchange, I leaned the seat back, closed my eyes, and continued to think. All of my past shortcomings, misdeeds, and bad fortune were just that. They were all a part of my evolving. Some of the finest fixtures were shaped and molded under extreme pressure, by fire, or both. With this knowledge, one hurdle was overcome, but my challenge would be to apply what I knew.

Once inside the Jewelry Exchange, we shopped around for the ring that would seal the deal. After about an hour or so, we finally found it. Just as the store employee shared her opinion of how nice a ring it was and asked who the lucky lady was, my phone rang.

"Hello?"

"Ay, Blood, we at the park and we need you here ASAP."

"Nah, go ahead and handle it. Me and the homie on something right now. We took a pass on this one," I replied.

"This ain't that, Blood. We need you here. On the 'hood, it's urgent."

"Aight, we on our way."

The urgency in the voice on the other end left me curious as to exactly what was going on. My mood changed. I rushed the jeweler to box up the ring. There was no time to waste. So Fat noticed my instant mood swing and questioned, "What's poppin'? Who was that on the jack?"

"That was the homies saying they needed us at the park ASAP."

We got to the park in record time. I could tell something transpired by the looks on the homies' faces. Federal documents state:

October 21, 2001—Murder Conspiracy in Oval Park

Later on the same day, Double II members called a meeting in Oval Park to address several pressing issues. First, was the stabbing in Club 1199. Second, the same people responsible for the stabbing were also reported to be selling drugs in Double II territory on 13th Street. So on October 21, 2001, the day after the stabbing of Devil and George, the members of the Double II Bloods plotted their revenge.

The meeting was presided over by Double II Bloods leaders Tewhan Butler (Massacre) and Quadree Smith (Trouble). George Brown and Red Dev were there to recount what had happened at Club 1199. Tewhan Butler and Quadree Smith admonished the group that they could not allow something like that to occur without retaliating. In regard to the stabbing of Devil and George, it was decided that a team of people would be sent out to shoot Jahfari Harrison. It was also decided that associates who sold drugs with Harrison would be shooting targets as well. Thirteenth Street and 7th Avenue was chosen for the shooting because Khalif and Jerome Lagin lived there and sold drugs for Harrison at that location.

The plans were set to shoot Jahfari (Harrison) and others. The Double II members broke into different teams to carry out the multiple shootings. Quadree Smith separated out the Double II members willing to engage in violence from those who were not. Specifically, Trouble said in substance and in part "if you're a vegetarian, sit on this side;" "if you are ready to eat food, sit on this side." Members of the Double II set, including Preston Jones and Howard Wright, volunteered to carry out the acts of violence.

That 13th Street beef only enhanced one's thirst for more. Everything in the streets from October 21, 2001, to about mid-2002 was deadly back and forth for months. Everybody was cautious, hiding behind tinted windows, bending corners with caution, and running red lights to avoid becoming a sitting target. In this short period the gang culture took off. Much work was put in prior to the events of October 21, 2001. However, after, it was total pandemonium. Bloods looked to kill Crips. Crips were out to kill Bloods. And the consequences, nobody cared. Go to prison for taking the life of an enemy and be treated like a king. A regular life doesn't matter to a hardened gang-banger. A real nightmare, played out as a dream.

Gang-bangers had become addicted to violence and death and, like any true addict, would do anything for the next high to be better than the last. For months on end, days seemed to repeat, yet during meetings I recall telling homies no run lasts forever and things would change. With our good fortune would come troubled times. All I asked was for everybody to be ready. Nobody feared the law, let them tell it.

During these same meetings I also had to hand down laws of my own and ban certain things, like smoking PCP and reckless gang-banging. Some had a high tolerance and others didn't. Homies would be high out of their minds doing things that, no matter how lawless we were and how callous the world saw us as, could not be ignored.

Before I knew it, the New Year rolled in and offered nothing new. For me the only thing that seemed promising was the expectant birth of my son. But before that, on April 30, 2002, the law grabbed me again—my sixth adult case.

It was the start of spring and the weather was just beginning to break warm. After a few blunts, I went on a long stroll around the 'hood with the homie Shorty Thug, a younger homie around my brother's age with hazel eyes, light brown skin, 'hood flash, and a bad attitude. He had come up since his days as a Young Buck. Later down the line Shorty Thug proved he wasn't the thug we thought he was, if you catch my drift.

We decided to take a trip over the water to New York to do a little shopping and cop a few bags of that beef and broccoli, what we called that combination of heavy brown weed and sticky green from Harlem and Washington Heights.

Still in Jersey, on our way under the Orange Street Bridge in Newark, we ran smack dab into the gravy train (a caravan of unmarked police vehicles). We were dirty (in possession of drugs) as usual, and there was no telling either of us that we were not about to be boxed in and carted to jail. The list would have gone: One Lincoln Precinct, then Green Street Precinct, and next the filth of the Essex County Jail. As luck would have it, we escaped the box-in. We stumbled upon a light fortune and decided to make a sharp detour to put up what was in our possession that would have guaranteed a prison term.

We arrived in front of Shorty Thug's grandmother's house on Murda Ave. Before we could even exit the tinted black Acura Legend a few of the young homies strolled up and wanted to kick it. We were on a mission and didn't have too much time to rap. We passed off what we had to the young homie who happened to be the younger brother of my homeboy and earlier co-defendant in the drug raid case, Too Gee (Omar Broadway).

Right after we passed off to the young homie, East Orange Police Department pulled up in a hurry looking to arrest anyone in sight. Too Gee's younger brother took the chase and it was off to the races. I sat trapped inside of the car. I knew if the law spotted my face there would be trouble, and I was in no way looking for another run-in with the law. Shorty Thug wasn't as worried as me and jumped out of the car and headed into his house. Lucky him, police didn't even notice.

I leaned the passenger seat back and prayed the police would continue searching for the homie who fled and overlook the vehicle. Minutes later, the young homie appeared in cuffs with his clothes dirty and sweat running from his forehead. He wore a look of failure on his face. Surely, police made him pay for running. The entire scene played out before my eyes, until the one super cop, and there's always one, came and peeked into the windows of the Acura. "We got one," he yelled to his backup. In my mind all I thought was, *Damn!* Guns were drawn. I was ordered to exit the vehicle with my hands in the air. I did not want to become law enforcement's shooting gallery, so I eased my way out of the vehicle with my hands up.

I was cuffed and thrown onto the trunk of the car. Lil Too Gee and I were left to deal with the police and their antics. In this incident, no news was bad news. I continually asked what the problem was and, continually, I got no response.

At one point, I glanced over my shoulder and saw another squad car pull up with someone in the back. I couldn't make out who the person was because of the way they had me pinned to the back of the car. From beside me, the police escorted a cuffed Young Too Gee to the squad car and did what appeared to be an on-the-spot identification. I thought there had to be something more going on than I was aware of, but whatever it was I wasn't worried because I had done nothing. After a positive ID on Young Too Gee, I all but pled with the law to allow me the chance to be ID'd by this individual. Whatever it was, they would not be able to say I had done a damn thing. I had just pulled up with Shorty Thug just seconds before the police ran down.

"No, you look too intimidating," the officer replied. I knew then I was in for the fix. I was stuffed into the backseat of yet another police car. And I found myself alongside Young Too Gee headed to East Orange's decrepit precinct.

We arrived to the precinct in minutes and were literally thrown into the bullpen. It was the same bullpen I was thrown into back when they charged me for the 2000 homicide. The same bullpen I was thrown into when East Orange's Task Force raided the apartment on 15th and William Streets a few years back. And it was the same bullpen where they had held my older homeboys when I was a child on Carnegie.

I was out of the loop as to why I was arrested. The police were no help, so I whispered questions to Young Too Gee in an attempt to find out exactly what was going on. After hours of being treated like trash, I was finally led to the lieutenant's desk and charged with armed robbery, possession of a weapon, a gun that was never presented, and aggravated assault. What type of pin the tail on the donkey type shit was this?

While we sat in the bullpen, many officers who knew me through previous run-ins stated they knew the charges were far from my M.O. As a hustler, robbery was something I never had a passion for. However, with smirks on their faces, they told me it's out of their hands and it was the lieutenant's call. During the strip-out process, the police learned I had $1,700 cash in my possession. You wouldn't believe with money in pocket I would've committed a robbery for a measly $25. But our law officials have learned many ways to manipulate the system. To substantiate their robbery claim, they allowed me to sign the money over when my family arrived, suggesting it would be of greater help in my family's hands to assist with my bail. Ironically, later, the money slip was somehow lost. If this was not testament to their manipulation, while stuck in the basement of East Orange's Precinct during the conversation between Young Too Gee and myself it was revealed he had exactly $25 cash. "Tewhan Butler we sentence you to . . ." was all I heard. After a day or two stuck inside the basement of the East Orange Police Precinct, Young Too Gee and I were transported to the Essex County Jail.

The next day I entered the courtroom to be arraigned. I hadn't showered in nearly three days. I was dingy and in cuffs. Just the way they want you to walk in front of the judge. I was unable to deliver retainer payment to my lawyer by court call, so I had a public defender standing beside me, and directly next to him were Young Too Gee and his public defender. For a few minutes or so our legal designees attempted to recount the ordeal, none of which I knew, while basically pleading for a reasonable bail. Almost in mid-sentence, the judge cut the proceedings.

"Mr. Broadway [Young Too Gee] your bail is set at $10,000 over a $1,000, cash or bond. Mr. Butler your bail is set at $250,000, bond only."

They say life isn't fair. The system ain't always either. An innocent man would now have to muster up no less than $13,000 cash in order to be set free for a crime he didn't commit.

After I was processed later that night, I called my mother in attempt to soothe her nerves, and of course to make sure the bail money was on its way to the bail bondsman. During our fifteen-minute phone call she assured me everything was cool and my name should be called before the final pack-outs, which were normally around 8 PM. With that news I hung up the phone and dialed Neisha, who had been staying at her mother's house.

My conversation with Neish was not as pleasant as the one with my mother. Almost immediately, Neisha began a rant about how my son was due any day and I was in jail as a result of my "not being able to leave them damn streets alone." I wasn't really in the mood to hear it. I sort of brushed her off and tried to lift her spirits and let her know this was the last time I would allow myself to get caught up. It definitely wasn't the time to profess my innocence. It was plain and simple—get my ass out of Dodge, and not worry about this problem anymore.

Before I knew it the fifteen minutes for phone calls were up, and the CO was yelling "LOCKDOWN." My number was to be called any minute. I dozed off and opened my eyes only to realize I was still in jail. I was beyond pissed. I exited my cell and headed straight to the phone. As soon after the operator said my name and I heard the button on the phone pressed to accept the call, I was on one.

"Why am I not out of jail?" the anger in my voice was recognizable.

My mother still knew how to get feisty from her days when she went by the alias Lateefah and kept my father in line, and shot back instantly, "Tewhan, I don't know who you think you're talking to, but I'm still your mother. First, if your ass would listen, we paid the goddamn bondsmen, but they put you on something called the Hot List [a list that alerts bond insurance companies that you are out on high bails and may be a potential flight risk]."

"The Hot List? Man, what the fuck? I knew this shit."

My mother interrupted to say, "Boy, listen, we have the bondsman on it, and what can be done will be done."

I fought off my frustration and responded, "Aight," before angrily hanging up the phone.

On the eighth day of sitting in jail mad at the world, and after dozens of arguments over the phone with Neisha regarding the ill behavior she felt landed me in jail, the CO yelled for me to pack out. A huge smile spread across my face. Not a minute later and my heart felt pain.

It was truly a moment of conflict. The smile was a result of my being released. On the flipside, it was painful to leave so many behind. One would be shocked at the camaraderie on the inside. My brothers were trapped behind these walls fighting the system for freedom that may never again be theirs. Time seemed to stop as I looked into the eyes of those who committed crimes and cared less about the court's comeback. Then there was the look in the eyes of those who stumbled into a life of crime, with little comprehension of the consequence known as prison. The silent delay spoke words we could not. We refrained from sensitive conversations in prison, but looks said enough. My heart cried for those who would never see the light of day again, and even those who would. Each day behind bars destroys another part of your person—sometimes to the point you become unrecognizable (not physically, but mentally and emotionally).

A CO interrupted the moment and yelled, "Butler, if you want to go then let's go. If not, you can surely stay here with the rest of your homies."

Men and women dressed daily in COs' uniforms and witnessed the abuse and injustices endured by prisoners and few, if any, feel even an ounce of compassion. Are they heartless, hateful, or is it just the power of a paycheck?

I left it all behind and grabbed my bedroll and headed toward the gate. One by one the homies took turns to holler things like don't come back, hold your head out there, and don't become a victim of circumstance as they had. I went through the discharge process (strip out, fingerprints, photo) and about an hour later I walked out of the County and into a 'hood embrace offered up by my homegirl Twin and the young homie Trillville.

When the homegirl Twin got put on the set we became inseparable. In my eyes, as well in everyone else's eyes for that matter, Twin was one down ass bitch. If the HBO series *The Wire* was an illustration of our 'hood, Twin would without doubt be Young Snoop.

Twin was the female thug who played in the streets more than unsupervised kids in the summertime. Twin was the epitome of a ride-or-die chick. This chick reminded me so much of a homie it was ridiculous. From the way she was gung ho when drama kicked off to the way she played dudes like two-dollar tricks. On more than one occasion I looked at Twin with "what if?" on my mind.

Behind tinted windows chiefing (smoking) on some loud pack (good weed) I would die laughing as she rolled from block to block setting up appointments with thirsty young hustlers. One after another the same silly smirk would cover their faces when they spotted me in the passenger seat all smiles. Too late and too fearful of what Twin might do if they declined, they would stand in shame as we pulled off.

There was so much more to Twin than what the streets knew. On the outside, she appeared tough as nails. On the inside, maybe just a hint, there was a soft spot. I'm no Dr. Phil, but I strongly believe a lot of Twin's feisty attitude was a result of her feeling alone. Both her twin sister and her older brother Al Kabir (Shot Box), who was also a member of the set, were serving stints in New Jersey's prison system. In their absence, here we stood joined at the hip and I would give her the moniker Mini Me.

Twin and the homie TrillVille hopped out of a new model Jeep Cherokee and handed me bags with an all-black Dickies suit, a pair of red Chuck Taylors, a fresh white tee, and a cherry red bandanna. Your boy was back!

I was released right on time for Troub's party at Club Gregory's at the top of Central Ave. This was the same spot where we had the run-in with the Pirus back in the day.

With Troub's party the same night I was released, I knew I was on my way to trouble of my own with Neisha. Over the past eight days we had been on the phone going back and forth about what I needed to do when I got out, and there I was entertaining the thought of getting out and running right back into the streets. Actually, it wasn't the streets, and I hoped she would understand. Hell, it was my road dawg Troub's b-day bash!

As soon as I entered the house Neish greeted me with an ugly stare, which for her was hard to do. I guess it was a woman's intuition. It was like she knew I had a trick up my sleeve. Maybe I needed to pass on the party. I was stuck and looked back and forth between her and the homies who stood in the doorway. If it wasn't for nonsense I believe I would have had no sense at all. I decided to go to the party. This decision was basically the beginning of the end for me and Neisha.

An hour or so later, we pulled up to Gregory's already high off weed and drunk off shots of Hennessy. As we walked in, a few looks on faces read, "How did he do it again?" Yeah, I was out and there to honor my homeboy Troub's b-day. Truthfully, I didn't have too much rap for anyone. I sat in the back of the club by the pool tables, enjoyed the sights, and took a few pictures in my cherry red rag, throwing gang signs high in the sky. We toasted the night's events and before we knew it the night had come to a close.

On May 26, 2002, Shalonda Princess Little gave birth. I didn't appear at the hospital. I still had no words for Princess and did not believe the newborn baby girl was mine. I did not want to end up playing daddy to the next man's baby, and we decided to have a blood test. If the test proved otherwise then surely I could not make up for lost time, but I would damn sure try. I can't ask to not be judged about my decision and the way I handled things, but this was who I was. In the 'hood many men were duped into believing a baby was theirs when it really wasn't. In many cases they were just the mother's choice. Women knocked up by a nobody, lying to a somebody that their baby was a blessing. This story might seem off to suburbanites. But show me one person in the ghetto who doesn't know a truth like mine.

On this same day, May 26, 2002, as fate would have it I presided over a meeting, as the Feds' informant delivered Confession #2. The law, still salivating and wanting more, sought to sink their teeth into me again. I still did not see the boldness of this confidential informant, who was right beneath our noses. In meetings to discuss Blood business, who knew someone was wearing a wire and we were under heavy surveillance? So while I was supposed to be off the radar, I was being recorded and photographed. According to Federal documents:

TRANSCRIPT OF MEETING IN THE

BACKYARD OF THE RESIDENCE OF NAFIS FLOWERS,

196. N. NINTH STREET, NEWARK, NEW JERSEY

RECORDED ON MAY 26, 2002

BEGINNING AT APPROXIMATELY 3:38 P.M.

PARTICIPANT: **(Names of 36 participants omitted)**

UM: Be that Bloody [UI] 2-35. I bang for my brother and he bang for me.

FRIEND LNU: I be that Bloody Friend, Double I, 235. I'm banging cause my set bang for me.

JAMAR HURD: Be that Bloody Fox, I bang cause this world don't give a fuck about me, [UI], I love you.

[LAUGHTER]

BAINES: Be that Bloody Beans reppin' that mother fucking Double I, 2-35 for sure. I bang for mother fuckin' brotherly love, overrides the oppression and destruction of society.

TONE: I be that Bloody Tone. Bang for 2-35, Double I. I bang cause I love you.

MOODY: I be that Bloody O, bangin' Double I 2-35, banging cause my homies bang with me.

BUTLER: I be that Bloody Mass, reppin' that 2-3-5, Queen Street Blood gang, Double I, Inglewood, Illtown. I bang for Blood, cause Blood bang for me.

S: WRIGHT: Hold, hold. Hold. Hold it. Hold up. I don't care if you know me or not! Know what I'm talkin' about? Be that Bloody, Bloody Bawnyea, know what I'm talking about. QSBG. I bang to override oppression and destruction.

BUTLER: Yo, more or less, the I's official, the I's gonna stay official. Niggas be banging, niggas don't know why they banging.

UM: Mm-hmm.

BUTLER: You know what I'm talking about?

UM: Uh-mm.

BUTLER: Shit's sloppy right now. Everybody looking at the I, like the I is tight. The I is not tight.

FLOWERS: Not at all.

BUTLER: I'm not feeling this shit.

FLOWERS: At all.

BUTLER: Know what I'm saying/ We not gonna be breedin' nobody, bringin' nobody home, for nothing. You know what I'm saying? Niggas is just out here running reckless. All this red. Niggas don't know what the fuck this red is about.

UM: [UI] know what the fuck [UI].

BUTLER: Niggas ready to die for this shit. It's more than just busting your gun.

S. WRIGHT: Straight laced.

BUTLER: Know what I'm saying? It's mind over matter, Blood, mind over matter. Know why you busting that gun when you go to bust that gun. Know what I'm talking about? Know why you jumping out on Brabs, when you go to jump Brab. Who the fuck in here know what Crip mean? Who in here know what Crip mean?

UM: [UI]

BUTLER: So why don't you like Brabs?

UM: [UI]

BUTLER: Why?

UM: I don't know. I just don't like them.

BUTLER: Why?

UM: Cause they ain't Blood.

BUTLER: Why don't you like Brabs?

UM: Because they trying to override what we stand for.

BUTLER: Why don't you like Brabs?

UM: They was riding on us, man.

BUTLER: Why you like, why, why you don't like Brabs.

UM: Cause they try to bring down everything we try to accomplish.

BUTLER: Why you love Brabs?

UM: I don't love Brabs.

                          [LAUGHTER]

BUTLER: Why you don't like Brabs, homie?

UM: I don't like Brabs cause of the simple fact that them niggas been my enemies since day one. Before Blood—

BUTLER: I don't like Brabs—cause they counter everything I stand for.

UM: Right.

BUTLER: I'm here to uplift my community, my black people have brotherly love. Brotherly love, meaning y'all and everybody else. I [UI] you a 550 you ain't my brother. I stand for black people and black people as a whole. You know what I'm talking about? Revolution. When niggas ready for the war, I'm there. That's why I bang. That's why I don't like Brabs. Crips, Counter

Revolutionary Intelligence Party of Society. Blood, Brotherly Love Overridin' Oppression and Destruction of Society. Know what I'm talking about? They counter everything I wanna do. Everything I stand for, they disagree with it. That's why I don't fuck with Brabs. I don't—I wear blue. I don't fuck with Brabs because they wear blue. You know what I'm saying? I don't fuck with Brabs because they don't stand for what I stand for. That's why I don't fuck with Brabs. You know what I'm talking about? Everybody got a proper understanding?

VOICES: Mm-hmm. Trills.

BUTLER: Well, you know what I'm saying? If it's about a blue and red thing, this, this shit don't mean nothin'. It don't mean nothin'. What it mean? What it mean? Everybody back here got some blue on right now.

UM: Trills. Trills.

BUTLER: Blue start with a B. So why don't you like blue?

S. WRIGHT: It ain't about the colors, Blood.

BUTLER: Huh? Blue start with a "B". Why don't you like blue? It ain't about that. Know why you banging. Know what the fuck you gonna bang for. I'm tired of nig—Fuck all this. You wanna hop out, you all up at East Orange High. You over here, you on Springdale, you downtown. You see a mother fucker with some flue shit on, you ready to get at him. Why you gettin' at him? Why you gettin'—That shit don't impress me. Half the mother fuckers back here broke. Broke. You wanna get at Brabs, you wanna jump mother fuckers, stab mother fuckers, shoot mother fuckers—now you stuck in jail.

UM: —no bail money—

BUTLER: Blood ain't got no use for you in there. We ain't got no use for you. Straight laced. Now you in there, it's fuck everybody out here! Cause you stuck in jail. Why? Cause you out here doing some dumb shit. Know why the fuck you banging. Know why you banging. Banging don't just mean I could fight, I could shoot. This is what banging the fuck is about.

UM: Trills.

BUTLER: This is what banging is about.

UM: Trills.

BUTLER: This is what the fuck banging mean. Using your mother fucking head. All you mother fuckers out here acting stupid off this water [PCP]—that shit is a no-no. I'm not beat. Niggas going off that water. Niggas is gettin' disciplined. If you can handle it, handle it. Do, yo. Do the drug. Don't let the drug do you.

UM: Trills. Trills.

BUTLER: You know what I'm saying? You can't, you, you can't handle it. Don't fuck with it.

FLOWERS: Don't fuck with it.

BUTLER: Don't fuck with it. Your pockets ain't right. Don't fuck with it. Don't fuck with it. Everybody feel me?

VOICES: Trills.

BUTLER: Everybody hear me?

VOICES: Trills.

BUTLER: I love y'all. I hope y'all love me.

VOICES: Trills.

BUTLER: I'm here, I been doing this shit—officially since 9-3. Everything I ever put my hands on dealing with Blood, I pass down. I pass down to each and every one of y'all. Why? Cause I bang for y'all. I put my life on the line for y'all every day. Every day. I'm facing the rest of my life in prison for everyone of y'all, including myself. Including myself. Do I regret it? Hell, no. Don't make me regret it. Everybody, niggas wanna come home. Niggas wanna be dawg. Little homies, y'all finally got y'all chance. Don't be reckless with the shit. Don't be reckless.

During this meeting, when I expressed that I faced the rest of my life behind bars for things I had done, in the law's eyes, it was my admission of guilt as it related to the October 19, 2000, homicide. Certainly, the comment was interpreted the way they felt would help rid the streets of the "problem." This excerpt would be logged as evidence, Confession 2. However, the rest of the recordings of lengthy meetings were deemed irrelevant because they did not corroborate the image that they set out to portray.

After all that happened in recent months, I remained in one of the most intense battles of my life with the one person I feared the most, me.

10

ONLY THE STRONG SURVIVE

June 11, after numerous false alarms, the running of red lights, and rushing through the hospital's hallways, doctors said the wait was over. My next up was ready to make his big debut. And at 11:14 AM, Tewhan Hakim "YahYah" Butler Jr. took center stage. I was right there, the proud father to welcome him into the world. I was pleased to have made it through the recent turmoil and be fortunate enough to bear witness to his birth. That day was extremely special for me. An extension of self was born with opportunities to break down barriers I had failed to overcome. The day marked the arrival of a better me.

When doctors handed my son to me, I stared deep into his eyes in hope that he could see my past did not have to be his future. When his baby eyes opened and he looked back, it was as if he knew all I had done wrong and wished to do right.

I had never known feelings of regret, but in that moment shame overshadowed my joy. Shame, due to a life lived where I feared the possibilities of change. I was unable to transform my tragedy into triumph and carried on and allowed circumstances to dictate my life's path. I used certain misfortunes as a crutch to justify my actions. I was ashamed because the things I came to value were of no real worth. I never wanted my life or my mentality for my kids. I wanted, as I'm certain my father wanted, and my homies' fathers wanted, for us to overcome the obstacles. Yet we were out defeating ourselves.

Our way of thinking had been selfish and in some instances, downright foolish. True enough, we didn't ask to be born at the bottom with the inherent disadvantages of poverty. But it was our actions, or lack thereof, that perpetuated the cycle as opposed to bringing it to an end. None of this made sense to me until that moment.

I knew I was not free. The demons within still had hold of me. Truthfully, I sought no escape from the evils men do. I knew regardless of how righteous I wanted to become, in the jungle animal ambitions are necessary. And as Dame Dash once said, "The food one kills is the food one eats." (Ecclesiastes 7:20: *For there is not a just man on earth who does good and does not sin.*)

The night I left the hospital, I left with a new outlook on life. For the umpteenth time, I had had it with the gun toting, all-night partying, and the B.S. Still, I wouldn't turn my back on my homeboys, and I couldn't give up my hustle. At the time it was what kept food on the table. But the hustle was to be as far as I would go. I even planned on gradually stepping away from hustling.

I had it all mapped out. When Neisha was released from the hospital with my son, I would hit the streets and tend to my business and by the time the street lights came on, I was to be in the house doing the family thing. This was the only way I saw to escape the madness. If I kept running, there was no denying the outs that were available—death or prison. Both were a loss I didn't want to take.

About a month later I was convinced things would eventually get better. Then, I received a court summons in the mail. I was somewhat pleased as I ripped it open because I expected it to be a court date. Trial would present the opportunity to close my 2000 homicide case and allow me to move forward. But anger crept through me like never before as I read the notice from the courts. "*Tewhan Butler to appear before the Honorable Judge Betty Lester,*" with a check next to bail hearing. The law just would not let up.

I immediately called Paul Bergin and asked exactly what it meant. He told me what I already knew, they wanted me behind bars. They failed to block my bail and now they were trying to flat out revoke it. Before I hung up the phone, my lawyer asked who I pissed off. I was at a loss. Aside from the bogus armed robbery charge,

I hadn't been in trouble since I maxed out on my weapons offense and was released on bail for the homicide case and the additional State racketeering charge. What was it all about?

It seemed no matter how I moved, the law countered. The law's tactics were discouraging. I began to wonder if the whole "change your life around" thing I was pursuing was all it was cracked up to be. According to them, the possibility of change didn't equate for a man of my caliber. In their eyes, the person who I was would forever be. It was a damned if you do, damned if you don't situation. I was stuck between a rock and a hard place.

I could walk into court and have my lawyer argue I had done nothing wrong. Still, I most likely would have been arrested and left to wonder if I would I ever see the free world again. Or I could take my show on the road and lack the freedom to live. The law would have definitely been in hot pursuit. The babies crawling around inside their playpens made either decision extremely difficult. I needed some time to think and think hard. Whatever I came up with would have to be squared away fast. I only had two days to decide.

After some heavy contemplation, I came up with a middle ground. Two days later, I walked into Essex County Superior Court casually dressed, trying to look the part. I wore a pair of soft black linen pants, tailor-made at Mamadou's off Market Street, a pair of black low-top Pradas from Neiman Marcus, and an off-white linen button up.

I entered the courtroom and assessed my surroundings, though I was no stranger to its detail. I took a seat in the last row. Neisha checked the roster to see when I was due before the judge. I already had an attorney, but I knew there would be a public defender on deck until the courts were notified.

When Neisha approached the desk and spoke my name, I saw a man in a suit greet her and ask where I was. From his demeanor, I couldn't make out if he was a public defender or a prosecutor. That's never a good sign. I looked him up and down fully aware of his pedigree—paid to defend the public while buddying up with the prosecutor to figure out ways to secure guilty pleas. I already knew what the day would entail. I did not want to let on I had him figured out, and I asked, "So what's going to happen today?"

With attitude in his voice, as if representing me was beneath him, he answered,

"Well nine times out of ten, they are going to lock you up and revoke all your existing bails."

"For what?" I asked.

"Obviously because you can't seem to stay out of trouble, Mr. Butler."

I laughed and asked if there was anything he could do. He cut me off with a wave of his hand while I was trying to explain my position.

"Not my problem. Just sit here, we're due in front of the judge in a few minutes."

Under a different set of circumstances, I would have thoroughly checked him on his disrespect, but I didn't need the unwanted attention. So in earnest, I played it cool until he disappeared behind the doors of the judge's chambers.

As soon as the door closed, I dashed.

"Meet me at the car," I told Neisha.

I took three, four, and five steps at a time. I was in the car with the engine running by the time Neisha walked up. As we pulled off, I couldn't help but feel like a man backed into a corner and left with no choice but to fight back or be eaten alive. And in this case, fighting back meant not losing my name to become a number. If I was going to be punished, it would have to be by my own unraveling and not simply because my face fit the frame for their anti-gang agenda. It was situations such as this that made a man feel hopeless. Every two steps forward, they would try their hardest to knock you three steps back.

The early stages of my transformation had begun, but now with the law breathing down my neck, it was back to square one.

To ease my nerves, I jumped on the highway en route to Short Hills Mall, an upscale mall about twenty-minutes from the 'hood in the affluent suburbs, for a little retail therapy and to do a little shopping for the newborn. Neisha and I were there only minutes before we had a brief argument over what to purchase and what not to purchase. I was already stressed from my earlier courtroom drama, and we stormed out of the mall with neither of us so much as breathing in the direction of the other. Our timing couldn't have been worse.

We rolled past a Millburn Police car on the way out of the mall's parking lot. I continued driving, easy on the gas. Out of my peripheral, I could see the cop breaking his neck in attempt to see who was behind the wheel of the tinted-out Grand Marquis. Something told me he would double back, and as soon as the thought entered my mind, I heard sirens behind me. Damn! It took everything in me not to take a page from O.J.'s book, but I knew I wouldn't be able to live with myself if I brought chase and the wheels got from underneath me with the mother of my child in the G-ride. Thugs feel too.

I wished I was riding solo. I started to fidget as I pulled slowly to the side of the road. I rolled down my window as the officer approached.

"License, registration, and insurance, please."

I had none of the three. My troubles were just beginning. After I revealed I didn't have any of the documents, what came next was to be expected.

"Can you step out of the car, sir?"

Before I stepped out, I stared back in one last attempt to savor the flavor of my child's mother. For this might have been the last time I got to see her without the restrictions of the Department of Corrections' rules and regulations.

Once outside the car, the officer began his charade. I quite possibly could have been one of the first black men he ran across in this town. The officer tried desperately to impose his authority. After I gave him an alias, he ran it over his radio. He proceeded to search my car while waiting on the record check to come back. He returned empty-handed after the search of my vehicle. He was also disappointed the name I gave came back clean. He expressed his disbelief. "With those tattoos on you, there's no way you have never been to jail before. I'm bringing you in."

This was a classic tale of the stereotypes thrown at young black men across America daily. Officials with their distorted views of reality, too warped to realize these forms of over-simplifications shine an even brighter light on what many like to call "The Invisible Line."

The Invisible Line is the rarely spoken of divider that silently screams of America's bias: A misconstrued right of belonging and an absurd right to culturally alienate, racially reject, and cast off classes of people. Further enhancing this invisible line is the crazed belief of superiority and inferiority and, if I might add, society's dejection and deception.

After I was brought to the police station, the few officers who manned their precinct went back and forth with threats to fingerprint me and uncover my true identity. I was unaware of how long the process took for a warrant to show, so I sat there and attempted to keep my cool and not give up the fact I skipped out on court earlier in the day. They say patience is a virtue, but I was running out of it fast. The longer I sat inside, the closer I was to being found out.

Finally, with nothing to book me on, they informed me my car was to be impounded and I was to receive a line of traffic tickets. None of it mattered, as long as I was free to go. The entire time they had been bluffing. With all of the money that flowed through Millburn, the taxpayers' dollars hadn't been invested in a modernized finger printer. I walked out of the station after a few hours and was met by Neisha, who was just as pleased to see me as I was to see her. The earlier disagreement had long been forgotten.

On our way to the train station, an unidentified number showed up on my phone. I answered and quickly realized it was my lawyer. He told me how he had been dialing me for hours, wondering why I hadn't showed up in court. I didn't share I actually did and left, nor that I had just been released from the Millburn Police Department. I disclosed only what he needed to know.

"I'm not trying to walk myself to jail for nobody."

My lawyer asked for my trust and promised he had my back and would not let me down. I wanted to believe him. I told him it was already too late. My failure to appear would have been logged before we completed the call. But at the courthouse, when he realized I wouldn't be showing, he was quick on his toes and worked it out with the judge to have the hearing rescheduled for the next day. It was definitely a good look, but there was still no telling what would transpire if I stepped foot into that courtroom. The attitude-wearing public defender already spilled the beans—they planned to arrest me. So what was going to change in twenty-four short hours?

Trust, the one thing I always had a problem with, is never to be given and always to be earned. I was supposed to trust this man who owed me nothing outside of confidentiality, and even that could be snatched if the law so deemed. I wondered, would he waver, or was it truth he spoke? I told him I'd show.

The next day I still wasn't sure why I put my trust in this "stranger." Nevertheless, my family and I paced the hallways of the court building, awaiting my attorney's arrival. When he appeared, he was more prepared for what was to come than I. "Not his life," I thought.

My nerves were literally all over the place. I couldn't wait any longer for whatever was to be, to be. When the hearing got under way, I couldn't determine which side the scales of justice were leaning. And then prosecution began ranting to the judge that my bail should be immediately revoked. Furthermore, it was stated I was and always will be a drug dealer and nothing else. To add insult to injury, the prosecutor began an unwarranted attack on my mother and how her financial records didn't show an income to support the bonds that were nearly three quarters of a million dollars. How if my mother didn't disapprove of my lifestyle, then she had to be a part of it. The sounds of deep gasps silenced the courtroom. Everyone from the bailiff down to the stenographer knew a serious line had been crossed.

When I heard the things the prosecutor said in attempt to crucify everyone, I thought back to the days when I lived on Carnegie and how the police would raid and arrest everyone, including those they knew were innocent, even when the guilty accepted the blame. The system was relentless. It never stopped, and didn't mind collateral damage to achieve a desired end.

My mother started to respond mid-rave but was interrupted by Judge Betty Lester, who politely informed her not to worry, that she would appropriately handle the situation. Judge Lester spoke firmly and made it clear she would not tolerate such unprofessionalism in her courtroom by either party.

"Let me remind you, it is Tewhan Butler who stands behind the defendant's table and not his mother; therefore he is responsible for his own actions and not Mrs. Butler. Furthermore Mrs. Butler, I would like to apologize on behalf of the Courts for such unwarranted behavior."

In addressing the prosecution, she went on, "If your office wants Mr. Butler off the streets so badly, convict him!"

The bail hearing was ruled in my favor. As I turned around on my way out, I caught the prosecutor staring a hole through me. In return I offered up a slight smile and casually strolled through the doors with my family and my attorney by my side.

I was free! I had managed to dodge a bullet. However, I couldn't shake the horrible feeling that the next one would seal my fate.

11

AND THE BAND PLAYED ON

IT WAS THE summer of 2002 and everything in the neighborhood was on full blast. Add in the heat, and Down the Hill was as hot and deadly as Afghanistan. Bullets would fly, heads were hit, and memorials were painted on walls, while the locals kept quiet and poured out a little liquor.

There was certainly a war going on, and not only between Bloods and Crips, and dope dealers and stick-up kids. In the same breath, law enforcement was waging war against us all. Numerous government-funded task forces attacked the streets, almost as if their intent was to push us deeper into the abyss. Millions of dollars spent to shackle the slums and not a penny invested to nurture the people who lived there. The despair in the 'hood was good at being hushed but the intensity of the determination in one's eyes spoke volumes. Sun-scorched skin and clothes drenched in sweat, who said the hustle wasn't work?

Summertime neighborhood events such as block parties and the park festivals were now gone and replaced with dice games, shoot outs, drive-bys, a steady variety of cars, hustlers, and hardened gang-bangers dressed in jean shorts, tank tops, and red fitted hats. Just about everyone's pockets filled with what it took to bring home the bacon.

Young girls plastered on porches, watching the young boys who ran in and out of backyards to their stashes like track stars. They didn't want the doctor or the lawyer;

this was the 'hood. They wanted a hustler, a gangster, the high and the thrill of being known as the Mrs. to one of the 'hood's bad boys.

Our old heads loitered inside and outside of our Middle Bar playing pinochle, downing six-packs, and passing around bottles of whiskey. This was most definitely the 'hood.

I loved strolling into the Middle Bar only to catch a jewel from one of our local old heads like C.C, Big Blue, Fred, and a few others. C.C would always tell me, "Mass, the sun don't shine forever you know."

In return, I would shoot, "It's already raining, old man."

Before I left he would call back and say, "I'm glad you noticed."

C.C. was the bartender who had been around for years, long enough to have seen the 'hood rise, fall, and rise again. Wise enough to know history had a way of repeating itself. He never passed on an opportunity to offer his wisdom to those who would listen. Right in tow was Ms. Cat, the owner of the bar.

On days when the neighborhood was flat, Ms. Cat and I would crank up the jukebox and play pool for hours. I enjoyed the presence of an older woman, and I would vent and share with her my many plans to get away from the life. Strange thing was, when I talked like this, she would give me this look, say nothing, and keep right on playing. Later, I figured, with her silence, Ms. Cat was telling me if I was so confident in what I was going to do, I needed to stop wasting time speaking so much about it and do something about it.

That same summer, after being around for longer than I could remember, the Middle Bar closed. It was most definitely a sign of the times. Some things were changing, others weren't. I wanted the change, but my fear of what lay ahead was my biggest weakness.

My years as a Blood totaled nine. Nine years and I had gotten nowhere. Nine years a nightmare and now reality had me dodging death. Enemies of all sorts aimed to end my life. I knew it was no mystery somebody or somebodies had a hot one (bullet) reserved with my name on it. Every dog has its day.

This summer was strange. Apart from the 'hood fixtures, whether drunk, high, or sober, whenever I closed my eyes three things were always there:

1. The life I always dreamed of

2. Death

3. Prison

The latter two seemed much closer, but I didn't stress. Death was promised. I always knew I'd never escape its grip. I simply hoped the summer would die before I did.

No matter what I did, I could never escape death. Subconsciously, I knew it could happen at any moment. You can't predict your fall. While I thought I had it all, I had nothing. My addiction to gang-banging took what little life I had. I would never let on how envious I was of the squares and the geeks. The "cool kid" I was hungry to be as a child was showing me its truth. Physically, I was free; yet I was trapped. I craved a "normal" life so bad it hurt. I wanted a life where I didn't have to look over my shoulder every minute and play the rear view every second. I had criminal cases out the ass I would eventually have to deal with. Since I turned eighteen, my adult cases went as follows:

Adult Case 1: Receiving stolen property

Adult Case 2: 15th Street raid case

(Both of which I was blessed to have run concurrent and received only 200 days in Caldwell's Annex.)

Adult Case 3: Possession of a firearm (364 days in the County Jail)

Adult Case 4: Homicide (open)

Adult Case 5: State racketeering (open)

Adult Case 6: Armed robbery (open)

I knew freedom wouldn't be mine for long. Like Beanie Siegel, "I could feel it in the air." I hadn't attended any family gatherings or spent a moment with my extended family in years. Everything was many miles away from normal.

I had escaped assassination attempts, overcome plenty of nights in grueling jail cells only to endure destroyed relationships and more self-destructive behavior. Because I grew up with a disdain for normalcy—wanting to be hella bad, hella fresh, and one hell of a hustler—I was hell-bound. People began to tell me my levelheaded demeanor was gone. Some accused me of change.

"Tewhan, don't let the devil get you, baby," my grandmother would say. Little did she know, I was already in his grips desperately struggling to break free. I wondered what life would be like without fear. I wasn't afraid of others. I was mostly afraid of myself. No guns. No drugs. No bandannas, just me living a normal life. I knew my mother and Neisha wanted a normal life just as much as I did. My lifestyle did damage to us all. I caused more pain than pleasure. I wanted normal but I did not know how to become.

A gang-banger's life silences any sign of normalcy. Your existence is centered on your gang, 24/7, and its livelihood becomes your sole purpose. Most often the actions needed to ensure the gang's longevity are on the far side of normal. When it was all said and done, I didn't want a million dollars and the glitz and glamour; I just wanted to be Tewhan, as normal as can be.

The subjective feeling that life was passing me by was becoming more vivid. I would watch attentively and see my own turf playing the game of life for keeps under laws of double or nothing: P-Funking in Prince Street Projects, New Community, and Amherst; G-Shining in Little City; Stratford, 18th, 19th, High and Spruce, Rollacking; 15th and Springfield sporting trench coats and rocking Brim hats; Avon Avenue hustlers toting like Billy Badass. There was a time when witnessing such would have sent a surge of energy through me, but that same rush was no longer found.

Normally, this was a part of the summer when things began to pick up speed. However, for me, life was slowing down. I attained a rhythm, sort of a harmonized feeling, with a more productive way of carrying on. Legitimate business proposition, real-estate investments, travel opportunities, and the works started to come my direction.

The way of life I professed to have wanted was now being presented to me on a platter. The fruits of my labor were allowing me to turn water into wine. How could I not see? This was my dream—the opportunity to live life under conditions that weren't as stressful and dangerous as slanging and banging. This should have been the easiest decision of my life.

"Go, Mass. Get away. You have far outgrown the life you're living. There is a thing in life called chance. Some people are presented with one and others none. This is your chance. If you fail to take advantage, I'm afraid you may never have another."

Time and time again, I heard these words. But I missed the message, under the impression I made the rules and could limit just how far and deep I ventured into the streets. Self-deception provided me enough room to lose myself once again.

We all were moving fast, but headed nowhere. Standing still were my surroundings and the people within them. Sickening, yet determined to find a cure. The years of misguided struggle and fight to overcome life's obstacles had led us to, a greater degree of despair: What were we to do? Society's rejection emerged as the greatest illness.

If psychologists suggest that a man's actions are determined by his character and his moral fiber develops from the conditions of environment, then maybe if we improve our environment we can conceive a more virtuous being.

Could it be said a lack of evolving in inner-city areas is a result of carelessness? From the outside looking in, it seems lower-class communities are filled with individuals who lack drive, determination, and focus. When in all honesty there is nothing further from the truth. But then again who cares?

Certainly, the gang culture had become more harmful than helpful. But before categorizing the outcome, one has to look deeper and evaluate what the cause is. I understood the pulse of my community: my neighbors whose dreams of success were shattered by society's shortcomings; a body of people held back and held down, then conveniently rejected for the life one chose.

If I was sincere and opted out, it had to be all the way or it counted for nothing. This I understood. The difficulty came in whether I could truly become open to a lifestyle I wasn't accustomed to. I continued on as a gang member, for it was never my intent to denounce what I pledged my life to, but no longer was I gang-banging. My mission of being known for things in life, which I now knew meant nothing, was being converted. But true enough, violence is not the only way to destroy your dreams.

Million-dollar strips; stakes were high. There were block-bidding wars. No more G-packs ($1,000 packs). Gangsters were flying birds—paper or plastic? Both! There were out of town trips and country vacations. Word was official—moneymakers were rubbing elbows with tycoons in the King's Court. We never knew what it was to make it rain. In the East, heavy snow was in the forecast and that made for a better situation to stockpile the blow and watch the money accumulate.

As we got older we learned the difference between dumb dollars and mature money. Sneaker money and upgrading the wardrobe were frivolous finances. Property owned meant the dough was well-developed. Nobody came from money, yet all were headed in its direction. Shoeboxes were traded in for pillowcases, and bank statements told the truth. Show me your friends and I could tell you who you were. If your man was broke and your pockets were empty, watch the company you keep.

I began to change my pace, to step out and try things a little differently; growing up and getting my grown and sexy on, so to speak. I was attending plays at the Beacon, enjoying top-notch restaurants and upscale functions, all courtesy of comrades who too were attempting to leave it all behind. This whole other world was beautiful. Not a worry in the first, at least not until the night was over and the destination was Exit 15W off the New Jersey Turnpike. Twisted, with all of these positive endeavors available to pull me away from self-destructing, I played on.

Among my generation, most were beyond our years. We learned from the best. Now, the elders were taking notice. I received a phone call and was offered the opportunity not to buy out the bar but to buy the bar. Jack's on Orange Street was on the market and Tarik—an Original Gangster in the 'hood who converted his past hardships into legitimate entrepreneurship—felt it was time I broaden my scope and stop seeing and thinking about the corner alone. We had a discussion, and I remember him telling me:

> These streets ain't forever. Fail to let them go and when they snap back I guarantee you'll regret it. You gotta know when to remove yourself from the equation or be subtracted altogether when the law rolls around. Chances don't come around often. When prison or a coffin turns out to be the only outcome then there is no way that you can suggest the end justifying the means. If you got it, then get it—or have it snatched away. How do you think people are able to properly support their families? Paper-passing from one generation to the next? Money making money. That's how. No matter how good a connect you got or how serious you think your hustle is or how many corners you believe you can flood—the game will not allow that to happen. Money handed over to bail bondsmen, lawyers, and other legal expenses ain't money well spent. It means you lost and it's time to pay the piper and give back what you thought was yours to keep. How foolish is that?

The talk with Tarik certainly opened my eyes and made me aware of how feeble-minded I was. A wise one would opt for international bargaining over 'hood celebrity any day. To finally be able to call something legitimately my own was a power move, one I had to make. But before I could lay down the groundwork I was back in the mix. I never got around to acquiring Jack's. It was one of many opportunities I let pass me by. Looking back, I see so much I could have done differently. The entire time, in one fashion or another, I was being sent the message—enough is enough! It's the same thing I see in many youths today. They get ahold of fast money, the luxuries, and the dressings and believe the moment will last forever. They make the money and have no clue what to do with it. Hundreds of thousands made, sometimes millions, and not a single investment. Not a dollar spent on good. What good is a baller with the cars, the big jewels, Prada and Gucci galore, and a child without a trust fund?

A hustler knows how to make something out of nothing, no matter the field. So, why are we under the impression a hustler is only one who stands on the corner from sunup to sundown ducking the law to eat? The picture of a hustler can be found on the Forbes List with tax increases as their only worry. Certainly, a far cry from the troubles faced by the illusionary, illegitimate hustlers in the 'hood who most often, along the way, lose the work ethic necessary to earn a legitimate lifestyle and build and maintain wealth. You have to be grown to have grown-up money. You have to be mentally sharp to manage and grow your money. Or you will spend your life chasing a dollar and unknowingly running from the dream.

Whenever I wasn't out flirting with the finer people, places, and things, I was right back on the block. Though my days of hand-to-hand, corner-boy hustling and chasing drug sales were done, conspiracy was just as wicked. I paid no mind to the everyday, all-day utility vans, construction trucks, and the constant patrol of unmarked vehicles. The daily grind continued with total disregard for what was right in front of our faces. With an attitude of "If a nigga don't hustle, then a nigga don't eat," struggling souls who didn't mind paying a price to provide for their families were out moving and shaking, and surveillance was tracking. From May 1 through July 29, the FBI kept track of it all: where, what, when, how much and to whom. From two bricks heroin on North 14th to one brick and two bundles on 19th north of Eaton. They tracked it all.

Dozens of other transactions were stockpiled in files no one would know existed until it was too late. Also corroborating these claims were statements made by their informant. This individual went as far as aiding officials in labeling their observations, matching government names to aliases, logging evidence, and building their case. This information, summarized below in Federal documents, would be part of the nightmare that consumed my dreams:

Tewhan Butler (Massacre) had several people working for him making heroin sales, including (1) (Twin), (2) (PB); (3) (Death); (4) XXXX; (5) XXXX; (6) Abe (LNU) (7) Ibn (LNU); and others. Also, at various times, (1) XXXX (Big Red); (2) XXX (Death); (3) XXXX (Murder); and (4) XXXX (Yuckey) sold heroin for XXXX (Floco).

The Double II Bloods' heroin business became a way of life for its members and a way of sustaining most of them financially. In order to assure fairness among the members and to keep the lucrative business running smoothly, Quadree Smith (Trouble) and Tewhan Butler (Massacre) instituted shift work. Each member had a designated six-hour time period during which he/she was permitted to be on the street selling heroin. The 6 a.m. to 12 p.m. shift was occupied by XXXX and XXXX. Anyone hustling for them could also be out at that time. From 12 p.m. to 6 p.m. was Tewhan Butler (Massacre) and XXXX (Bad News) shift. XXXX and XXXX worked the 6 p.m. to 12 a.m. shift. The last shift, from 12 a.m. to 6 a.m., was a free-for-all shift, during which anyone permitted to sell in the area could come out and try to make some money.

So just when things were beginning to look good, as if sensing a long-overdue smile on my face, the law came out of hiding determined to make its presence felt. I began to notice I was being followed. I also began to take notice of the funny faces posted around my place of residence and the out-of-pocket comments made by patrol cops. My mother began to notice the sounds and sights of helicopters hovering overhead just before I would arrive at her house. Things had gotten to a point where the jump-out boys would hit the block, and without frisking or even record-checking me would say, "You could let him go, he's clean." I was happy to avoid the hassle, and I brushed it all off. In reality, this should have been all the more reason to disassociate myself from the streets.

I remember the day Troub, almost in a panic, called me to come pay him a visit. When I arrived, his uneasiness was clearly visible. He was hiding behind a screen door, pacing and peeking up and down the street. What was going on? When I stepped into the house, with seriousness in his tone, he stated, "The Feds are on us; it's time to go."

The Feds, I thought, no way. During my upbringing, the Feds weren't as common in Jersey as they were in other states. I could count on one hand the times when the Feds made a big bust in Jersey. Besides the early 90s case with our old heads from The Block (18th Street)—Mook Daddy, Lil Steve, and Ski—the only two other noteworthy Federal cases in New Jersey were the Zoo Crew case out of Newark and Elizabeth's E-Port Posse. With none of those individuals around due to mandatory minimums and maxes, their primary accounts of the perils and pitfalls that come with the drug game were not shared. We learned as we went along and shot from the hip.

Years later I would learn that the Feds had begun swarming many cities and states, particularly poor and minority communities with what was labeled "The New Jim Crow Law"—a conspiratorial plan to disenfranchise a people through incarceration.

Troub's paranoia was beginning to rub off on me. I questioned if the funny business taking place was the work of the Feds. Without a doubt something was going on. Still, I couldn't place my finger on it. The State's Gang Unit and Drug Task Force were just as deliberate in their surveillance, but I needed, or better yet, I wanted, just a little while longer.

The comfort of the truth is nothing in comparison with the crippling creations of ignorance. And because I was blinded by Blood—gang, money, power—I was entrenched in poverty. This lack of regard, where both men and women shut out truth and opportunity and neglect their own potential, is devastating. The eyes can't see what the mind does not know, and within the minds' of poverty-stricken youth, no one had the slightest idea of reality other than that which occurred in their daily lives. Personal experience seemed to be the only teacher. If not concrete, oftentimes things seemed irrelevant. If we knew better, we could've done better. But most didn't know better until it was too late.

There was very little social awareness of life outside the 'hood because in the 'hood people were trapped in a world only they knew. People appeared to pay little to no attention to the ways of the world, which didn't relate to the story of their life. This lack of exposure and disregard for anything and anyone beyond self resulted in a sickening disadvantage that plagued us all like a debilitating illness. It was destructive, and I too was not above it.

Despite my ill temperament, my eyes were continuing to open and a newly emerged self was attempting to shine through. I wondered if this "new me" would be the result of natural progression or if change would be forced upon me. I would find out the answer a lot sooner than I hoped for.

12

NO WAY OUT

September 28, 2002. Time found one more way to haunt my every day. The summer was over, and I made it through unscathed, playing this dangerous game called life two-fold, with one foot in and one foot out. The one in was in deep enough to have me tied into yet another case. This time it was double murder.

Another day in the 'hood, standing guard in front of 13th Street's townhouses, huddled around a case of Coronas and a half dozen Dutch Masters and enjoying the last of the warm weather, my older homeboy, who almost never stopped on 13th Street's strip, pulled up and hopped out of his G-ride and motioned with his finger and a slight head nod for me to part ways from the crowd. I did as told, and we met in the street. What he told me instantly filled my head with unachieved dreams and awaiting nightmares.

"Listen, homie, I just got a call and was told to tell you them people got it out for you for that situation that jumped off a few weeks ago." No need to go into detail; I knew just what "situation" he spoke of.

A few weeks prior, a reputable old head and his associate had been murdered in what was labeled a robbery gone bad. Middle of the night, on-the-scene investigators questioned a couple of bystanders. One was an admitted drug addict and the other a supposed 'hood tough guy. Both fingered me as the man they witnessed fleeing the backyard, smoking gun in hand, seconds after two men had been shot and killed execution-style. No time to ponder, I knew pleading my case would be of no use. More than likely, it will never be admitted, but in lower-class communities where criminal activity is higher than average, once fingered by a "witness," credible or incredible, willingly or forcefully, the case was yours to fend off. Tell it to the judge.

The actual night of the murders, September 11, I was, along with a little under a dozen of my homeboys in about three to four vehicles packed up and rolled to the after-hours spot on Norwood Street. The after-hours spot was nothing more than a garage stacked with wholesale liquor from the local retailer Home Liquors, half-naked strippers, 'hood-hoppers, and thugs of all sorts who would much rather spend their late nights chunking cash on five-dollar shots of Hennessy, smoking weed, and bagging females instead of getting a good night's sleep.

On this night, I received a phone call from my mother that my younger brother was to be released within the next hour or two from the County Jail. With just about every other block manned by a different set or gang, traveling to your 'hood alone after release was a good way to come up missing. So we took the party to the gates of the County Jail to await my lil bro's release.

Outside the County Jail, we turned up the music in our cars, popped bottles, and put on a show for the homies who weren't fortunate enough to enjoy the freedom of the night. Time passed and the wait became frustrating. We sent in our homegirls Lee Lee, Big Hak, and Kee Kee to find out what was going on. They returned minutes later only to say, "No more releases tonight." Out of our control, we threw up the "B" and hollered "SuWoop" to the windows of the jail, jumped back in our whips, and burned out. It was back to the after-hours spot to party like rock stars.

All the while, in a different section of the city, a home invasion had taken place. Yet and still, murder was the case they gave me.

In spite of all the times I woke up in cold sweats or could not sleep at all, too tormented by the naked images of despair, the words "Just a little bit longer" still echoed all around me. I was too hungry, too selfish, and too foolish to understand enough was enough. Now, life was showing me its strength.

The night of September 28 I kept my cool and jumped straight on my cell phone. First call was to my lawyer and the second was to my mother. I instructed both to call Robbery/Homicide to see what they could find out and if in fact the law was hot on my trail. I knew the next person I dialed would be just as stunned by the news:

"Hello?"

"What's poppin', Blood?" I whispered into the receiver.

"You already know. You, me, the 'hood," came the voice on the other end.

"All the time. But listen, I just ran into a problem"

"A problem? With who?" he asked.

"Easy, homie, not that type of problem."

"Then what type?" he snapped back.

"Dig, homie, being judged by twelve is running too much of a risk."

"Damn, Blood, I told you to be easy. You see that shit I'm going through."

"I already know. Thing is, this ain't my beef, but somehow my name got tangled up and the rest is history."

"Aight, listen. You know how to get here. If I'm not around when you arrive, the key will welcome you home."

"Say no more. No later than tonight I should be in your presence."

As soon as I hung up the phone, I felt it vibrate. With a mixture of anger and concern in her voice, my mother kicked in:

"Listen, son, I don't know what's going on, but I spoke to the people and one of the detectives recognized your name and assured me that you were not on their list of suspects or wanted for questioning in relation to anything in their department."

This was good news in part, but I knew there was only so much information they would give a suspect's family if they really were on to him. My mother continued:

"Tewhan, you sure you're okay?" A question I seemed to be getting asked a lot lately.

"Yeah, I'll see you later," I responded in an attempt to rush her off the phone.

I knew if the law wasn't looking for me yet but word was in the streets, it wouldn't be long before they were.

Months had passed of me telling myself I wanted a better life, one where I could parlay in peace, worry-free, and inhale the beauty of life—and still my faults got the best of me. The tug of war—should I or shouldn't I—was over and no longer of any significance. All at once, I was to disappear and assume a new identity and give everything up.

I found it incredibly difficult to put it all behind me. While I had the power of choice, my right to the effective application of that choice was chained within the prison of my mind. The consequences of isolated thought limited my potential and left me mentally arrested. No one was to blame but me. When the door was open, I was too afraid to step through. Things finally caught up with me at a time I least desired.

My twenty-third birthday was just three days away and there I found myself scrambling to gather the necessities to begin a new life underground, alone!

Time definitely was not on my side. I knew detectives could swarm at any minute, ready to take me to jail. I knew they would be prepared to shoot if necessary. I contemplated what I would do if I was trapped in a corner. Would I surrender, or would I cock, aim, and shoot? No easy decision. Both would basically be the ends of life as I knew it.

With so much going on in the streets, it was virtually impossible for me to snatch up my possessions and collect outstanding debts without drawing suspicion. I needed a few days to wrap up all the loose ends in the streets—and I didn't need too much of anyone in my mix, so I postponed my departure until Monday night, October 1, 2002—my twenty-third birthday.

September 30, twenty-four hours before my born day, was to be the last night my face would ever be seen in these streets. I only shared the drastic turn of events with a select few of my homies. Most didn't know of my plans. Some took turns chauffeuring me around to collect the pay from the last of the work I trickled out to the streets. I crouched low in the backseat, out of view to any passing pedestrians, and attempted to memorize each street and every block. It would surely be a long time before I saw any of it again. Hopefully, my name would be cleared and I could return to the place I called home. It was just a thought but highly unlikely. During this last minute, I needed a little time to myself.

"Bump J, drop me off, homie, I'm trying to catch a few Zs," I requested through a mouth full of weed smoke.

I had known the homie Bump J for years. Those days he was on the 'hood like us all, yet most of his time went into writing rhymes that I might add would outdo most of the rappers of my time. His style reminded me of something like Kanye West and his verses were spit with precision.

"Go ahead and nap back there. I got you. A nigga trying to rock with you for your B-day, Blood," Bump J replied.

"Trillz, we gonna do that, so don't trip. I just need a quick hour or two to regroup for the night. I already know y'all planning to get a nigga faded," I shot back.

Bump J smirked and replied, "Aight, Skoob, but we'll be back around 8."

I was happy to steal some alone time but once at home I didn't sleep. I just pondered life and its happenings, which just so happened to be my unraveling. I took into account the commonality in hardship among myself and my community and questioned if genocide was taking place in America. I wondered if our plight was carefully calculated behind closed doors in an America where we are not in favor. Was there actually some bold plan we failed to see that skillfully manipulated our acceptance of mediocrity and took advantage of one's fear to stand upright and ultimately led us to shield our potential from even ourselves?

Born and raised in surroundings full of neglect, along with thousands, I existed as a consequence of social immobility and mental neglect. Physically, I was able to move but mentally I could not make out the direction I wanted to travel. It was stagnation in its truest form. And just as stagnant waters surely spoil and become the source of disease and sickness, I watched myself and many of those around me wither away in a corrupt environment contaminated by decades of social stagnation and decay, leaving those of us in the ghetto saturated in the filth that inundates the slums to endure the misery of poverty. It's not only those who reside in the 'hood—this harsh reality of the social stagnation of the economic underclass has now gone global.

"While in the evil streets, time goes by you're puffing on lye, hoping that it gets you by. The entire time you're going crazy."—Tupac

My pleas for sanity were spoken softly. Did I really wish to be heard? My dismissive eye created tunnel vision and led to destructive behavior. My life was robbed of pleasure and compensated with pain. I had to deal.

America's competitive nature rewards us with loss in a huge number of ways. When will we learn? How many must we lose? Do we at the bottom count for nothing? Questions posed to those who condemn the people and places they keep a safe distance from. Only if I could have seen this all sooner and not allowed my natural abilities to be downplayed and dictated to by those who could never understand.

My phone rang and broke my train of thought. It was 8 o'clock on the dot and Bump J and the homies were ready to get back to it. What I knew was what I knew. However, it would be difficult to apply now that my life no longer belonged to me.

Night fell, and I could relax a little with my person less visible in the streets. I sat up and exchanged swigs of Hennessy and tokes of chronic with Bump J and Young Odie. The homegirl Twin was on the wheel as we cruised the town.

A little before midnight, I got an unexpected phone call from Neisha. Lately, Neish and I had been on the rocks, and we were no longer staying together, largely due to my inability to leave the streets behind. When I answered, her voice was just as I remembered,

"I know you're not going to bring in your birthday without me," posed as a question, but sounding more like a remark.

I was happy whatever the disagreement, we had worked it out and replied,

"I'll be there to get you in a half hour. Be ready."

Before disconnecting, she called out,

"Massacre, I love you."

I shot back, "I love you the same," and felt in my heart exactly what I said.

I hung up and wondered if the love she had would remain the same or continue to grow when she learned this was to be my last night in town. Would she question my love for her and my son? Would she understand and vow to ride under the laws of forever?

Later that night, I picked Neisha up and we pulled in front of the Patio right before the clock struck 12. My birthday had the bar more crowded than usual. Outside sat an assortment of whips, hoopties to foreign cars, females in everything from Payless to Prada, and 'hood reputables in Timberlands and sweats, Evisu jeans, and button ups, to sidewalk soldiers in army fatigues, red rags and Gore-Tex boots. Really, it was just another night, with the exception of my life being turned upside down a few days prior. But, all in all, I couldn't allow myself to get caught up in the troubles of tomorrow. I threw back shots, laughed and joked, you know, party and bullshit, feigning the impression life was picture perfect. Had you seen the façade I put up, you would agree I could have been nominated for an Oscar.

The one thing I remember most about that night was, even with all the drama and distress, there was harmony in the 'hood. Our hardships united us in a way I didn't even understand. We argued, we fought, everything you could imagine, yet we loved one another. Crazy, but true, and it was a sight to see.

Bloods and Bloodettes from all around the town packed inside and outside a tiny hole in the wall to celebrate the birth of one of their own. It was moments like this that made the bottom feel as if you were on the top. That togetherness, that camaraderie, that sense of family was intoxicating. But it was bittersweet. I knew for reasons beyond my grasp, the journey of self-discovery would continue and I would remain lost.

My thoughts were interrupted when in walked who I thought of as "the last of a dying breed": Dough Boy, Young Kwame, Flock, Bat, QB, TB, and a handful of others with whom I spent many days and many nights chasing dreams. The same dreams I imagined as a child, the big ones of making it out the 'hood. After they entered, a crew of my homegirls came smashing in, Big Sha, Dira, Bree, Trina, and Tawanna. They all approached to wish me a happy born and the night kicked up.

I was already faded out of my mind and knew another shot would take me over the limit, but I couldn't refuse as homeboys and homegirls alike ordered the bartender to keep 'em coming—shots and more shots; double shots and more double shots. This was 'hood love! The remainder of the night everything and everybody stayed the same—all the way live!

"Last call for alcohol. You ain't got to go home, but you got to get the hell out of here." The crowd chimed in midway to finish off Larry the bar owner's favorite saying.

After chilling outside the Patio for a few, a gang of homies suggested we hit up the after-hours spot to keep the night rolling. A suggestion that under other conditions I would have accepted, but I didn't want to risk such a hostile environment with the mother of my child. If something kicked off, it could have easily created a tragedy none of us wanted to endure. Some were disappointed, while others understood. Either way, as much as the liquor was talking to me, I knew I couldn't chance it. I handed Neisha the car keys and in a drunken slur, I requested, "1 & 9, shoot out to 1 & 9, so we can get a room."

"1 & 9" was a local highway lined with dozens of motels, hotels, strip malls, and restaurants. There, I knew it would be hard to track me and I would have plenty options. With the liquor in control of everyone in the car, nobody felt confident enough to make the trip. In that instant, with every bit of sanity I possessed, I should have demanded we find a willing homeboy/girl to make sure I was put away safe for the night. The mind is a terrible thing to waste. I found every excuse not to do exactly that which I should have never second-guessed.

Maybe the law wasn't on me yet. Maybe they found out I had nothing to do with it. Hell, it was Monday; raids normally took place on Tuesday and Thursday (TNT). Either way, I'd be out early enough and no one would notice. So, "Fuck it, take me to my mother's over on Arsdale Terrace." As soon as I spoke those words, I knew somehow I would regret my decision. It turned out to be a dumb decision. My mother's address was on every bail slip I ever had, and trust I had more than a few.

Once at my mother's, the rest of the night was a blur.

I was awakened the next morning by straight ruckus. First thought was it was death approaching, the Grim Reaper coming to collect his debt. Retribution for the inexcusable acts I committed over the years. There was no way around whatever it was. The screams were right beside me and in the adjacent room. I feared if I opened my eyes, the man or men in the house would not hesitate to send me home. The thought:

Ecclesiastes 9:2: *The same destiny ultimately awaits everyone, whether righteous or wicked, good or bad, ceremonially clean or unclean, religious or irreligious, good people receive the same treatment as sinners.*

I took a few deep breaths, shook off the effects of last night's partying, and prepared to meet my maker, fully aware. I opened my eyes and stared down the barrels of the pistols pointed at me and realized it was not an act of revenge or stick-up kids looking for a come-up, though just as bad, if not worse: It was the law.

Aside from the yells and screams, I heard nothing until this point.

"Don't move. Let me see your fucking hands. If you move, I'll blow your fucking head off."

It was every intimidating remark imaginable, when in all actuality at that point, they were more afraid than me. They dragged me out of bed and slammed me straight to the floor. My hands were placed behind my back and cuffed simultaneously. I attempted to raise my head from the ground and witnessed the remaining officers handcuffing Neisha. As if this was not enough, when I was led into the living room so they could search the apartment for any evidence related to the crime I was accused of, there on the couch sat my mother and brother, both in cuffs. My brother had just been released from the County a few weeks earlier.

Tears just about filled my eyes. Never in life did I entertain the thought of things going this far. All I felt was shame. The people who I loved the most, I somehow caused the most pain. I could search a lifetime and still not find a forgivable reason. Is this what they meant—"the typical male is one so afraid of life and love that he discovers ways to damage not only his own but the lives of those who have brought nothing but affection into his world"?

The woman who brought me into this world and to whom I owed my life was hurt, with a look in her eyes that pleaded for help. I, the man who had this false belief that I was in control, could do nothing to help her.

Reality opened my eyes in ways I never imagined. No matter how fearless or tough, any man who can witness any form of injustice inflicted upon his first lady is a coward. My heart was broken. I never felt so small. My head hung low. The remainder of my family had no clue why the police kicked in the door executing a no-knock search warrant. I began to prepare them for the troubles of tomorrow. With feelings of hopelessness I stated, "You know, I'm never coming home from this. Ma, I love you. Neish; it was always real, however, move on with your life."

To my younger brother, I encouraged him to do right by the family.

For me, there was nothing left but to measure the endless array of abnormalities that assault you in prison. I knew the search would result in nothing incriminating, so I sat patiently and waited to be taken to the place where they shackled lost souls.

Twenty minutes or so, into the living room walked a white detective whose name I do not recall who asked, "Is there anything in the apartment we should know about?"

"No, not at all," I answered.

From behind his back, he revealed a brown paper bag, and asked, "So what is this?"

Damn, another blow, adding insult to injury. I totally forgot the day before, out of fear for being recognized while driving, I decided to take a taxi. There was no guarantee the cab driver would take the chase if necessary, so I opted to keep the bag stashed and planned to return later that evening to pick it up. I got sidetracked and never made it.

"Arrest everyone," the detective demanded.

"For what? Whatever you found belongs to me."

There was no way I was going to see my family destroyed by an unsparing and merciless judicial system. Yet as a tool to divide and conquer, they knew with the contents of the bag they had leverage and could threaten and scare my family into giving them information they, or I for that matter, didn't have. Even after I owned up to their findings, they still wanted to put the sack on everybody.

What was found was of little to no value. Besides, with what had led them to the door in the first place, it could affect me none.

A black male detective stepped in next. I later found out he headed the case. "No, that won't be necessary. Arrest only those who were in the bedroom," leaving my mother out of the equation. Though we were on different sides of the playing field, I respected his decision and was grateful my mother was not arrested.

Once we arrived at Robbery & Homicide, which was a single floor inside the Essex County Courts building filled with tiny cubicles, mug shots, and coffee-drinking detectives, I knew all was very much real. While waiting, I witnessed detectives lead Neisha into one of their many interrogation rooms. She was already threatened with our child being taken away, so I could only imagine the things about to be said behind closed doors. Still, I had faith she would *never let them see her sweat*. A quote, I would repeatedly tell her whenever things got rough. While I figured her to be going through that fiasco, I was in another interrogation room:

"OK. Mass, isn't it? Or should I call you Massacre?"

With sarcasm in his voice the detective went on.

"One hell of a birthday, huh?"

"To save us all some time, I'll make this clear: Not for one second do we believe you didn't take part in what transpired on September 11. I know better. I know when you were there. I know you pulled the trigger. And I am going to personally see to it that you rot in jail for the remainder of your natural life."

Almost in a single breath the detective began recounting his perception of what took place:

"So, Massacre, on September 11, S.D. and his Spanish drug connect sat in S.D.'s basement [a converted studio] discussing what was to be their next move in regards to wrapping things up in the streets and getting serious in the music industry. While the two sat alone, accompanied by one other who was in the adjacent room, the door went flying open and before anyone knew it they were at gunpoint while you demanded the goods. More concerned with the boss himself, the third person was able to escape while S.D. and his connect could not. Little words were exchanged. No time was wasted. The studio was rummaged. Drugs were found and you were fearful of being later identified or sought out for revenge, as S.D. was surely a reputable individual in the streets. Before fleeing the scene two gunshots brought this story to a close, or so you thought."

When the detective was done giving up what he believed was a play by play of the unfortunate occurrence, I was led to a holding tank and left to sit. An hour later, I was escorted to Essex County Jail, where I sat on the second floor and waited to be processed.

"Butler," I heard my name called. "Come to the gate. Put your hands behind your back." I never went through the process in this fashion. My antennas were up. I had not even changed into my County attire. I was handcuffed and led into a little room. First thing to mind was the law and their antics. I sat in the room, when polished shoes and a Mafia-sharp suit came strutting in, briefcase in hand.

"Hello, Tewhan. My name is Michael Robbins. I'm a criminal defense lawyer. I have been informed by a few friends of yours, some of whom I have represented in the past, that you may be in need of legal assistance."

I was somewhat shocked Robbins managed to arrange an attorney visit so soon. I liked his style. A little more than thirty minutes and we were done. A fee was set, and I provided the contacts needed to secure the funds.

Back in the bullpen, it wasn't long before another CO approached the gate.

"Butler, you must be a very important person. You have another visit."

Already tired of the runaround and no fool to the trick, I knew this wasn't a visit I would enjoy. Cuffed again and led off, this time we passed the attorney/client booths and continued the length of the hallway until we reached its end. A knock, then the door opened. Inside were three white males, dressed in plain clothes. It was the County Jail's Internal Affairs Squad (SIS). I most definitely would not enjoy this visit.

"No need to be seated. This will only take a minute," stated one of the three from behind a desk stationed in the far corner. "So you're Mass?"

Never in denial about who I was and what I represented, I stood there with a look that said, "Aight, now what?" but said nothing.

"Well, listen closely. We know all about you. Here, you will follow the rules and regulations of the institution. If you think for one minute you are going to come in and run the show, we have a place for you. You have heard of Trenton State Prison's MCU [Management Control Unit]?"

Indeed I had, but at the moment I didn't care where they sent me, so the idle threats did not move me in the least. I was already fighting the gas station murder case and here it was not even a full two years later, and the law had piled on two more. Since the system was adamant to demonstrate I couldn't win, I carried it as if I couldn't lose.

"Take him back where he belongs," ordered the officer who stood before me.

As I was led back to the holding tank, I thought of the nerve of such characters. My freedom was just snatched and they were under the impression I was so closed-minded to have been focused on running somebody's jail—a clear indication of what they thought about gang-bangers. Our minds were not respected because they thought most of our resolve was attained through force as opposed to reason. I hated that we couldn't see we provided them with this notion we were nothing more than our physical.

Later that evening, I entered the dayroom, bedroll in hand, and was received with looks of disbelief, disappointment, and disgust by those who knew me. They had no knowledge of my current situation. Many were counting on me and others to represent and make it to heights they were unable to. It was almost as if, especially for those from my neighborhood, that a part of their dream vanished when I walked in. It was an honor to be viewed in a light where others would choose to live vicariously through me. Truth be told, I was having enough difficulty succeeding from one victory to the next.

Normally, homies were shunned who made it home, failed to take advantage of their opportunity in the free world, and returned to jail. After the initial shock subsided, I explained I had been mixed up. That wasn't hard to believe given more than a few of them were wrongly accused. Afterward the homies on floors six and seven of the County Jail showed me what we cherished, Blood love!

During the months of sitting in the County Jail awaiting trial, I stayed on a strict militant-minded grind, focused only on what I needed to shape my mental and physical. My daily regimen was working out during the day and studying during the night. I became obsessed with political history, stories of people, struggle, and so on. Fidel, Che, Mandela, down to Marx and Lenin. But my pending cases weighed heavy on my mind. I wanted another shot at life. Just one more chance to apply the knowledge and wisdom I now possessed and display full understanding. I was convinced it was now or never.

Along with Banga, Petey I, Ohs, Grimy, Al Wild, and others, I took to our adverse circumstances as we prepared one another for higher ground. While we attempted to soar above the conflict-filled conditions of a life behind bars, COs and the County Jail's administration alike remained persistent about ridding me from their custody. Given I was now using more of my mind, as opposed to my body, the only way for them to demonstrate just cause was to fabricate my sentry file.

Every incident concerning the Bloods, minor or major, direct or indirect, my name was linked though I was never involved. Certain COs who respected the manner in which I carried myself began to warn me and let me know I was the topic of roll call and other staff meetings. It was said I was more influential than the administration and whether this "influence" was for good or bad, it could not be tolerated.

With the heads-up, the only way I figured I could fight was to stay as low key as possible, but that proved to be more difficult than I thought. Every time an incident occurred, I was summoned to settle it. I could not lie back and watch internal confusion, not for their sake but in the name of our cause. I knew my proactive approach was working against me, yet I remained fearless of any consequence.

While bidding and accepting whatever my fate was to be, life was finding a way to catch up with those within my circle. Every time I turned my head, another homie was entering the system.

Over the nine months I was in, my younger brother had caught some time, Nas had been arrested and charged Federally, Troub's stint on the run ended, and newspapers claimed Flock was captured returning from the NBA All-Star Game in Miami.

Flock had been running from an earlier homicide, which he later pled guilty to. Flock was accused of murdering another member of the set, Shot Box, the brother of our homegirl Twin. When this incident occurred I was already serving time. Rumor had it Flock and Shot Box had been beefing over money. Whether there was any truth to the story, I do not know. The streets were no joke and when a person was trying to eat and another got in the way it was all she wrote. However, I will always wish it never happened. The incident did irreparable damage to my relationship with the homegirl Twin, my Mini-Me.

The law bit J-Rock, and Bito was picked up on a minor offense turned major. Everyone I grew up with was falling short to a lifestyle there was obviously no way to win at. My experience made me a believer. What was real could not be denied and so I accepted that every beginning is preceded by an end.

One year following the day of my arrest, a gang of my homeboys woke me up in the jail wanting to bring in my birthday. Not too much celebrating could take place inside the County Jail, yet despite the down side of being incarcerated for my birthday, sharing it with my comrades was enough. Nine o'clock in the morning partying had me ready to take it down before lunch. Unable to maintain any longer, I went to my cell and dozed off. With no clue of how much time lapsed, I was shaken out of my sleep.

"Ay Blood, they calling for a lockdown," B.G. from Brim Gang informed me.

In the background I could hear the CO yelling, "Lockdown! Lockdown! Do not miss your gate, gentlemen."

I wasn't fully aware of what was taking place and didn't want to make a call that required physical altercation with the staff when it could've been avoided. I ordered, "Stand down, lock in, and see what's up."

Once inside our cells, I went back to sleep, unconcerned with anything besides the safety of my homies. Next thing, I was awakened to, "Goon Squad. Here they come, Rosko."

I realized I wasn't dreaming and got up in a hurry. The sounds of bump, bump, bump, bump, as boots slammed the concrete floors, left to right. A dozen or so of the jail's biggest officers rolled in prepared to do their do.

I knew nothing that warranted the squad had taken place and was confused. I posted up at my cell gate to see what was happening. My intuition was telling me I was part of the reason for the invasion. I was three cells in from the end of the tier between K.O. from Valentine Bloods and Al Wild from G-Shine. The squad continued in our direction. Evident one of us three was their target, I prepared for the outcome.

Just a few days before, during a weeklong lockdown, I sat in my cell reading when a CO pulled up to my gate and whispered, "They're trying to get you out of here." It was another reminder the administration wanted me out of their facility. I guess this was it. The squad stopped in front of my cell.

"Austin, turn around, lie on the ground with palms up."

Austin, I thought. So they weren't there for me. They were for the cell next door. They extracted the homie K.O. and left.

A reasonable amount of time passed and I figured they would not return. I kicked off my boots and went back to sleep, waiting for the tier to be reopened.

"Butler!" Boom, boom, boom; the banging of clubs against my gate.

"Butler; turn around, lie down, palms up."

Groggy, I rolled out of bed and reached for my boots.

"Do nothing other than what we said. Get down now!"

I did as told and was cuffed and led to R & D, where I was met by a group of officers I had never seen during my stay in Essex County Jail.

Videotaped, I was told to strip. Handing over one piece of clothing at a time. When completely naked, I was ordered to lift, squat, and cough. Degrading was a life behind bars. I was handed back a pair of pants, one T-shirt, and a pair of socks. No shoes, no slippers.

I was surrounded, then feet shackled, hands cuffed, belly-chained, and guided into the back of an armored DOC truck, where I could see absolutely nothing. The interior was all metal. The cuffs were so tight, after minutes I lost all feeling in my hands.

"Happy birthday," I thought.

My only wish was wherever I was headed we got there fast. We shook back and forth from the speed as we pulled off. I couldn't see where I was going, yet I could hear the sirens. After what I believed to be just about an hour, we came to a stop. Next, I heard the clanging of gates opening and closing. My destination had been reached. I stepped out and when my eyes adjusted to the light, I knew exactly where I was.

There were only two prisons in the state talked about with an anxious uncertainty, alarm, and admonition. From the outside I could feel the horror that infected this place. I could smell the blood and hear the fight of those struggling not to be forgotten—sacrificed souls with their sanity slipping away.

It was New Jersey (Trenton) State Prison, Units 4B and 3B, North Compound, home to the State's infamous Management Control Unit and Death Row. This was prior to Governor Jon Corzine signing a bill to abolish the death penalty in New Jersey in 2007.

The North Compound held hundreds of serious offenders—murderers, bank robbers, and serial killers on down to rapists. Each compound was just as dangerous as the other. The West Compound was General Population and Administrative Segregation. North Compound was General Population, Management Control Unit, and Death Row. South Compound was General Population and a lone female Administrative Segregation Unit and Protective Custody for those who could not handle the pressures of prison. My stay at Trenton State Prison was an around-the-clock lockdown in the North Compound's Management Control Unit.

I entered the prison and was greeted by a line of officers, nightsticks in hand.

"LT to control, cease inmate movement in the North Compound."

Seconds later, I heard the same repeated over the intercom.

"Move," commanded the white shirt.

Still shackled, I hobbled to the elevator and read the numbers as the car went to its top floor, four. The steel from the ankle cuffs cut into my skin, the moisture of blood dampened my socks.

When the elevator doors opened, a nightstick to the back urged me forward. The MCU at Trenton State Prison was asylum-like. The cells' were all white, and the unit was overcome by a scary silence. The lights were blindingly bright. There were two parallel tiers with twelve cells on the flats and twelve cells on the upper deck. Both sat in front of "The Bubble," an officer's booth shielded with Plexiglas. There was a shower and a conference room.

The MCU's caged recreation yard was shaped like a triangle. The only thing other than the jungle's concrete was a pull-up and dip bars and a single basketball rim. Everything was jammed in between a twenty- to thirty-foot brick wall and the rectangular windows of the North Compound. There was nothing other than a pantry separating us from men sentenced to Death Row.

MCU looked neither comfortable, nor accommodating. It was obvious the unit was made to hide men whom the New Jersey Department of Corrections classified as ill-suited for even a glimpse of general population.

After being buzzed in, an officer from within the control booth stepped up and announced:

"Welcome to MCU," a cordial reception in the least, I thought to myself but said nothing.

"Cell 8, men," booth control instructed.

I stepped into the cell through an iron-clad door with a 6- x 24-inch window made of wired Plexiglas. All there was inside was steel, cement, and solitude. The sink and toilet were one piece, similar to those in the County. Step outside of your cell three paces, and more cage. There was a metal-caged fence separating the cells from the remainder of the unit. The gate provided a barrier between convict and prison guard. At no time in MCU was there to be unrestrained contact between officer and inmate.

When the shackles and cuffs were removed, it was all I could do not to yell out in relief. He who has the right of mind to kneel before God can stand against anything.

I had no idea how long I would be held on MCU, and I just sat and stared at the wall. I shed so many tears in the silence of the night, I could cry no more.

"Mass! Mass!" I recognized the voice and limped to the door.

"Yo," I called out.

"They got you too," hollered K.O.

"Yeah, I guess so. Who else they got down here?" I asked.

"Me, you, Zak Brim in cell 10, and Al Wild in 6."

"Damn," I whispered.

Not too sure who was in my immediate surroundings and drained from the day's events, I cut the conversation short.

"Aight, Blood. I'll get with you later, East to da West."

"Ay, Mass."

"What's poppin'?"

"Happy B-day, Blood."

A smirk instantly appeared on my face. Yeah, happy birthday. I hit the rack.

When I woke up in the morning, it took a few minutes to register exactly where I was. The sharp pain in my wrist, back, and ankles served me a reminder. I sat in my cell and just a little after breakfast two prisoners approached my door.

"Ay, young Blood," said one, tall and slim built, with dreads down his back; the other was short and stocky. Both were older, and you could tell had been in for quite some time and took good care of themselves over the years. In prison, it's said that if a man's sanity stays intact and he stays active with the physical, jail preserves his youth.

"There's a bag out here for you with the things you need to get yourself situated."

I knew to be careful of what I took from anyone in prison. However, by their demeanor I could tell they were good-natured and had good intent. They gave off the aura of some of the black militants I read about during their run in the 60s and 70s, especially when addressing me as young Blood.

"Also, there are a few books out here to help you keep your head in the game."

"Aight, thanks," I said.

In response, the shorter one said, "No need to thank me, young Blood. You just be sure you do the same when the next brother comes in. Besides, 'thank you' shows a sign of separation and we're one, comrade."

I didn't even know how to respond. I had never been hit with such a subtle jewel. I simply nodded my head while they walked away.

That brief conversation made me wonder. I knew I was in MCU but really where was I? All that seemed to be housed here with the exception of those who arrived with me were a generation or two before my time. The words they used (young Blood, comrade, brother), and what did he mean by "thank you shows a sign of separation"? We *were* separated. I didn't know him and he damn well didn't know me, so how could we be anything other than separated?

I had studied history and though I believed it to be on a large scale, in all actuality, my studies were minimal. I paid more attention to specifics and overlooked a people's universal connection and how we bleed the same: the truths found in unity as opposed to the falsehoods of hatred and division; the rhythmic heartbeat that moves us all, though it may not be recognized. I hated to admit it, but my time in solitary confinement in the MCU just might have been the cure for my ailing psyche.

I was constantly in and a part of nonstop action on the streets and in the County. A much-needed rest from it all would help me get me right. I never had a clear second to think or sit still and enjoy silence; some say I was near insanity and knew no calm. I behaved as if Satan was more friend than foe. I needed a rest. Maybe it would be granted via solitary confinement, courtesy of a Higher Power in order to provide clarity.

For days on end, there would be silence, except for when food slots opened and closed and the few times cell doors were busted. Other than that, there was nothing but time to rid yourself of worry. For the strong, MCU was a breeding ground for solidarity. For the weak, the MCU was a closed casket. I was at ease, knowing tomorrow would bring only that which my shoulders could bear.

When I retrieved the bag, there were hygiene products, a box of Buglers, and two books, Geronimo Pratt's *Last Man Standing* and George Jackson's *Soledad Brothers*. Just as I thought—these brothers were conscious descendants of the struggle for justice and liberation in the 60s and 70s. You may call them revolutionaries; others may mark them as criminals or terrorists. As for me, I honor them as freedom fighters. The two comrades were Gumu Infumo and Massai Khaban.

While housed in Trenton State's Management Control Unit, I not only learned universal law and how it applied to man, but also I was informed of how fearful the government is of those who develop such awareness. One of the criteria for MCU states "*He/She who poses a threat to inmate population and/or staff alike.*"

Conscious comrades housed here for decades with no institutional infractions, spoke to me of the threat. I was added to the list, stripped of privileges, and subject to recreation in spans of eight, nine, and ten days apart justified through the quoting of 10A Law,

In controlled units inmates are to receive up to 5 hours of recreation per week, unless it interferes with the orderly running of the institution.

How could it not when the prison is to cease movement any time a controlled unit prisoner leaves the block? All about control, 23 & 1 lockdown often swapped out for 24 & none. No movement without the accessories, two correction officers, a lieutenant, cuffs, and waist belt. Confined and carried in the way of the wretched.

While in MCU under the bright lights, I felt beneath a cloud of darkness. Prison began to dig its claws into my flesh. I would fight to get away, but I had no control. I wanted desperately to live beyond these prison walls, on the other side of these steel doors, away from the barbed wire, outside of isolation, and so close to freedom, but on no day in MCU did it arrive. All elements of normalcy for me were defeated. The strain and pressure of the MCU was like a fifteen-year-old child attempting to bench press 650 pounds. Long nights, and I do mean long nights, in my ravenous dungeon-like cell with nothing but the echoes of emptiness and the shadows of my past demons. The unusual punishment was everything including cruel and inhumane. I relied on brief physical workouts to release built up stress, pinned up frustration, and a lifetime of bottled up aggression.

This was only a small portion of what I had to face while in MCU:

In the MCU we were babysat by men who found pleasure in dehumanizing us beyond the physical circumstances of the unit. There were regular cell shake-downs that could result in officers destroying personal property. There were strip searches in front of dozens of other inmates, as well as female COs. And being held captive in a shower stall for hours was a form of punishment, as was being left outside in pouring rain and snowstorms. "You asked to go outside" would be the staff's response when questioned about it. All communication was monitored and heavily scrutinized. Prison isn't about privacy, and certainly not the Management Control Unit.

It was here under these conditions while serving time under black militants, including BLA (Black Liberation Army) members, ex-Panthers, and New Afrikan Brothers in the likes of Ajani, Ubay, Bomani, Yeru, Ojore, and Kisu, to name a few, my eyes began to open. Thanks to their mentoring I learned to embrace struggle and learned the importance and value of intergenerational camaraderie. I remembered the days when they would pass down kites (letters) recounting historical events the blind failed to acknowledge. Their pens bled stories of Assata Shakur's escape from Clinton (New Jersey's women's prison), to the MCU's middle-of-the-night assas-sination attempt and shooting of Sundiata Acoli in the prison by COs prior to him being taken to the Feds, and the murder of Little Bobby Hutton, Eldridge Cleaver's exile, and the Free Huey P rallies. They wrote about the days when they donned black berets, black leather jackets, and with one fist in the air, echoed "Power to the People!"

The world had advanced but the MCU was still defined by the culture and men-tality of the 60s and 70s. Many seemed to have forgotten, yet those within the MCU remained extraordinary examples of sacrifice and struggle. In my immediate sur-roundings stood men, shackled as a result of being fearless in their quest for justice.

In and out of prison, they wanted to be free. How could any man rooted in truth not identify?

Back to my days as a youngster and the police raids, the homeless, the drug addicts stretched out in the streets, the mothers struggling, and the missing fathers: it all made sense. I felt the need to act. I was these men. These men were me. Their belief that as long as it remained one man, one woman, and one child presented with struggle, then we all struggled was also my belief. However, my inability to tap into these feelings and beliefs until that point is what kept me off balance over the years. I had been defeated, seduced by the material world, and tricked into believing a few more dollars made, a fancy car, big rims, and flashy jewelry placed me above the struggle. My struggle was so much more. It was psychological. To survive I had to strengthen my mind and overcome my own thinking habits.

My battle to leave it all behind now made sense. It wasn't because I was foolish, naïve, or incompetent; it was because subconsciously a part of me knew the happiness I pursued could never be as long as others were left behind to navigate poverty's matrix.

Through illegal means, I secured an out for myself, but what was I to do? If I stayed, I could only teach what I knew, "the game." If I left, I still influenced others, as it was evident I preyed on weaknesses to enhance my strength. The mental medication I was receiving in MCU was right and exact. My only fear was now that I gained such knowledge the system would prevent me from passing it along. My mail was already being opened. I had no phone privileges, and all visits had to be pre-approved. I couldn't do anything without scrutiny. I was gaining in certain areas, losing big in others—yet this was my life.

During my stay in MCU, I noticed more and more homies from different sets coming in. G-Shine's Laydown and Stack-A-Dolla, 9 Trey's Tec-Tutt, and others. Previously, the law had us stationed in different sections of Jersey, presumably to keep us apart and dilute influence. But now, it seemed the law's strategy shifted to long-term isolation. Everyone was making their way to the Management Control Unit in Trenton.

Gangs had become so political it was ironic that all roads led us to Trenton, New Jersey's capital. I guess you could say we were all off to join the political bosses who robbed generations before me blind and helped perpetuate the cycle of poverty in New Jersey's cities. Check New Jersey politics during my lifetime. Politicians and their bosses literally got rich off exploiting residents of cities like Newark, Jersey City, Camden, Trenton, Orange, and East Orange. Very few were ever held accountable and even fewer have gone to prison. Do you think there could be a link between the political corruption over the years and the fact that these same cities where kids like me grew up have historically had some of the worst public schools in the state, some of the most violent, drug-infested streets, and were the first and most deeply affected by drugs, guns, and gangs?

With much of gang leadership locked down, on the streets Bloods of all sorts attempted to pick up where we left off. From the confines of my cell I shamefully watched the daily news flashes as gangs spiraled out of control. Bloods were killing Bloods. There was reckless shooting and false flagging. Imposters posed as gangsters, corrupting a cause that was sacred to many, but how could I blame them? Much of what was going on was a twisted attempt to imitate the Bloods of my era. Regardless, if one was to accept it or not, we contributed to what could arguably be viewed as the beginning of the end.

In turn, I also observed carefully the mind games played by our government. Suddenly, around election time, a local Newark politician looking to capitalize from another's struggle played front-page headlines with the words, "Bloods and Crips Form Peace Treaty." But who were these Bloods? Who were these Crips? It was pure exploitation for political gain. And with all due respect, the treaty was needed, but in my heart of hearts I knew it could never work. For one, it was not manufactured by the people. Two, the people behind it who "supported" this movement never dug deep enough to touch those who were suffering as a direct result of gang activity. And three, this problem was beyond colors and gangs, red and blue.

Take away the colors and the bandannas and rid the city of its gangs; fail to correct the horrific conditions that plague the community and what you have is the same result, if not more severe. People tired and turning against one another, willing to do whatever is needed to get ahead.

Public Service Announcement!

Dear Mr. President,

Now that my eyes are beginning to widen, I ask, do you see what I see? An America thriving on misunderstanding where our kind—white and black, Muslim and Christian, rich and poor, Republican and Democrat, Red and Blue, Blood and Crip, Have and Have Not—remain divided. Since the inception of "our" fair country, division has been pumped into our homes, schools, jobs, and even places of worship. Allow me to remind you of the Constitution of the Unites States of America and quote: "We the people of the United States, in order to form a more perfect union, establish justice, insure domestic tranquility, provide for the common defense, promote the general welfare and secure the blessings of liberty to ourselves and our posterity..."

Union, domestic, common, ourselves, posterity. Why so much division? But back to our treaty, agreement, contract, constitution in which those it is made for are bound and those it is made by have room to deviate. Trickery, once again in its highest degree, and we wonder why we are faced with extreme proportions of rebelliousness.

All of this I became aware of simply by paying more attention. It was lessons of the sort that encouraged me to embrace my struggle. There remained one thing I hadn't fully learned to accept: my legal woes. And other than the State's racketeering case, I had not been spoken to or confronted about the double homicide case that led to my current incarceration. Additional frustration rose from the fact I had not heard a single word from my attorney Michael Robbins. How in the world was I to defend myself when I hadn't the slightest opportunity to prepare a defense?

Slowly but surely, time was passing by. One year, two years, then unexpectedly one day at 5 AM inside the year of 2004, my door in the MCU shook.

"Butler! Shower, court today."

Unprepared and still half asleep, I gave the thumbs up through the window of my cell's door. My door was opened, and I went to shower. While showering, I thought to myself, *Which of my many cases would I be going in front of the judge for today?* I knew it couldn't have been the State RICO case because two of my co-defendants on that charge were also housed in MCU and were not awakened for court. I hoped it was my latest charge, the double homicide. I had the other homicide case to fend off and remaining drug cases to resolve but their bails were all valid, and I had a clear path to freedom once I got the other murder monkeys off my back. It was a joy to get some movement outside the MCU. It was another step closer to the door for good, yet a hassle in getting there.

On previous court dates, I was always transported in the same armored truck with no view of anything, inside or out. This day was slightly different. The truck had been tweaked or was in disrepair, and I was able to catch a nice visual through a tiny crack in the window block. The past three years, I had seen none of the free world, so I was thrilled. While we sped through traffic lights with sirens screaming, I was able to steal a view of what became of the streets I once ran. Neighborhoods as I knew them no longer existed. They were torn down and replaced by government-subsidized homes with "curb appeal." On every block, there were rows of townhouses. Had I not known, I would've thought different, but I knew better. What I knew was no matter how much makeup is applied, what's underneath doesn't change. In this case, the pretty townhouses couldn't cover up the ugliness of the streets.

During my minutes of reminiscing, I felt the truck come to a stop and its doors open. I peeked out and what I saw left me flabbergasted. There were vehicles assigned to seal in the truck. From within one of those vehicles out hopped four SOG (Special Ops) officers, assault rifles in hand, who brought all traffic to a complete stop. Maybe something had happened. Surely, what I was seeing couldn't have been for me.

After stationed securely behind the gates of Essex County's Courthouse, I learned that indeed, I was the reason for all of the hoopla. With a scene like that, if the people inside the courthouse got wind I was the one responsible, the impression in their minds would be damning. In the court of law, perception, at times, was enough to seal your fate. All I wanted was a fair shake.

I was led to the jury room, which was the only place I could be held without revealing the SOG officers who hovered around me like I was the president. My attorney Michael Robbins walked in. His presence confirmed this court call was for the double homicide and exactly what I hoped for. Confident, maybe even cocky, Robbins approached with a swagger of his own as if I shouldn't have been upset about not seeing or speaking with him in over a year.

"Tewhan, you ready?"

"For what?" I asked.

"Well, I already spoke with your mother, and they brought your clothes down. Today, we're beginning jury selection. You nervous?"

The nerve of this man! My life came down to this moment. No timeouts, no do-over; just the now. Was I nervous? Hell yeah, I was nervous! In addition, I was angry. He spoke as if I should have had no worries with my life in the hands of twelve and two (twelve jurors and two alternates). Yet, with the best of game faces, I told him I was cool and shared my desire to put the whole ordeal behind me.

Next, I was unshackled, allowed to dress, and led to the courtroom to begin my jury sequester. In days, we had the jury and were ready to roll. Those chosen were supposed to be my peers, with the responsibility of weighing the evidence, or lack thereof, and ruling without prejudice.

"All rise!"

Opening arguments weren't even complete before the prosecutor came out scratching and clawing. Two weeks straight, repeatedly back and forth, the process became routine. Then, there came a delay in the proceedings that left me curious.

Robbins stood beside me, seemingly less confident than usual. Maybe my talks of how the system had it out for me were beginning to show more clearly. During our conversation, he informed me that two special investigators assigned to watch over the courtroom from beginning to end conferred with prosecutors on what was said to be a conspiracy of some sort between me and a juror. We were said to have been exchanging secret gang signs. And the juror was accused of wearing clothing outside of court that symbolized affiliation with the Bloods street gang—a red belt and San Francisco 49ers Jerry Rice jersey assumed to represent a Blood symbol.

With no proof, other than the word of special investigators and prosecutors, both of whose jobs were to secure a conviction, they backed the judge into a corner. Adamant the juror had ties and must have been lying about his true identity, he was forced to submit to fingerprinting. The court's instructions were followed. Prints returned; indeed he was a law-abiding citizen with no affiliation to any gang and/or association.

Wait, the plot thickens.

The system only trusts in the system when convenient. He was removed from my jury and replaced by a middle-aged white woman. *A jury of my peers.* Perception! And if that was not enough, the following day, I was presented with yet another obstacle. To prevent the jury from having knowledge I was already incarcerated, when recess was called, I had to sit back until the courtroom emptied out. While everyone else filed out, the judge ordered my attorney not to leave. A sidebar was needed.

This time, the prosecutors brought to the court's attention that one of their key witnesses no longer wanted to testify out of fear for herself and her family. Prosecution requested witness protection for the family.

My lawyer questioned the reason for the witness-protection request, fearful that along with yesterday's event, not to mention the heavy security throughout the courthouse—metal detectors strategically placed in front of the courtroom and requiring identification to enter a courtroom normally open to the public—would begin to raise the eyebrows of the jury and possibly bias their ruling. Perception!

Prosecution's argument said the witness's child had been threatened by a group of Bloods who promised death in return for any testimony. It was said I ordered those threats. This information prompted certain individuals to be barred from the court proceedings. Those who did attend were subjected to all kinds of prejudicial treatment and harassment.

Even after presenting identification, the court had one homegirl, Toya, escorted out of the courtroom and arrested, all in an attempt to discourage my support system. However, their antics proved not enough for my family.

Day in and day out, each time I hobbled into the courtroom, there sat my mother, Aunt Ann, her son Shaquan and daughter Sheyeast, my cousin Lynette, and my son's mother Alneisha Hall. During such a critical time in my life, I was grateful to be understood by those who mattered.

We resumed court proceedings and tried to make our way through the hurdles. The complete trial lasted a full two weeks, including closing arguments. Throughout the proceedings there were moments I couldn't help but feel like a spectator in one of the world's greatest legal demonstrations. The display Robbins put on compared to nothing I had ever witnessed in a courtroom. Now, I see why he strolled in with such confidence.

We hadn't spoken. But when it counted most, Robbins knew every little detail of my case and pinpointed every little mistake of law enforcement. Each day he picked away at the inconsistencies of witnesses' testimony and all but crucified the prosecution for a shabby investigation.

"The waste of taxpayers' hard-earned money is what this is," he yelled, before presenting the jury with that he called the scales of justice.

It was over. The look of defeat found its way into the eyes of the prosecutor. But of course it was a decision to be made by the jury. Deliberations. Would their decision be based on evidence or perception?

After the courtroom cleared, not even a full hour later, forty-five minutes to be exact, the bailiff announced the verdict was ready. It was one of two things: the State's case was either extremely strong or extremely weak. I was led from the bullpen into the courtroom, uncuffed, and told to take my position next to my attorney behind the defendant's table. My family was two rows behind me. I had so many mixed emotions, but I had to keep my composure.

I whispered to my attorney no matter the outcome I felt he did a wonderful job. I then turned in the direction of my mother and mouthed for her not to cry. I needed her strength now more than ever. She nodded her head in response. But her eyes already began to water. In walked the jury, one after another until the jurors' box was full.

"All rise, the Honorable Judge Harold Fullilove," said the bailiff.

The judge took his seat on the bench and situated the paperwork before him and asked, "Does the jury have a verdict?"

"Yes, Your Honor, we do," replied the jury foreman.

For a little over a minute, although words were spoken, I heard nothing until the ruling.

"Not guilty on all counts."

Screams of joy emanated from my family.

Judge Fullilove announced, "Mr. Butler, your matter before me has resulted in a full acquittal. You are hereby free to go."

I had been granted the one last opportunity I craved. All the things in life I never had the chance to do were about to be done. But my first line of business was to get my arms around my kids and assure them I would never leave them behind again.

Then, suddenly, the courtroom became so quiet you could hear a pin drop. I was unsure what happened. I followed the direction of everyone else's attention. I locked eyes with the prosecutor, who was in turn staring me down as if to say, "Not so fast."

"Your Honor, if I may bring it to the court's attention, Mr. Butler here has a Federal detainer."

The courtroom erupted.

Never let them see you sweat. I smiled, nudged my lawyer before they cuffed me, and asked him,

"Now you believe me?"

Special Operations escorted me out of the courtroom to the sounds of my family crying.

13

JUDICIAL GENOCIDE

BACK IN THE MCU, I wracked my brain trying to figure out what the detainer was all about and what the Feds could want. No matter how many times I pulled at my hair, nothing came to me. I remembered the rumors of the past, but as far as I knew nothing solid ever came of them. I had been in prison since 2002; it was now 2005. Why the wait? Was it last resort? Only time would tell.

With nature's course taking on a shape of its own and none other, I decided to rest and let it all be. Finally, after sitting around with no knowledge whatsoever about this new case, I received what was said to be an attorney visit. I quickly learned differently. As I entered the room, I immediately recognized the two men who sat before me. These were the same two men I saw trying to disguise themselves during my double homicide trial.

"So, Mass, we finally meet."

Both agents gave their names. The lead agent made clear his name was John Havens and the other I can't quite recall. He was more reserved and pretty much let Havens do all the talking. To my surprise, they weren't hostile, yet they were firm in making it clear they possessed the evidence needed to secure the death penalty for me.

I feared none of their rant of how witnesses were more afraid of them than what I could have done and how they'd been around since '99 and knew just about my every move. They told me they knew of my possession of cell phones within the prison and the creation of a new structure and even confessed to have been the ones behind the heavy scrutinizing of my mail. Over the years I had mail turned around, opened outside of my presence, and destroyed. Other times I was forced to read my mail and reply in the presence of investigative officers. Things were now beginning to make sense, but since the day of my arrest, I was resigned to the notion of never touching the streets again, so all of what was said held no bearing on how I was to proceed.

All my years of slanging and banging, trying to ignore this end, and the moment had arrived. On numerous occasions, meetings were held discussing loyalty, honor, and sacrifice. A sixty-eight-count Federal indictment would test those waters. I stared into the faces of both agents and gave up my life for those I loved.

"Whatever was supposedly done, I will take the weight for. You can cut everyone else loose."

In response, one agent stated, "My assessment of you was correct. I knew you would attempt such a thing, however, the only way for your homies to get away from this is by providing us with more information on you."

"Then so be it," I stated.

With cuffed hands, I wrote, "I'm never going home. Tell them whatever you want about me and only me, Mass."

Just like that, I ended the visit.

Back in my cell in the MCU, a whirlwind of emotions overtook me. Was I stupid for offering up my life? Would the same have been done for me? Didn't I owe it to those who walked beside me on this journey through life, or did any of it even matter? Most may not understand. I don't expect you too. It was what it was. Eighteen co-defendants bundled up into one big Federal RICO case.

After I found out the Feds placed a sticker on me, I sat alone in my cell unable to control the feelings of lonesomeness. Unsure of who to turn to I sought refuge in the one man I knew I could trust. I wrote a letter to my deceased father.

The exact date I can't remember. All days had begun to look alike. The only change was each twenty-four hours seemed to bring about a greater struggle than the last. Seated atop my rock-bound prison bunk, dressed in full prison gear (khaki top and bottom and beige prison-made state boots), I wished I was headed home. I used toothpaste to fasten newspaper to the light fixture to lessen the cell's bright light. This afforded me a glimpse of my shadow as it danced off the wall and played treacherous tricks with my mind. It was the only company permitted inside this hellhole. Still, there was silence. I couldn't hear the desperate cries of the convicts around me. It had been a while since I confided in anyone. I had grown leery of even my own conscience. I was alone, not a soul in sight, and filled with so much emotion. A lone teardrop cut through my reserved emotions and echoed within the silence and stillness of my surroundings. After pacing the floor for nearly an hour, I reached into one of my four bins we were allowed to store our personal property and pulled out a composition pad and pen and began to write:

Dear Dad,

Man, how I miss you. For some odd reason I feel like if you were still here my life would somehow be different. All of my life I've felt like I've been alone, forced to face the world all by myself. You were my savior. Everything you used to tell me seems to becoming into fruition. I remember you telling me the streets were no good, but I was too stubborn to listen. I see now your experience made you worthy of the advice you gave. The knowledge I felt I had was no match for your wisdom. Look at me now.

Dad, I pray that even with the decisions I've made I will not lose your love. I know we'll meet again, and I promise with the remainder of this life, and the next, to be the child that you created. After all, I am "YahYah's son."

Changing the pace, do you remember the day I came to Little City after having received news that Troub (Quadree) had been shot, and I had basically pled with you not to grab your gun and go out retaliating? I always knew you were down for whatever. I never told Troub how hyped up you got, but I'm sure he knows. We used to get our fair share of stories about you and Dip [Troub's father] back in your heyday.

But look, before I venture off, allow me to bring you up to speed on the latest. OK, I know you're curious but don't worry, mom is still holding it down. It took me a minute to get used to you two not together and imagining her move on, but I must admit she's still riding. Me, right before I came in I had a handsome son and a beautiful daughter—Tewhan Jr. and Zamel. They're not twins. They're about a month apart. Yeah, yeah I know. I managed to get caught up thinking with the wrong head. Stevie had a son—Little Quanir. Though prison has kept me away, I hear he's just like Stevie—bad as ever.

The jewels you also gave me regarding friends and how far and few they come— again, you were right. My incarceration has run many away. Thus, among the pack, still rest a few good men. If you remember (Lucien) Dough Boy, heavy-set kid with a swag something like Biggie Smalls who I met at Clifford Scott? Turned out to be one of my closest roadies. Since I been knocked he's kept my books fat, looks out for moms and, more importantly, he does what he can to keep the little one out of harm's way. A genuine, stand-up dude. [Years later Doughboy would be found dead inside his home. Home invasion. The truths as to what happened would never be discovered— to the law, just another case closed.]

On another note I can't give you too much on the extended family, Butlers or Smiths. This unit I'm in only allows selected visitors. To be honest, I can't say that I would request visits anyway. Don't want to be seen like I'm calling for family now that the road has gotten rough. My apologies. You taught me to always keep family first, yet I let my foolish pride keep me away. Dad, I feel like I've been losing it. I hadn't had a peaceful moment in what feels like forever but the solitude is somewhat pleasant. However, there is a little too much time to think and I feel like every day my room gets smaller; the walls close tighter. John Baines in *Morals for the 21st Century* states, "We only see what we expect and wish to see and close our eyes to the rest." This secluded and forsaken cell forces man to defiantly face exactly what he created. Ran around like my shit didn't stink and now I'm buried in it.

Apart from that, I'm not sure if I ever told you? Probably not, as our relationship lacked in-depth conversations, but I always sought power in the streets to mirror your image. When I was a kid and we would pull up at the projects, bumping oldies mix-tapes with the O'Jays, The Temptations, Luther Vandross, and others. As soon as your clean Cadillac was spotted overtop of the music, I could hear nearly all we passed shouting, "YahYah." The recognition you had made me feel important. So as I grew older, maybe for some of the wrong reasons, I chased power. I'll tell you this though, when I finally captured what I believed to be power, the responsibility that came with it seemed to suck more life out of me than it did to enable me. I never got around to asking you what exactly defines power. Surely, being trapped twenty-three hours a day in a cell wouldn't have been it. I won't deceive you. If anyone knows me, it's you. I lost myself in the chase. The image began meaning more than the reality. Now, my inescapable reality is prison. Locked away for years. I just recently was acquitted of two counts of felony murder. Now, I have the Feds on my back screaming forever. Through other means I've been able to shoot back and forth with Troub, who, as you can imagine, finds himself as one of my many co-defendants. We decided that if we could get our hands on twenty years, we'd take it. Sounds crazy, huh? Fishing for time like that. We've been hearing everything from LIFE to multiple LIFE sentences to the death penalty. We'll see.

Almost forgot, not too long before I got locked I had gotten engaged. Yeah, I was ready to throw in the towel. Sad to say, she left me. I paid more attention to the streets than I did home. Although I never knew you for doing time, maybe you can help me to understand how the lifestyle is cool until the consequences roll around? Then it becomes, nothing you were doing was enough and everything you had done was the opposite of right. Crazy, huh? I guess all around the board it's a lose-lose.

OK, one last thing. Do you recall the day I slipped up trying to play Romeo and left school early with a female friend and, for showcase purposes, had left my pistol (.38 Special) atop the dresser in plain view only for you to spot it as soon as you entered the bedroom? Bad enough I was skipping school. My heart damn near jumped out of my chest when you walked in. I just knew you were going to yell, punish me, whip me, something. Instead, you turned around and left like it was nothing. Having had you do nothing pained me more than any discipline you could have ever given. That day I knew you had let go. I have to ask, did that moment change your life like it changed mine?

On that note, I leave as I came—in peace.

I love you Dad.

Your son,

Mass

That night all that wasn't revealed to me by the agents was plastered on every news station. Fitted onto the screen sat me and Troub's mug shots, side by side, with the intersection of North 15th Street and William Street sprawled in the backdrop. News reporters, channel after channel:

"LIVE—BREAKING NEWS: U.S. Attorney Christopher Christie set to make an announcement regarding the sweep of eighteen members of New Jersey's largest, oldest and most deadly street gangs, the Double ii Bloods, led by the two men you see here, both of whom are already housed in New Jersey's prison system, Tewhan Butler and Quadree Smith."

Next, a copy of the Federal indictment filled the screen.

With this came everything I should have been leaving behind.

Attempted murder of another person, Racketeering Act 5
(A) Conspiracy and two attempts to commit murder (B) and (C) Racketeering
Act 6, counts 7, 8, 9, 10, 11 and 39 (924c)
Conspiracy to murder, murder of _____ and 3 attempted murders,
Racketeering Act 7, counts 12, 13, 14, 15, 16, 17, 18, 19 and 20
Conspiracy and attempt to murder _____, Racketeering Act 8, counts
21, 22, and 41 (924c)
Robbery of _____, Racketeering Act 9, count 42 [924(1)]

Conspiracy and attempt to commit murder of _____, Racketeering Act 10, counts 25, 26, 27 and 43 (924c)

Attempted murder of _____, Racketeering Act 11, count 28 and 44 (924c)

Attempted murder of _____, Racketeering Act 12, count 29, 30 and 45 (924c)

Murder of _____, Racketeering Act 13

Attempted murder of _____, Racketeering Act 14

(Information from Federal Indictment CR. No. 03-844)

Down the list the reporter read: murder, robbery, kidnapping, arson, drug conspiracy, gun trafficking. There was no need to see any more. If I didn't believe the stories then, I did now. I decided it was best I reach out and see what was circulating in the town. I worked my hand and was able to place a call to my mother. She answered the phone in tears and told me people had been calling all day, suddenly masters of the law and how it all applied, and were way too generous with their opinions. Most were judgmental people who posed as friends but really had little to no genuine concern. They simply wanted the inside scoop. Too much for her to take, it brought her to tears. I told her the only thing I could:

"I love you, Ma. It's okay."

I had failed. I was soiled in the streets, blinded by Blood, red-ragging, and toe-tagging. There's always a price to pay.

If clearance came back from Washington, D.C., to pursue the death penalty, I was sure to be fighting for my life, literally. In no way was it okay. In no way was it okay to leave my son and daughter to grow up without their father, and my mother to have both kids buried in the system. And me, well, I guess this was what I wanted, my dish served cold.

Shortly thereafter I received a visit from my state attorney, John McMahon—a cool yet conservative white guy, glasses, with a light sunroof haircut. McMahon seemed to really care about the oppressive nature of injustice and those to whom it was prejudicially distributed. He informed me via video-conference that the state was prepared to do away with the 2000 gas station homicide. They wouldn't drop it completely but were willing to downgrade it to manslaughter, leaving me with a seven-year sentence. I was already in for just under four years, most of which I spent in the Management Control Unit. Another three years was cake. I told him I'd take it.

"OK, just give me a few to notify the courts and I'll set up another visit to have this issue squared away. By the way, good luck with the other thing," stated McMahon.

"Thanks, I'm sure I'll need it," I replied.

The other thing he spoke of was the Federal case, which was a hot topic on the street and in legal circles throughout the state. Good thing it took some days to resolve the state matter. I learned it was all legal strategy concocted by the Feds. The plan was to offer me a number small enough to jump on, keep me off the streets, and provide them the opportunity to secure a conviction later down the line through a superseding indictment. Double jeopardy did not apply. The Federal courts and the state courts are two separate jurisdictions. This valuable information came by the way of my newly appointed Federal attorney.

For the third time in a matter of weeks, I was shackled and led to an attorney/client visitation booth. I sat back and waited, figuring it to be McMahon. The door opened and this was certainly not John. It was a sister. One who obviously ignored the "No you can'ts" in life and grabbed hold of her "Yes you cans." She had a 2000 swag with an Afrocentric twist of the 70s. I felt her confidence before she reached out to shake my hand with a friendly face and a hint of no-nonsense in her demeanor. I knew she was a winner. One whom I felt would fight to the bitter end; just what I needed to go up against the Feds, who around this time had about a ninety-percent conviction rate if not higher.

My new Federal attorney's name was Wanda Akin. After we worked through the brief formalities, she wasted no time and got right down to business. In comparison to the streets—Ms. Akin was getting her grind on and hustling hard. In a short period, we managed to cover plenty of ground. She revealed to me, as she said, "What

I didn't want to hear." They had people, supposed friends of mine, on their side. Still, determined to fight and win, she gave me my arraignment date and began adjusting her schedule to do what was needed to prepare our defense. (*Hustle, hustle, hustle hard!*) Maybe, just maybe, things were going to be okay after all.

A brief forty-eight hours later, I stood in Newark's Federal Court and listened as prosecutors, I suppose for shock value, read off all sixty-eight charges one by one along with the maximum time each carried. My big dreams of getting my loved ones out of the 'hood had gotten me stuck. What was to be the end for me was only the beginning. But on the bright side, we learned Washington shot down the death penalty. I was left facing a total of six life sentences, plus 130 years. Talk about overkill!

Looking back on that day, the court proceedings were a circus. There was no space for all eighteen of us to occupy one courtroom, and they were fearful that if we did, it posed greater security risk. We took back hallways and rode in double-door elevators. The courtroom was surrounded. In addition, squads of Marshals were assigned to oversee certain inmates. I knew then, we were in for a long ride.

Still tightly fitted inside the Management Control Unit, with more than enough time to think, I looked at the vast number of gangs spread throughout New Jersey—predominantly Bloods, Crips, Latin Kings, and Netas, in places like Asbury Park, Camden, Elizabeth, Jersey City, Paterson, Plainfield, Trenton, and the entire Essex County—and wondered how many gang members were already sentenced to a similar fate and didn't yet know. But why? Was it because we, as a people, fail to accept responsibility for providing today's youth with not every answer, but at least some direction so that they could find their own? Why have we gotten away from the days when the village raised the child?

The current of the sea dictates the direction of a boat until someone takes control. The same things apply with the lives of our youth. Did you know evaluations are being done on elementary school kids to determine how many prisons need to be built in the future and why? It's statistically proved that we tend to give up on our own at the first sign of trouble.

Just as I had been informed by my attorney, on January 5, 2006, the Feds came with their superseding indictment, adding to it the 2000 gas station homicide. Stockpiling charges on top of charges figured for better headlines and could help sway public perception.

In 2006, the Double ii Bloods case became the benchmark for just about everything wrong with New Jersey's cities: guns, drugs, and gangs. But what was not mentioned was the meticulous group of self-serving politicians who failed to address the problem in its early stages. Many of these same politicians held office and did nothing to seriously confront the gang issue in its early stages. It seems it only became a problem years later when gangs entered the suburbs. Once that happened, suddenly gangs became the platform to secure points for the political elite. And there you had the impetus for shallow strategies to destroy the rabble. It became one wrong move, association, imprudent conversation, or the use of slang such as *homie* and *what's poppin'*, that made you a prime candidate for a life sentence under the general description of "Federal racketeering." Once you were on their radar, it was watch you, arrest you, and prosecute you. Next, you were locked up, deemed a threat and hidden within the Department of Corrections' and Bureau of Prisons' Security Threat Group Management Unit.

It was all very similar to today's heroin problem in the suburbs. Heroin in the inner-city meant little, but once this ever so powerful drug reached the suburbs it compelled immediate action from politicians.

In the pages of the indictment, I learned the Feds had been watching for years. Certain counts dated back as early as 2000. They had been everywhere, providing us just enough room to box ourselves in. This entire time we had fooled no one. Things we believed were done in the dark were actually on display, being recorded, logged, and sealed as evidence. Much of this evidence, even after formally charged, was hidden from my attorney and me. Each time we addressed the court with legal motions and pressed for discovery, our requests were shot down. My lawyer kept on. (*Hustle real hard!*)

Finally, when the courts did decide to reveal some of what they had, months had passed and their disclosure was nothing more than a chip off the block. Most of which on my behalf were hundreds of letters written to me by other Bloods throughout the prison system and transcripts of a meeting held where they planted a recording device on one of our own. It was nothing to really give up the impression of defeat.

They offered thirty-five years. It was most definitely a drastic change from the six life sentences plus 130 years I faced after the superseding indictment. But there was no way I was going to sign away the next thirty-five years of my life. The typical threats began through emails, phone calls, and at times, court appearances. Take a plea or go to trial, where the maximum sentence would be sought. It was a no-go. The way the game was normally played was different this time. Out of the eighteen indicted, only two had copped (Anthony "PB" Ward and Jamal "J-Rock" Coward) and the original trial date set was nearing.

Court call!

The Feds did not want to appear as if they were losing control of the situation and made room for us all in the courtroom for an evidentiary hearing. They lined us all up in the rows of the jury booth, and it was like old times. We were back together. The worries of what we were facing vanished. The power of togetherness is amazing. Over the years, the prison system had separated us all. Most, I hadn't seen in years, but before the reunion got too out of hand, Assistant U.S. Attorneys Serena Vash and Mark Agnifilo walked in. Behind them were men carrying boxes with what seemed to be some difficulty. Next, came a few more men who began to fiddle with wires and set up what I believed to be a projector and screen. At this point none of us knew this was an evidentiary hearing, so what we saw raised eyebrows and led to whispers back and forth.

I had already learned the Federal process ran differently from what I was used to in the State. Everything with the Feds was for shock value—the big bang, intimidation, and dramatic. In a sense, all of my State run-ins now seemed somewhat generic. The Feds were putting on.

When you entered the courtroom you instantly felt the scales were weighted in their favor. There were all sorts of subliminal and overt psychological tactics that were hard to overcome. I wanted to believe, but the reality of the obstacles before me kept optimism at bay.

Even the Federal courtroom's decor was over the top. It was like an elegant ballroom of sorts, complete with statuesque columns, state-of-the-art equipment for the stenographer, and wall-to-wall carpet. I guess so the high-priced lawyers and death-seeking prosecutors wouldn't scuff their thousand dollar loafers. What wasn't carpet was marble; paintings that in my eyes resembled Mozart; and the untouchable and, in their eyes, priceless, gavel. Above it all was the Seal of the United States as if to say in this room YOU will not win.

Once the Feds were set up, our lawyers were granted access to the courtroom. By this time, Ms. Akin and I became quite familiar. I had developed a high level of trust in her judgment. She knelt beside me so not even the men next to me could hear, and she instructed me to pay very close attention and say nothing. As my lawyer, she could not have cared less about my friendship with others. She always made it clear she, at all times, had my best interest at heart. On occasion, we would have brief disagreements as she would ask, "Do you trust so and so?" She had seen it all before and would simply end the discussion with, "I hope you're right." Though I never showed it, I did as well. My loyalty was often times blinding. I learned pressure busts more than pipes. With naiveté, I acted as if everyone could handle the hardships of incarceration.

The hearing began. Assistant U.S. Attorney Mark Agnifilo stepped in front of the jury booth where my co-defendants and I were seated and proceeded to call out names, aliases, dates of crimes committed, and not only how they occurred, but a step-by-step rehash of events as if he was there.

"That's not all, gentlemen," Agnifilo spoke. "Those boxes you see over there," pointing to the prosecution's table, "are filled with an assortment of guns and heroin confiscated and purchased from each and every one of you during our investigation. If for one second, you guys believe we don't have enough evidence, you're sadly mistaken."

When done, almost as if on cue, the lights dimmed, speakers began to crackle, and the projector lit up. My voice blasted over the speakers and throughout the courtroom:

"I'm facing the rest of my life in prison for each and every one of y'all, including myself. Do I regret it? Hell no!"

I could do nothing but shake my head in disgust. The moment grew still. Seriousness overtook the room. There were no longer questions. Answers were laid out. The stakes on our freedom just doubled. My face showed calm but, internally, my heart was on fire. What we all just heard was clear evidence somebody, one of our own, stooped so low as to wear a wire in attempt to crush his own gang. The finale came when the inside of an all-too-familiar apartment showed up on the screen and revealed a group of homeboys discussing a murder plot. For this hearing, the Feds had pulled out all the stops.

"Today and today only, do these offers stand," said Agnifilo.

Down the line, pleas were called out—ten years here, fifteen years there, and so on. For me, and a few others, the offer was thirty-five years. Take it, or leave it!

There's always a trick. In closing, it was said that the pleas were global. Meaning, if all refused to agree, the plea was of no use to anyone. It was an underhanded tactic. They knew the likelihood of us all taking a plea for thirty-five years was slim; it left us in a position to be crossed out by those who knew no better. Still, everyone refused. Court was adjourned.

The following afternoon, during a lawyer visit with Ms. Akin, she relayed a message to me, sent directly from the Federal prosecutors themselves.

"Tell your client if he thinks he has more power than we do, we'll show him."

Calls were already placed to my co-defendants' lawyers to inform them the global plea was off and their defendants could now cop as they pleased. For some strange reason beyond me, prosecutors were under the impression I stopped others from pleading out. A case that should have been based solely on right and wrong had now become one about power—a continuance of fear for that they didn't understand. This battle was one I wasn't willing to entertain. If they felt it enhanced their chances for conviction to lessen the years of incarceration offered to others, it was fine by me.

The pleas were non-cooperational, so they obviously presented no greater difficulty in defending my case. However, I found humor in the fact government officials were in a *tit-for-tat* with a twenty-six-year old kid from the slums of dirty Jersey.

I prepared for trial, or, at least, that's what I liked to call it. Still, the government had refused to hand over any true material evidence, using the excuse that the Double ii Bloods had no hang-ups with "hushing" witnesses. Ms. Akin and I made best of what we had. Before I knew it, I was transported to court and told we were to begin jury sequester the next day. I hadn't even realized how fast time flew by. I had grown accustomed to the timeless isolation of the MCU.

I had recently wrapped up the double homicide trial, and I had some idea of what to expect. I arrived at court ready as ever. By this time, many of my co-defendants had pled out. There were seven of us left (Troub, Flock, YG, Death, SP, and James Dillard) to fend off a sixty-eight-count indictment. I still had no clue how were we going to do it. Our ability to mount a defense was minimal. The courts granted the prosecution the right to withhold certain discoveries up until, basically, hours before a witness was to testify. How do you prepare? Your guess is as good as mine, yet the game must go on.

For the remainder of the week, our lawyers filed one motion after another (Writ of Habeas Corpus, Limine, Bill of Particulars, Discovery, Objection to Photograph Submitting, Severance). We repeatedly made attempts to level the playing field. Motion filed, motion denied. Trial hadn't even started and already I felt I was losing. I felt I was fighting an uphill battle and covering little to no ground.

July 7, 2006, was the actual day of jury sequester. If any questions remained, they were soon to be answered. Surely, as I recount this particular moment, I want to feed you a story of how we all sat around the L-shaped defendants' table with an immeasurable amount of bravado, but to do so would be awfully misleading. Our pre-trial motions had been shot down. Prosecution, in a last-minute attempt to remedy the case, offered us thirty years, which we all refused. To our surprise, we were informed our jury would be picked anonymously. There was certainly no time for carelessness.

Trial was scheduled to last anywhere between four and six months. Any single one of the sixty-eight counts was capable of finishing us for good. We were at war. For weeks, my co-defendants and I struggled to read the every move of those who would issue judgment on our case. And though no one dared say it, worry and frustration overran us all. We never discussed if we had a legitimate chance at winning. Perhaps, nobody wanted to be the first to admit defeat.

With the pressure on, prosecutors angled to apply more. They squeezed.

"Today, Your Honor, we would like to bring it to the court's attention that we are currently contemplating superseding this indictment, adding to it, one, a conspiracy to commit murder, where we have evidence proving defendants Butler and Smith were overheard discussing a plot against Your Honor, and, two, tampering with a witness, as we have been notified that both defendants sent threats to the Passaic County Jail to a defendant they believe to be cooperating." (Passaic County Jail held additional units for Federal detainees.)

In unison, Troub and I looked at one another and knew there was no truth to such claims. We also knew our odds for victory dropped drastically. The offer of thirty years began to sound more and more tolerable. But that offer was off the table. However, we knew if we decided to plead out, the courts wouldn't refuse. No one looked forward to a lengthy trial. We slept on it.

Not even twenty-four hours later, we were back in the bullpen, dressed to the nines. Beside me in one pen was Troub, beside him was the homie YG, and across the hall sat Flock, Death, and S.P. James Dillard did not have to attend for medical reasons.

During our court proceedings I learned that Mr. Dillard had passed away due to health complications. With all due respect, maybe his death resulted from his legal troubles. Whether innocent or guilty, Mr. Dillard had been accused of distributing firearms to the Double ii Bloods. The law's assessment was he desired a few extra bucks and had now received more than he bargained for.

The decision to be made was in no way a walk in the park. To sign your life over for any amount of time was difficult. Let alone thirty years. The next three decades in prison or life could be seen as a no-brainer, but for some, thirty years was the remainder of their lives. As for us, we were still relatively young, so if we decided to take a plea, daylight would still welcome us home.

"Sweeny [a name given to me by my homeboy Tall Dawg from the set's Steel Click and used only by those in my inner-circle], you got thirty in you, Blood?" A question we were all silently asking ourselves.

"Ay Blood, I got whatever they throwing," I replied.

"But damn, thirty?" Troub asked.

"Yeah, homie, that shit heavy. Under different circumstances, I couldn't see it, but you already know if we go the distance they gonna smoke us."

"Ay, YG, what you think?"

YG was as loyal and committed as they came. This is the same Y.G. who the media in its deceitful and sensational ways went on years later to give a false account of his offenses on the History Channel's *Gangland* series, in which they stated he killed a father who supposedly confronted the gang for recruiting his eight-year-old son.

"Dig, homeboy, I'm riding with y'all. Whatever y'all want to do is cool with me," YG replied.

A decision was made. The courts were informed, and we were brought in the courtroom to begin the proceedings.

"So, Mr. Butler, is it true you are willing to admit to the 2000 homicide you have been charged with in this indictment?"

Pause . . . I conferred with my attorney though the decision was ultimately mine to make. I answered with a simple, "Yes."

Assistant U.S. Attorney Serena Vash questioned again, "Also, it is said that you are willing to admit in detail the manner in which you committed the crime."

"Yeah," I stated, with anger in my tone.

"So do you mind telling us what happened October 19, 2000?"

I had them figured out. In doing so, it would surely corroborate the ills propagated about my character. I hated I had put myself in such a situation. Free of outside incrimination, I described the fashion the crime was to have been committed. They were already under the impression they possessed the motive as legal documentation states:

Days before the murder, RDT (victim) contacted the Essex County Prosecutor's Office and informed an unidentified detective that he had a verbal dispute with me over drug sales in which I stated I had an itchy trigger finger. With this testimony to corroborate the homicide, they chose to look no further for a suspect.

"Okay, we are willing to accept your guilty plea and will request to the court the same."

After it was all said and done, I was unsure as to what to feel. All I knew was I was ready to receive my sentence and move on. To begin a new chapter of my life, I needed to bring the current one to a close. Consequence: 360 months spelled it out perfectly. My dues for a life I failed to take better care of. Satisfied with a lifestyle full of todays, I discontinued my search for tomorrow. I sold myself short and this was what it all amounted to.

With nothing left to do but read over the terms of the plea agreement, sign, and get my show on the road, I entered the courtroom the next day only to be met by disbelief. Prior to the courtroom being filled, my attorney exited the judge's chamber. Alongside her, in perfect stride, was Assistant U.S. Attorney Vash with a look on her face I'll never forget. It was a look of war, revenge, no mercy, and no compassion. You know how the saying goes, "If looks could kill." Seconds later Judge Katharine Hayden walked in and took the bench.

"I've been made aware that there has been a problem regarding the pleas of the remaining defendants," spoke the judge.

I thought, *A problem? How could there be?* Just yesterday, we sat here and discussed the terms that resulted in me admitting to a murder charge. I looked at Ms. Akin and asked, "What problem?" feeling my temper beginning to rise as I inquired about the supposed issue prosecution had with the mutually agreed upon deal.

"Your Honor I have been informed by my superiors that we will no longer be accepting the guilty pleas entered yesterday," said Assist U.S. Attorney Vash

Here were the courts playing with my life as though it was nothing.

"Just a minute, Tewhan," mouthed Ms. Akin, trying to keep her focus on what was being said by the prosecution.

I had grown tired. There was no minute. In any second, I was going to blow! For months I was forced to sit by quietly while prosecutors, the media, and others ran my name through the mud as if I was nothing more than a monster without a conscience. I blew!

Rising from my seat, I yelled out, "I got something to say!"

Shock pervaded the courtroom. Special Ops guards and Marshals alike rushed toward me, uncertain of my next move. Before things got too far out of hand, Judge Hayden intervened.

"Okay, Mr. Butler, what is it you have to say?"

So much was bottled up inside, I had no clue where I would begin or end. I simply spoke from the heart.

"Your Honor, it's clear that everything in one's power is being done to twist us out of a fair shake. Yesterday, prior to me admitting guilt, I was told our pleas were good. Now today you tell me they no longer stand. How am I supposed to go to trial when everyone in the courtroom heard me say I did it?"

"Well, Mr. Butler, that information will not be used against you; therefore, the jurors will have no knowledge of it."

"But I know, you know, and the prosecution knows. Now I'm forced to trial and to prove innocence when it's clear I'm guilty. I'm asking for one thing, Your Honor."

"And what is that, Mr. Butler?"

I replied, "That you stop signing writs for me to attend. I waive my appearance. Just send my guilty verdict to the prison."

Conspiracy theorist or whatever, I felt the justice being dished out was biased. I wondered if justice just some of the time could be seen as justice at all. Well, this system of ours—yes, yours too—believes so.

"Are you sure that's what you want?"

"Yeah, I'm sure."

"Okay."

Prior to taking a seat, I looked at my co-defendants and told them straight up, "I'm done with this shit."

The track had been laid and I sure as hell felt railroaded. I did not know the next time I would see any of my co-defendants or if I would ever see them again. Physically, for us, the buck stopped here. Our ties were to be severed. In my heart and mind they would forever accompany my every step. Neither struggle, nor time would alter that. But this day the system was forcing us apart. I only knew my fate. I could no longer protect them. They could no longer protect me. Love was the only thing to keep us connected from here on out.

What I failed to see in the past was now right before my eyes. There was no winning in this game. No matter how long you shake the dice, it's only a matter of time before you lose and lose big. My lifestyle was a gamble and from the day I entered the streets, I was one roll away.

When the day's proceedings were complete, I did away with any emotion I held and set my sights on the discomforts of a lifetime in the penitentiary. There was no doubt in my mind the verdict would read guilty. Did I need to hear them say it? Absolutely not.

There was too much riding on the outcome of our case. The media-loving U.S. Attorney's Office pumped and primed the public with the Federal government's position that the Double ii Bloods case was to be groundbreaking and would serve as a wake-up call and warning shot to other gang members throughout the state. To allow us the chance to walk free was a hit you could bet your bottom dollar they weren't going to take.

War had been declared when I was first made aware of the Federal RICO indictment on October 1, 2004, ironically my birthday. One thing guaranteed in relation to war: death or submission is always responsible for its end. A valuable lesson I picked up studying books like *The Art of War* and *The 48 Laws of Power*.

Following the prior day's mild outburst, I was awakened at 5 AM.

"Butler, shower. Court call."

Didn't I make it clear I wanted no part of the tyranny? I knew what needed to be done. Today was definitely going to be the last time they transported me to Federal court.

On my way, all sorts of thoughts ran through my mind. Whatever action I was to take would have to ensure my point was made: I would not be attending.

When we arrived at the courthouse, I noticed a quick deviation from the regular routine. Instead of changing out of our prison clothes for civilian clothes and waiting to be called up, we bypassed all bullpens and headed straight to the courtroom. As we rode the elevator up, I wondered what awaited me when we got there. I entered not sure what to expect. My eyes peered around for my attorney. I spotted Ms. Akin already seated behind the defendant's table, skimming legal documents, and jotting notes on her pad. I casually took my place beside her.

I realized things changed. From what I saw, the plea agreement was back on the table. I felt like I was standing on the edge of a cliff with no parachute, no safety net, and wind everywhere except beneath my wings. I read the plea agreement again, word for word, page by page. Of course, it meant I would be incarcerated for an estimated 10,950 days. However, what was not in writing was that if it wasn't life, it wasn't long. I would still see daylight. And if light symbolized knowledge and light travels at 186,000 miles per second, 11,160,000 per minute, 669,600,000 per hour, and 16,070,400,000 per day. In time, knowledge acquired would bring about under-standing—an understanding that would come only in time and illuminate a pathway out of the darkness. Knowledge and understanding would bring me peace.

"Good morning, Tewhan," Ms. Akin greeted me and handed over the documents I saw her reviewing when I approached. "Read through this carefully and when you're done, you and I will go through it again."

I signed the plea agreement. And finally felt I could now focus on self, most importantly for me. Second, for my family and comrades who matter the most. No later than the dawn of a new day, as to be expected, the headlines they so desired were printed.

"BLOODS GANG LEADERS ADMIT MURDER"

April 16, 2007, was sentencing day, and the courtroom was filled with many unknown faces. No cameras, yet plenty of news reporters were seated, pens moving, documenting every move and every word. Nobody wanted to miss a thing. Everyone was there to witness what was considered to be the fall of the man held responsible, in large part, for the gang epidemic that had plagued the state and now had grown up and down the East Coast. Federal agents who dedicated years of their life to the case sat in anticipation of the moment their investigative work paid off. Finally, the case was coming to a close. I was the first of dozens of defendants to be sentenced. For them it was a show. For me it was my life. The curtain was raised.

I stood shackled and expressionless. Would I address the courts? What would I say? How would I say it? How much time would I get?

A variety of conversations were taking place at once, with me at the pinnacle of them all. Today there was interest, and tomorrow it would be yesterday's news. In the exact place I was standing, there would be another stranded, left to fend off the vultures who saw such a critical moment as nothing more than an opportunity for a pay raise and personal advancement. What if it were their child?

Who would be next to benefit and profit from the sun, moon, and stars being snatched from another's sky?

The Court: "Good afternoon. Are all here and ready?"

And just like that, the courtroom quieted down and the proceedings were underway. Much of what would happen next was understood, yet there was still a chance things could change for the worst. Even though I signed to a stipulated thirty years, it was still at the discretion of the courts to adhere to the recommendations set forth by the U.S. Attorney's Office. Under Federal sentencing guidelines, my offense level was at forty; 360 months to life across the board. That left plenty of room to shake things up if the judge so well pleased. Thus we knew to tread lightly in the deep waters of justice. After the prosecution and my attorney's response, the judge went on.

The Court: "All right, we are here in the matter of sentencing of Mr. Tewhan Butler. May I have counsel's appearances, please?"

Ms. Vash: "Good afternoon, Your Honor. Assistant U.S. Attorney, Serena Vash for the U.S. Attorney's office."

Ms. Akin: "Wanda M. Akin, Your Honor, representing Mr. Tewhan Butler."

The Court: "I should say at the outset—you can be seated Ms. Akin—that I have received very full detailed submissions from all parties entitled and obligated to make submissions. I don't have everything on the bench with me that I have been going over, but you could assume that the robing room is littered with quite a few documents that I have had the benefit of receiving, reviewing, and taking to heart. So I am prepared for the oral arguments and presentations on the part of counsel."

My attorney, Ms. Akin, then took to the podium, prepared to present the legal niceties associated with the state of affairs.

Note: the following is condensed to minimize the proceeding and to give prominence to certain issues.

Ms. Akin: "I come to you today, saying that it's a lawyer's job to zealously represent the client's interest against all the world, and at the same time to respect the dignity of the court. So keeping that in mind and realizing that today which starts the closure of this entire case with respect to forty-five individuals, not Just Mr. Butler, I would indicate that emotion is first and foremost for the victims and their surviving family members . . .It's an emotional day for Mr. Butler, the self-professed leader of this gang, and he is being sentenced first. And it's emotional as well because of the sentence that's agreed upon and that sentence contemplates thirty years . . .Continuing on . . .minus some technical adjustments that we'll discuss and that I'll embark on here today, that this is for Mr. Butler, a man of twenty-seven years, this is tantamount to a life sentence, given the actuarial research that we have done . . .On Mr. Butler's behalf, I have sought to find effective ways to communicate in this emotionally charged environment to the court how Mr. Butler feels in terms of his acceptance of responsibility . . .

"He says 'I'm definitely remorseful for any and all violent acts that took place throughout the course of the time that I may have had a part of, directly or indirectly. I am definitely remorseful for the people that lost their lives. I am remorseful to the people who lost their family members. Kids that no longer have parents because of certain acts that was committed. Mothers and fathers who no longer have children because of certain acts that was committed. I have a son of my own now. I left my son when he was three months old. There's a strong possibility that the next time I get to lay hands on my son, he will be my age now. I haven't been able to touch my son since I have been incarcerated. I have been incarcerated for the last four and a half years. My son is still alive, but I feel like I lost my son. My son doesn't know me. I can't really sit here and say that I know my son. I can only imagine. There are times I can feel the pain of what certain people go through when they lose members of their family, their companions and loved ones for life. I can write my son. I took that away from other people. I can call my son. I took away a big part of their life.'"

Ms. Akin resumed, "Also with respect to Mr. Butler's written letter to the court, I wanted to highlight that he said in that letter, *'I stand before the court today in remorse with great embarrassment, remorse for the victims whom I have aggrieved directly or indirectly, regret for my actions and poor choices. And finally, embarrassment and shame for the hurt and pain I selfishly imposed upon my family. I apologize open-endedly to each and every one of the parties mentioned. Sincerely.'*

"And lastly, Your Honor, in conclusion and just stressing to the court that Mr. Butler is not asking for any special consideration or certainly not any favors in the sentencing by the court here today. He acknowledges that he's not finished yet; he has a long ways to go and that his transformation has just begun. Thank you, Your Honor."

The Court: "Thank you, Ms. Akin."

Following Ms. Akin's emotionally driven presentation on my behalf, what was to be expected clearly made its way into the room. A picture, painted with a stroke of genius to outshine Picasso. Enough was never enough.

The Court: "Thank you, Ms. Vash."

Ms. Vash: "Thank you, Your Honor."

Now in the courtroom as opposed to the media, the Federal government had the opportunity to once again give form and motive to their case against forty-five lives (eighteen indicted and the forty-five total connected to the case). First Assistant U.S. Attorney Vash addressed a few legal issues related to the plea agreement and sentencing. When complete, she took flight:

"First, as Your Honor is well aware, as we all, there are two sides to every coin and the government has no doubt, I have no doubt that Mr. Butler is loved by his family, loved by his friends and that he is going to be missed by his son. I have no doubt that he's intelligent. And I submit to Your Honor in part that's what made him so dangerous . . . Tewhan Butler, known as 'Massacre' on the street, also known as 'Mass,' was the 101 of the Double ii Bloods street gang; the first Bloods set on the East Coast. He ordered disciplines and he beat people into the gang. Tewhan Butler single-handedly is responsible for spreading the Double II Bloods throughout East Orange and now Trenton, throughout New Jersey. And for over decades, he and his fellow Bloods members committed the most heinous acts of violence, plagued the streets with drugs. They took hold of and terrorized East Orange . . . His own parents taught him that you work hard; you get an education. And what—instead, what Tewhan Butler is that he saw the opportunity for power; power through the Bloods gang—he was the leader—and he seized that opportunity. He committed violence, he preached violence and he destroyed people's lives . . .

"He could have succeeded. He could have given back to his community. Instead, he preyed on his community. If anything, he failed his community. And he sought power for power's sake . . . I fear Your Honor, that his participation and his leadership will continue both where he is now in Trenton [prison] and wherever he goes. I hope I'm wrong. I hope he really has taken the first steps of transformation. I hope he really was blinded, but I have no track record to suggest that . . . And I would like to let Your Honor know that the victim of every shooting, every stabbing, every slashing in the Double II Bloods case was a young African American. And every one of the homicide victims in this case was a young black man. Most of them were fathers who left their children fatherless. All of them have families who loved them and families whose lives are shattered now, Judge, forever. These young men, the victims, left great goals unattained, great dreams unrealized and their boundless potential dies with, every one of them was killed in the street . . . Your Honor, it is the government's position for his crimes, Mr. Butler should be sentenced to a period of incarceration of 360 months and not a single day less. Thank you."

Ms. Vash continued, and we all listened. I thought of everything I wanted to tell my homies but had failed to verbalize; like life being a reward or a consequence of one's actions and inactions; how we had allowed circumstance to affect our self-esteem, alter our sense of security, and feed us misconceptions of manhood; how we all had within us limitless potential but how we must not be afraid to believe in ourselves; and how despair had stolen our lives and now it was time to reclaim them.

I read that men and women are like caterpillars and they become beautiful butterflies when their potential is recognized. And with this, as a butterfly aimlessly flaps around unsure of his or her power, they do not understand their strength and purpose will someday become powerful enough to foster a tornado, pollinate pastures, and travel the world over. Still in a whirlwind of my own listening to the half-truths that were being spoken, I did what I could to make sense of it all.

Ms. Vash's job was to send bad guys to jail. However, I do feel her words to the court shed light on her and a much greater disconnect from the things that actually took place in the streets, which she and others are strangers to. This disconnect made it easier for her and others not to feel for us, for her and others only to see us, a part of us, in a certain light through their own lenses. In essence, she too was blinded. Not necessarily in the same fashion as we were, but a blindness that prevented her understanding a life dynamic which lacked similarity.

Where there is no understanding, there is no equal playing field, and where there is no equal playing field, there lie superiority and inferiority complexes. So out of the gate, there was a predator-and-prey mentality based on one's thoughts and perceptions of another. This authority complex is played out daily within our communities as each side seeks to make their presence felt and get the other to understand their position. But since you stage and flaunt your "superiority" with new laws, flashy new cop cars, and fancy new police stations, as opposed to building relationships and investing in the residents of the community, we are left to attack one another.

Are we to sit in court and attempt to justify wrongdoing on anyone's behalf? Maybe, maybe not, but the one thing I did know was as Assistant U.S. Attorney Vash ranted and raved about black-on-black crime and us being unremorseful I knew firsthand these weren't just innocent victims. In many events triggers were pulled in the context of life-and-death situations. I can speak for the masses when I say that no one I knew attacked the streets with racial motives. Race played no part. In the jungle animals kill animals. Lions attack zebra, tigers prey on pigs, bears kill deer, and snakes suck the life from whomever.

The redundant references to black-on-black crime made by Ms. Vash were only half-truths made to cast us as selfish, self-destructive, and ultimately self-sacrificing mad men. Here, I do not dispute the claim as a justification of wrongdoing. However I challenge such a claim on the basis of at least limited awareness.

Nobody wants to understand the need for survival in inner-city America. Take a trek in any ghetto in America's cities and nine out of ten residents will tell you the gun is their friend not their enemy—a tool to keep away the evil and ugly demons lurking in their neighborhoods in day and night. They may tell you drugs are evil, yet drugs put food on the table. I guess everything finds its purpose in the context of circumstance.

In most cases drugs were sold to help quiet hungry babies in the home crying for milk. In other cases men's hearts went cold as a result of feeling like nobody else cared about them and had cannibalized their hope, faith and esteem. I bet if I was to reverse roles for only a moment, grab a pistol and point it in the Federal prosecutor's direction, she would blow my brains away without second thought if she had what was needed to knock my head clear off my shoulders. It wasn't all they were making things out to be. It was strictly about what they wanted to see or not to see.

If we have a community full of blacks strung out to the point of murder, who else is there to harm but blacks? When you get off work and want a cold beer, do you go to the farthest liquor store you can think of? Absolutely not. You hit up the one closest to you. Why? Because it's logical, and while all murder or killing can be deemed sense-less, if a person has bad intentions on their mind, or an "I'm hungry and I must eat" mentality, who would be the logical target? Where would be the most logical place to find food? It's not a black on black thing, a white on white, or even a black and white thing, it's neighbor on neighbor.

How about a hard look at and the correlation between the prevalence of guns in select communities where "ironically" there just so happens to be a deluge of drugs that raises the stakes? Does this have anything to do with race? Does it have anything to do with the murder rate in these cities and neighborhoods within these cities?

When you have a community with everything except diversity, fed up with lack of opportunity, crippled as a direct result of the throw-away being consistently slam-dunked onto their front porches and back yards, when tensions rise and frustrations flare who is the aggressor? Who is made the victim? A case can be made that while our dollars and ignorance purchased the guns, we were still far from the source. In order to purchase there first must be a supply. A supply that in no way did we manufacture.

In the same tone, would it be fair to categorize the actions of gun manufacturers or distributors as premeditated acts of genocide with the intent to kill blacks? Could we say that the Columbine shooters targeted whites based on race, simply because the majority of their victims were white? Could we say that today's American justice system is a form of judicial genocide, the manifestation of a scheme concocted to replace slavery and enable large-scale indentured servitude and separate and oppress generations of black families? Or we could look at why young black males continually find themselves at the mercy of the criminal justice system. I thought to myself about the government's sentencing argument—enough of the race-baiting.

What ultimately led us all here, prosecutor included, was poverty—the desire and struggle to rise above and remain above the poverty line—and the pursuit of prosperity. Poverty afflicts all colors and the afflicted all fight the same struggle.

The prosecution's shameless effort to misinform and mislead people and members of the jury to believe there was a conscious effort on our behalf to purposefully kill, harm, or target anyone based on race is false, inflammatory, and perpetuates the idea of the black race. And not only us who were shackled to the defendants' desks, but all black men who are made to suffer from such sensational mischaracterizations, as barbaric and full of self and cultural hatred without acknowledging collective social responsibility and the failure to uphold a quality of life acceptable to all Americans. Still, it is easy for those who do not live it on a daily basis to not realize they cast stones from within a glass house.

But a Federal prosecutor would never take the courtroom floor and speak out about our failing American public institutions, education and law enforcement included, depressed economies, political absenteeism, corruption, and exploitation.

The media were equally sickening with their sensational ways. I saw firsthand how the Federal system uses the media to make its case and mete out justice in the court of public perception before trial with judge and jury.

Before I was set for trial my case had already been plastered on multiple news broadcasts, including an ABC network special titled *Gangs in Paradise* and multiple others. The effects of perception and public opinion in the court of law were and can be overwhelming. Any impression on the mind undoubtedly affects one's perception. The government repeatedly drove into the minds of the masses that we were "allegedly" responsible for New Jersey's gang problem. Allegedly was always there for legal protection for the sensationalizing media and crusading politicians who generate and benefit from such headlines. It's the same word used to give reason for war in the Iraq—"allegedly there were weapons of mass destruction." And it's the same word used today as they continue to attack the streets.

It was then, sitting at the defendant's table, in that moment, that past truths began calling my name. I began drifting in and out. Each time I would blink flashes of my life as a kid crowded my vision. I saw visions of the days when my mother would feed me a woman's wisdom as she prepared me for school, stressing the importance of not falling weak to the 'hood and its many trap doors. I saw visions of all the times when my proud father would cheer me on from the stands each Sunday I ran out on to the football field for the East Orange Rams. I remembered the teachers, the coaches, aunts and uncles who all told me I would grow up to be somebody special. A portion of my innocence was broken to pieces by experience. Then came the flashing lights, police sirens, gun smoke, and red rags.

The Court: "Mr. Butler, please stand. Pursuant to the sentencing reform act of 1984, pursuant to the court's review of the stipulations in the plea agreement and the stipulation that a sentence of 360 months is deemed to be a reasonable sentence under the guidelines—the guidelines' range being 360 months to life…"

...Sixth-grade graduation cheers from family and friends...

"...pursuant to a finding of the court that adjusted offense level of forty is the proper guideline to follow..."

...hugs handshakes and high fives; securing of the Little League Pop Warner Championship...

"...and that the advisory guidelines do carry forth the requirements of sentencing law under Section 3553 (A)..."

...Skipping school to hit the block, burning books to be a banger...

"...to wit, that the sentencing would be sufficient, but not greater than necessary to achieve the purposes of sentencing..."

...unforgettable, holding my son in my arms for the very first time...

"...which are to reflect the seriousness of the offense, promote respect for the law, provide just punishment, afford adequate deterrence to criminal conduct and protect the public from further crimes of the defendant..."

... "Homie, I'm telling you, that was the Feds. They're on us. It's time to get low..."

"...and in that fashioning the sentence, the court considers the nature and circumstances of the offense..."

... "Don't move or I'll blow your head off..."

"...and the history and characteristics of the defendant..."

... "Butler, you're never going home. We have a needle waiting on your arm..."

"...it is the intention of this court that Mr. Butler be imprisoned for a term of 360 months for the offenses to which he has pleaded guilty to under Criminal No. 03-44-05..."

Damn! I ignored truth and chased lies, yet ignorance can't be the excuse. If only I saw then what I was seeing now, instead, I snubbed the weight of callousness and consciousness, lawfulness and inequity, further damaging my dreams.

The Court: "This matter is concluded."

In a hurry, no time for farewells or goodbyes, a hand immediately made its way to the back of my belly chain and gripped tight. Instantly, Special Ops officers and U.S. Marshals alike crowded around and rushed me out of the courtroom in hope I would never be heard from again.

An hour or so later, I was back in the MCU left to complete the remainder of a five-year term for the drug possession charge in 2002 and the State's frivolous attempt to produce a racketeering case. I pled guilty to both and was now on the last leg of that stretch. I would exit state prison, only to be delivered to a Federal penitentiary.

January 2007, still in the MCU with a handful of months before I packed out for a flight across the map courtesy of the Federal Bureau of Prisons, I received a visit from a beautiful young girl named Zamel. This pretty little princess was my daughter. My daughter and I were meeting for the first time. There were no hugs, no touching; only a brief conversation through inches-thick Plexiglas. Sitting there, I found it hard to see my little girl stare at me through a window and know exactly who I was but no clue as to why I couldn't be around. I desperately wanted to explain. Tattooed tears fell from open eyes. How many children are penalized by a parent's absence and placed at a disadvantage? I felt not only for my kids, but also for the young who scour about just outside the palaces of prosperity, battling mission impossible.

Months passed. September 30, 2007, I was awakened by a heavy knock on my cell door.

"Butler, pack up. It's time to roll."

"Aight, give me a minute."

"There is no minute; they're calling for you now."

I was in no rush to meet the unknown. What were they going to do, leave without me? I took my time and tended to my hygiene. I got dressed in my prison browns and stuck my hands out of the food slot one more time to be cuffed and belted. It was sad to part ways with men who groomed me mentally and spiritually. I walked to the gate handcuffed and turned around. The CO tightened my restraint belt around my waist, keyed the gate open and spoke into his CB:

"Cease all inmate movement in North Compound."

It was just the same as when I arrived in MCU five years earlier.

One final thought came to mind, exiting the MCU:

2 Corinthians 6:4: *Here we have endured troubles and hardships and calamities of every kind. We have been beaten, been put in prison, faced angry mobs, worked to exhaustion, endured sleepless nights and gone without food. We prove ourselves by our understanding, our patience, our kindness, our resilience, and by our sincere love. We are ignored even though we are well known. We live close to death, but we are still alive . . .*

14

THE GRAVEYARD OF POTENTIAL

NINE MEN, HANDS and feet shackled, inside the all-white van with deep tinted windows. Everyone was quiet; no one even had a clue about where their troubles were taking them. "Let's roll, men," the lieutenant ordered. Personally, I could not wait to roll. There was nothing to eat with the exception of two stale pieces of bread and two slices of bologna. Hunger pains mixed with anticipation's butterflies. Almost there... In walk three officers. The clanking of chains filling the room with their noise... One by one we are cuffed, shackled, waist-restrained, and leg-ironed; each with a tightness to numb whatever they touch. Again, my mind tells me that I'm almost there... The bus ride was painful as the iron dug into my skin with each bump in the road. How refreshing were the sights. One never knew when would be the next time the free world would be seen. I cherished each passing car, pedestrian, building, and home. The small things removed from my life for years, I stare out the bus window wishing I had understood then the importance of freedom. It had been mine to lose, and I lost it. Before I knew it, we were pulling up alongside maybe a dozen or so Greyhound buses with escape-proof tinted windows, their interiors fitted with bars and gates.

Speeding down the interstate, departing from Newark's Federal Court building and on our way to one of the many airlifts stationed around the country, reserved to swap out thousands of Federal prisoners daily. Like me some were here for the very first time, others were victims of penitentiary violence, but most were disciplinary transfers. Pulling up, the scene was one I could have never predicted. Dozens of minivans, penitentiary busses, Greyhounds, and police vehicles scattered about the runway. U.S. Marshals, assault rifles in hand, rows of inmates standing single-file, exiting and waiting to enter what were rumored to be confiscated airplanes from the once-legendary kingpin Manuel Noriega, which were now being used by the government to transfer Federal inmates.

Here, be it rain, hail, sleet or snow, while the remainder of the world was in steady rotation, men held captive by the Bureau of Prisons endured the pains of a life lived that could have somehow been avoided but wasn't. October's chill on the metal chains made the moment that much colder. I sat tight in awe and anticipation of my name being called and my destination revealed. In recent talks with my attorney, it was brought to my attention that the possibility of landing in Florence, Colorado's, ADX supermax prison shouldn't be taken lightly.

"Butler, Kentucky USP Big Sandy. When you step off, give the Marshal your name and number." Seconds later, the sounds of metal clanging against itself could be heard as I slowly hobbled off the van and onto the concrete beside and behind men of all races, colors, and creeds. Murderers, bank robbers, drug dealers. You never knew who you were in the presence of. Instinct told you to proceed with caution. Though there was calm in cuffs, when removed, panic buttons were hit and anything was possible.

"Your name?" demanded the Marshal.

"Butler, 268520-050."

"Stand there," directing with the point of a finger.

Back and forth traded like chattel, identified by a number, stamped from this day until. The stories told of Fed life and the golf courses, tennis courts, and swimming pools. The truth could not have been more shaken and stirred. Replace such tales with cement, steel, barbed-wire fences, and gun towers. This was to be life in the penitentiary and it all started here.

The all-white Federal plane lands moments later and out come United States Marshals with shotguns and automatic rifles in hand. The perimeter is heavily secured.

I stand among the other men and women dressed in pumpkin seeds, paper pants, dingy t-shirts, and shackles. The sight before me is one I could have never imagined. I'm almost there . . . We enter the plane. Hundreds of prisoners packed like sardines. Prepare for takeoff. In case of emergency do not panic. Listen to the Marshal's instructions and you'll be fine. A man with his wrists strapped to his waist and his feet chained together could never be fine in the case of emergency... We are in the air. Next stop FTC (Federal Transfer Center) Oklahoma City. One would never know what the outside looks like because it's located on the fringes of an airport and the plane pulls up directly to the building like they do the terminal at the airport. My feet never touch the ground. It was straight from the plane into the institution's corridor. Corrections officers line the walls of a corridor, which is about half of a football field's length. The lights were bright and everything was white. One by one, led down the hall where my ankle irons are removed and the black box capped around my cuffs lifted. The game is now one of patience.

"Butler, step to your left."

The room I entered was shielded in glass and inside were four other prisoners. Their tattoos told it was not their first run. I did not appreciate the way we seemed to have been singled out and separated. I inquired, "What's this all about?"

"Ay young Blood, we're on our way upstairs to the SHU (Special Housing Unit)," answered an Arizona native I had been seated beside on the flight who was also in the room with me. The SHU generally housed inmates who failed to abide by the rules and regulations and had been subjected to disciplinary action. The response left me baffled; this was only my first day in Federal custody. Already, a tag had been attached to my chart. So much for flying under the radar.

After what felt like an eternity, I was finally led by two officers and a female lieutenant to the top floor for my first in a series of trips to the Special Housing Unit. After weeks spent 23/1 in Oklahoma City's SHU, though in possession of no personal property, I was told to pack up and that I was to depart within minutes. My next stop within the Federal prison system was identified as USP Atlanta's transit center.

USP Atlanta was horrendous and comparable to none. To say the least, it was filled with gnawing rodents, roaches, filth, and disease. As if that wasn't enough, the screaming negligence on behalf of the bureau's staff was disastrous. Safety was your own concern. Two-man cells overloaded, perfect strangers forced into the same space. Prison gangs had wars on sight when paths crossed. Eminent danger. If searched for, you will find that many men have been lost here.

Truth be told, the majority of these gangs were new to me. Things were actually the opposite in New Jersey's state prison system. There wasn't much gang diversity. Surely there existed gangs like the Bloods, the Crips, Netas, and the Latin Kings. But most gangs (organizations) formed based on geography or alliances among people from the South, the Midwest, or white supremacist groups for that matter, were non-existent in the New Jersey state prison system. I had no clue how we all were to co-exist. At that moment I prepared myself for the inevitable, and I knew fresh off the bus when arriving at USP Big Sandy I would make certain along with my care package (hygiene, supplies) to request a weapon. I didn't want to do it, but, obviously, it would be needed.

At long last, along with a bus full of others, I was on my way to USP Big Sandy in Inez, Kentucky.

What I would consider to be the longest ride of my life provided my moment of clarity just before entering the depths of disarray. The ride for me was one last opportunity to reflect. I used every minute to ponder past experiences and missed opportunities, while other inmates rapped along to the sounds of the music played by the Marshals—anything to escape reality. I sat and listened to the many prisoners debate who was the best rapper alive. Already caught up by penitentiary politics, everyone's favorite happened to be from out of their own geographical area. New York spoke of Jadakiss, Jay Z, and Nas; Dirty South held Young Jeezy and TI; California repped Snoop Dog; and the Midwest shouted names like Twista, Common, and Kanye.

As for me, I kept quiet, sitting on a mixture of disappointment, anger, and curiosity. I would stare into each car we passed by, imagining me on my way to anywhere other than where I was headed. I pictured family trips as a child and how my face would be frowning as I preferred to run the streets instead of exploring possibilities. If only.

Still, I listened to other inmates as they dropped names and thought to myself about these rappers they were talking about. What I caught that they seemed to overlook was these were "rappers." I take nothing away from the art or the artist, but what I did know was the life I was living was not for entertainment. The life I was living would destroy you for throwing up gang signs, B-hopping, and Crip-walking. Meanwhile these rappers/entertainers carried on as if losing homeboys and homegirls was urban fantasy straight out of a 'hood novel. Maybe these "rappers" think they are representing, but trust me I know many who have been forgotten about by these so-called rapping gang-bangers. Street life, maybe, but for true gangsters gang-banging in no shape, form, or fashion is a fad. One can't dress up in colors, tie a rag around a pair of skinny jeans and consider himself a part of something that is to be stood on forever. These same rappers/entertainers imitated and referenced a life that had us on this very bus ride. If these rappers experienced an inch and a second of what life behind bars was like, or had to duck non-stop bullets thrown at them by the enemy on the street and bury loved ones on the regular, I seriously doubt they would be so joyous about it all.

No disrespect to any of the official artists who moved on from a hardened life, and have found a better way and use the microphone as a way to tell their stories and highlight issues that would otherwise be unheard of. To them, the few and far between, I tilt my hat. But for the majority, these nondescript wannabes, who have been run out of their own 'hood and portray to be affiliated, associated, or a part of today's struggle, don't let it catch up to you. We'll be waiting.

We had been on the road a few hours when I heard an inmate yell to the front of the bus, "How much longer?"

"A long way from here," responded the Marshal.

And with that, I closed my eyes and took a ride of my own. This trip was one engulfed in grief as I scrutinized my life and the many opportunities I let get away. The way I envisioned the state of affairs growing up was difficult to accept and so I gave the world my middle finger. The trappings of a broken-down society had snagged more than its fair share, millions of people were being affected. Out of sync with my emotions, the entire time a quiet storm was raging within. The insensitivity of America was sickening. It left me disgusted.

Still to this day, I hated the way the smell of blood and gunsmoke permeated my neighborhood like morning dew. I hated the way blocks in my neighborhood were full of abandoned buildings, and our streets exhibited a sequence of shattered homes. I hated the way a dark cloud seemed to hover on top of my city, casting a darkness that appeared inescapable. I hated that I was born into the struggle and had yet to understand a better way of combating it until already boxed in. I hated the way I wanted success but was afraid to succeed. I hated how my fear of failing lowered my expectations, and I settled for a life beneath me. I failed because of fear. Seeing as if almost for the first time the possibilities I passed up, my jaws clenched.

How did I get to this point of my life? How had I fallen so far after flying so high? I hated that when I approached the inevitable fork in the road that we all encounter along the way, my choice was one of using the rules to break the rules, and the laws of life had gotten the better of me. Why is it that my intentions were good, yet my actions misunderstood?

Was it because I lacked the willingness to break the pattern that led to self-destruction or was it because I preferred to die like a man than live like a coward? I even thought of a question once posed to me by another, after being pulled up on as I stood on the block of North 15th and William Streets. One of my older homeboys who had clutched millions back in his heyday asked, "Is this what you consider living?" Then, absolutely. Now, on a half-day prison ride from Atlanta, Georgia, to Inez, Kentucky, clothed in paper pants, pumpkin seeds, and a worn-down T-shirt, I knew I had been all wrong. Ignorance and illusion led me to this stage of nothingness. I had to find the avenue that made me better.

The bumpy ride continued. Now we were passing through the state of Tennessee. All around us stood law firms, doctor's offices, and day-to-day civilians living the simple life, one without consequence. Things were beginning to click and as I witnessed the world in cuffs it registered: validation in the streets can never be found.

I was furious with myself that it came to this prior to me grabbing truth. But in some instances the greater the obstacle, the greater the awakening. Now, opposed to submitting to a life behind bars, I can freely pursue life, a life with meaning. The most challenging feat of my life thus far was the way I saw the world having grown up in the ghetto. One's mental condition controls everything. For me, overcoming impulse would allow exactly who and what I was born to be to shine through the dark clouds parked atop the 'hood. No more isolated thoughts, only a broader vision, a guarantee to pick up the secret gems carefully hidden from the mind's eye.

This saddened story is beyond me. It also applies to the scores of kids who didn't realize the negative results of growing up so young and the damages of rushed responsibility. There is a false belief that necessity negates negativity, and we lose our children because of it. Starved for so long in this cold world our children become unreceptive to helping hands and trust only their instincts. Our children are enrooted with coldness, lack guidance and do not want it and are left to experience the paradox of a two-faced America all by their lonely. Trust is unquestionably a luxury they cannot afford.

While on the bus to Kentucky, I realized my life resembled those of millions scattered around and within urban communities and jails, prisons, and penitentiaries everywhere. We all wanted more! But we had no actual idea how to grab it. The search became backbreaking and nearly impossible to recover from. Those who did survive the jagged experience forfeited the authenticity we needed—self-love, recognition, control, respect and reliance. While living the life, there was *no* understanding, nothing but blurred images to obstruct our vision.

"Welcome home, men," shouted the Marshal. I wasn't too sure as to what he spoke on, because I looked to both sides and saw nothing. I looked up and there it sat, a maze of a mountain, almost as if on top of the world. In the distance, you could see a cement building hemmed with yards of shock-ready fence and razor-sharp barbed wire.

USP Big Sandy, Level Six, feared by inmates and staff alike for being one of the most dangerous Federal prisons around. Minutes after entering R&D to be processed and assigned cells, the deuces (prison slang for panic button) went off and the staff all went running out on to the mainline.

It was obvious something occurred. The ten remaining inmates out of twenty, the other ten having checked in to protective custody as we exited the bus, looked at each other and wondered just what that something was. The mystery was short-lived. The door to R&D came busting open. Nurses, doctors, and COs covered in blood rushed through, pushing a stretcher with a man on top who looked to be hanging onto life by a thread. Through the mumbles of staff and voices busting through walkie-talkies, we learned the man on the stretcher had been stabbed repeatedly with a homemade shank and needed an airlift to the nearest hospital immediately. I thought to myself, *Was this what lay ahead?* One never knew. And just as if what we had seen was make-believe, a CO opened the tank like nothing happened and commanded, "Okay, men. Grab your bed rolls and let's make it."

Exiting R&D, the corridor was empty with the exception of a blood trail that was unmistakably freshly spilled. With bedroll in hand, I continued my long journey down the hall and to the left where I found my unit B-2, Cell 121 Upper. As I neared the unit, I could hear the commotion of men who were no longer considered to be faithful and loyal to the laws of the United States. I pressed the buzzer; in seconds I heard keys opening the door. I entered and handed over my ID card to the unit officer and without a word, he pointed in the direction of my new home, Cell 121.

Later, I learned the officer's silence was fear. This was often the time when a new arrival, no idea of what he was walking into, was spotted by an enemy or rival gang and was all but slaughtered—thrown right into a pit full of hungry wolves. As a result of the earlier stabbing, the jail was in the process of locking down. Tired after the long day of traveling, all I wanted to do was rest my eyes. Finally, I was in the cell and the CO made his rounds to secure each and every cell door. He seemed pleased nothing else kicked off on his shift. When he passed, I hit the rack and closed my eyes, bringing the day to an end.

When my eyes closed I thought to myself again of the three things that always were somehow present: prison, death, and the life I had always wanted to live. Yet, prison and death always seemed more vivid. Maybe it was the time I gripped the shot-gun and, not knowing it was loaded, aimed it at Oop and almost killed us both. Maybe it was my twisted train of thought growing up wanting to experiment with prison. Maybe it was talking to the rude-boy weed connect years ago and him telling me, in so many words, he knew I was destined to be a hustler. Maybe it was the summer I decided to step out on my own and head to New York to try on the hat of a juvenile drug kingpin, or maybe it was my donning of the red rag. Whatever it was, on this day the hard-metal bolted-down bunk I laid on miles and miles away from home and the constant clanking of steel cuffs and iron doors banging against each other made it obvious the life I always wanted to live was gone. Prison and death stood before me. With nothing and no one I had to do this time on my own. I reached at faith, not yet prepared to give up. I wanted to live. I had to live. I had to show the world what I knew and know to be as my truth. I brought yesterday to a close and today a new beginning. For I am . . . everything other than *Massacre*.

('mæs ə kər) n. the act of killing many humans indiscriminately and cruelly. *syns: bloodbath, bloodletting, bloodshed, butchery, carnage, pogrom, slaughter - mas'-sa-cre; v.

LIVEFROMLOCKDOWN.COM

In late 2010, I was blessed with the opportunity to start Live from Lockdown, a blog to offer the public an unvarnished view of the harsh realities of prison. This endeavor has grown beyond me to include influential gang members from across the country from all factions. Rather than glamorize street gangs, LIVE's mission is to influence a positive culture shift away from gangs and violence.

From the blog:

First day on the prison yard- Inez, Kentucky, USP Big Sandy, Level 6- it happens here. Unexpected word was delivered from a rival gang member out of my state, who I had been warring with since the day Watts' Grape Street Crip Gang made its way into Essex County and the surrounding area. Message was for me to meet him on the prison yard on the 9:00 AM recreation.

I thought what could he possibly want with me other than war. Where I'm from Bloods and Crips did no talking. Things were simple- on sight, bust first- no need for questions. So, why would he give me a heads up by sending a message? The moment was beginning to take on the feel of school days when you sat quietly anticipating the outcome that waited when the clock struck three. Difference here, there would be no fisticuffs. Fights without weaponry in the penitentiary are almost unheard of. Clearly, there were to be shanks (prison-made knives) and a fight for life. To survive the scandalous ways of the streets, only to lose self in the pen must be a hell of a thing. No way! With avoiding the issue out of the equation, I strapped up and made my way to the prison yard. Mind made up . . .

The slightest move . . . Shoestring tightly wrapped around my wrist. Ice pick firm in the grip. Do or die!

The metal detector guarding the yard's entrance rung as I attempted to keep my cool and casually stroll out as if my heart wasn't racing a million miles a hour. My adrenaline was revved. Kill or be killed! A new life with a new beginning, over and done with by a past I couldn't cut loose.

Slow motion around the track. My hands concealed. Spot on. We locked eyes. What was running through his mind, I wondered? No crowd. No gang. Just him and I. Certainly, he was strapped. His reputation preceded him. This would be no easy feat. However, neither would fall short. My gang, his neighborhood, with no knowledge as to why, other than colors, would forever be pitted against one another.

I approached. He spoke . . . Already, the unimaginable was happening. What was discussed shall remain between us, two men. Not gangstas or gang-bangers but men. Years of misunderstanding, shootings, stabbings, killings, and senselessness all overcome by struggle. On this side of the wall our fight was the same. Our stories understood. From that day forth I was able to see beyond color.

AUTHOR'S NOTE

AUGUST 2014, I find myself back in the midst of solitude; locked down twenty-three hours a day, or more, on my second stint in the Federal Bureau of Prisons' Special Management Unit at United States Penitentiary Lewisburg (Pennsylvania). A program designed for inmates whose incarceration requires greater management to ensure the safety, security or orderly operation of bureau facilities, or protection of the public. Following a blatant violation of my hearing rights, as an upshot of the program's referral criteria, I was transported here to spend the next eighteen-to-twenty-four months prior to my being allowed the "privilege" to re-enter general population. One mountain after the next, yet with the exception of physical restriction, I can honestly say I have found peace and my eyes are open.

To contact author: You can visit www.bop.gov and search by name, Tewhan Butler, or by BOP Register Number 26852-050.

CPSIA information can be obtained
at www.ICGtesting.com
Printed in the USA
LVOW12s1201200316

479958LV00006B/563/P